PATTERNS
for
PRAYER

A Daily Guide for
Kingdom-Focused Praying

ALVIN VANDERGRIEND

2402

PRAYERSHOP
PUBLISHING

Terre Haute, Indiana

Prayer Shop Publishing is the publishing arm of Harvest Prayer Ministries and the Church Prayer Leaders Network. Harvest Prayer Ministries exists to make every church a house of prayer.

Its online prayer store, www.prayershop.org, has more than 600 prayer resources available for purchase.

ISBN: 978-1-935012-00-9

1 2 3 4 5 6 7 8 9 10 | 17 16 15 14 13 12 11 10 09 08

Original contributors to this prayer guide include Edith Bajema, Dian Ginter, Joan Huyser-Honig, Don McCrory, Laurie Quist, Al Schaap, Mark Timmer, Alvin J. VanderGriend, and Jean Westenbroek.

TABLE OF CONTENTS

PREFACE

T his book is designed to help you develop a meaningful and disciplined personal prayer life. I have heard people say, "I'd like to pray more, but after five minutes I run out of things to pray about." Most of us know what that's like. *Patterns for Prayer* is for all who have "run out of things to pray about."

Regular use of this prayer guide will help you

- learn to use the language of Scripture in prayer
- use all of the elements of prayer regularly
- claim the promises of God with confidence
- keep your thoughts from wandering during prayer
- pray expressively for friends and family
- release God's power and grace for your church and the kingdom of God
- develop the habit of praying for unsaved friends and acquaintances

You'll discover a weekly cycle in these pages as you pray for the leadership and ministries of your own local church. You'll pray about worship, church leaders, outreach ministries, church education, world missions, caregiving and fellowship, and financial stewardship.

This guide is meant to enlarge and deepen your prayer life. It is not intended to be the whole of it. Let these prayer suggestions trigger prayer expressions from your own heart. Where they do not fit, customize them to your own situation. Space is provided on each page for you to keep a record of further petitions and intercessions.

The Heidelberg Catechism reminds us that "God gives his grace and Holy Spirit only to those who pray continually and groan inwardly, asking God for these gifts and thanking him for them" (Q&A 116). I pray that you may do just that and, in so doing, find that your life is enriched as you grow in intimacy with God and receive a generous amount of his grace and Spirit.

—Alvin J. VanderGriend

JANUARY 1

Personal Prayer

Praise God for his creativity. Give glory for the unending variety exhibited in his creation. Thank God for the wonderful way you have been made and for your unique personality, gifts, and talents. Confess any dissatisfaction you have had with the way you have been created. Commit yourself to serving God with your gifts and talents. Ask that God may reveal your spiritual gifts to you and give you opportunity to use them for him.

For Your Family and Friends

Pray that family members and friends will be a source of joy and blessing to each other and that together they may experience the joy and blessing of the Lord.

For the Church

Pray that pastors may speak the Word of God with power and conviction so that God's people may hear the Word and do it, be equipped for discipling, and witness boldly to the good news.

For the Kingdom

Pray that the gospel may reach, touch, and renew the hearts and minds of people without hope in our world today so that there may be a great harvest of souls brought into the church.

For the Unsaved

Since "no one can come to [Christ] unless the Father . . . draws him" (Jn. 6:44), pray that God will draw your unsaved relatives, friends, and acquaintances (it's best to name them) to himself.

JANUARY 2

Personal Prayer

Praise the prayer-hearing God that his ear is attentive to your prayers. Give thanks for the privilege of coming into God's presence and conversing with him through prayer. Confess any personal failure in your prayer life that you are aware of. Commit yourself to being a faithful intercessor. Ask that God will strengthen your prayer life and help you to pray in the Spirit with all kinds of prayer, on all occasions, for all God's people (Eph. 6:18).

For Your Family and Friends

Pray for unity in the Spirit. Ask for a deep love for, and understanding between family members and friends, and for reconciliation where they are at odds.

For the Church

Pray that your church's leaders—pastors, elders, deacons, and others—may be filled with the Spirit and be effective in the ministries to which they are called.

For the Kingdom

Pray that the leaders of your denomination will clearly discern God's will and vision for your churches. Ask that they will use their spiritual gifts to lead the church in that direction.

For the Unsaved

"The harvest is plentiful but the workers are few. Ask the Lord of the harvest, therefore, to send out workers into his harvest field" (Mt. 9:37-38). Pray that God will send helpful believers (this could be you) to unsaved persons you care about.

_____

_____

_____

_____

_____

JANUARY 3

Personal Prayer

Praise God for his matchless grace. Give thanks that his grace is sufficient for you in every situation. Confess any do-it-yourself efforts in which you have rejected God's grace and tried to go it alone. Commit yourself to being a channel of that grace to others. Ask that God will meet your needs according to his glorious riches in Christ Jesus (Phil. 4:19) and that his grace will be poured out abundantly.

For Your Family and Friends

Pray for the salvation of each family member. Ask that children may come to trust Christ at an early age and may desire to become part of God's forever family.

For the Church

Pray for each of your church's outreach ministries, for the leaders, and for those being reached, that God will use all these efforts to bring people to himself.

For the Kingdom

Lift up the names of the leaders of your nation, state/province, and community, asking that the Lord's strength and wisdom come to full maturity in each one as they learn to rely on him.

For the Unsaved

Pray that the unsaved persons you name before God may seek him, reach out for him, and find him, since he is not far from each one of us (Acts 17:27).

Prayer Pointer

"Our business in prayer is not to prescribe, but to subscribe to the wisdom and will of God; to refer our case to him, and then leave it with him." —ANONYMOUS

_____

_____

_____

_____

JANUARY 4

Personal Prayer

Praise God for his limitless power. Give thanks that God is willing to strengthen you with power through the Spirit within you. Confess any time that you have been weak because you did not avail yourself of his strength. Commit yourself to serving in the strength of the Lord. Ask that out of his glorious riches God will strengthen you with power through his Spirit in your inner being (Eph. 3:16).

For Your Family and Friends

Pray that your family and/or friends will experience rich times of praying together, playing together, and worshiping together.

For the Church

Pray for your church's teachers and counselors that they may communicate Bible truths clearly, live holy lives before God, and be Christ-like examples to those they lead.

For the Kingdom

Pray for small group Bible studies as they meet weekly in homes and churches all across the continent. Ask God to change hearts and lives through the Word.

For the Unsaved

Pray that unsaved persons you know may receive the free gift of God, which is eternal life, and may not have to receive the wages of sin eternally (Rom. 6:23).

Prayer Pointer

"When you pray, rather let your heart be without words than your words without heart." —JOHN BUNYAN

_____

_____

_____

_____

JANUARY 5

Personal Prayer

Praise God for his unswerving faithfulness in keeping all his promises and never forsaking his own. Give thanks that God gave his only begotten Son that whoever believes in him should have everlasting life. Confess any unfaithfulness on your part to God. Commit yourself to being faithful to all your loved ones and to keeping all the promises you have made to them. Ask God to fill you with the Holy Spirit and to give you the confidence that you are a member of his family and know God as "Abba Father."

For Your Family and Friends

Support family members and friends in their work or studies and pray that each may be diligent in pursuit of God-given tasks.

For the Church

Pray for your church's missionaries (by name, if possible), asking the Lord to encourage and strengthen them and to keep them from loneliness, discouragement, spiritual attack, and burnout.

For the Kingdom

Pray for your denomination's world mission efforts as missionaries are recruited, trained, sent out, and supported. Pray for adequate funds to carry on and expand the work.

For the Unsaved

Pray that unsaved persons who hear the Word of God will receive it and accept it not as the word of human beings, but as it truly is, the Word of God (1 Thess. 2:13).

_____

_____

_____

_____

_____

JANUARY 6

Personal Prayer

Praise God for his unfathomable love. Give thanks that he will let nothing separate you from that love. Confess to God any lack of love for him. Commit yourself to loving the Lord with all your heart, soul, mind, and strength. Ask that your love may grow and overflow to others just as Christ's love does to you (1 Thess. 3:12).

For Your Family and Friends

Pray for family members and friends to have a strong and growing love for God and for others.

For the Church

Pray for your church's caregivers that they may be gems of Christ's love and compassion and may be his hands and feet to reach out to many human needs today.

For the Kingdom

Pray that God will bless the efforts of relief ministries throughout the world as they help the church to motivate and empower members for works of mercy so that hurts are healed and needs met.

For the Unsaved

Pray that the Holy Spirit will convict unsaved persons you know (again, be specific), bringing them to repentance and faith and guiding them into all truth.

Prayer Pointer

"I have lived to thank God that all my prayers have not been answered."
—JEAN INGELOW

JANUARY 7

Personal Prayer
Praise Jesus Christ for his incomprehensible humility. Thank him for humbling himself to die on the cross that you might be set free. Confess any pride, egotism, or boastfulness you find in yourself. Commit yourself to doing nothing out of selfish ambition or vain conceit, but in humility considering others better than yourself (Phil. 2:3). Pray that you may have the mind of Christ in all matters such as priorities, goals, time management, vocational choices, relationships, and recreation.

For Your Family and Friends
Pray about weaknesses you see in family members and friends, asking specifically that God may overcome each weakness by his strength.

For the Church
Ask that God's people will give generously and cheerfully, according to the blessings they have received, that the financial needs of your church will be adequately met.

For the Kingdom
Pray for the church throughout the world that its divisions may be healed, its leaders endowed with the Spirit's power, its people filled with zeal for the cause of Christ, so that the church may increase daily and the kingdom be advanced.

For the Unsaved
Pray that the Holy Spirit may give you a burden for lost people like that of the apostle Paul, who expressed "great sorrow and unceasing anguish in [his] heart" over lost people (Rom. 9:1-3).

JANUARY 8

Personal Prayer

Praise God for his inexhaustible goodness. There is nothing lacking or defective in him. Give thanks for all the pleasure and blessings which flow from God's goodness. Confess any ingratitude to him. Commit yourself to God-like goodness. Ask that today you may grow in the grace and knowledge of the Lord Jesus Christ (2 Pet. 3:18).

For Your Family and Friends

Pray that your children will grow up in the training and instruction of the Lord and will learn to walk in his ways (Eph. 6:4).

For the Church

Pray that all who proclaim the gospel today may be clothed with power from the Holy Spirit (Acts 1:8) and may preach the Word of God boldly and clearly. Ask that worshipers may have open ears and attentive hearts, and that they may experience God's presence.

For the Kingdom

Pray for the unreached people groups worldwide to be reached with the gospel. Ask for laborers, open doors, adequate funds, and a positive response.

For the Unsaved

Pray that those who seek the Lord will seek him with all their heart and will find him (Deut. 4:29).

Prayer Pointer

"When you go to your knees, God will help you stand up to anything."
—ANONYMOUS

JANUARY 9

Personal Prayer

Praise God that he knows everything in every age. Give thanks that he knows you by name and that you matter to him. Confess any attempt to conceal things from God. Commit yourself to openness and honesty before God. Invite him to search your heart and life (Ps. 139:23-24). Ask to be protected from the evil one and kept from a spirit of worldliness.

For Your Family and Friends

Pray that each family member and friend may be responsive to God's grace and may live a life pleasing to him.

For the Church

Pray that your church leaders may grow in grace, in knowledge, and in wisdom as they continue in the Word of God and prayer.

For the Kingdom

More than 100,000 persons are added each day to the church worldwide. Pray for new converts that they may stand firm in the faith and may grow spiritually strong.

For the Unsaved

Since faith comes by hearing, and hearing by the Word of God (Rom. 10:15-17), pray that your unsaved friends, neighbors, and relatives will hear the Word and respond in faith.

_____

_____

_____

_____

_____

JANUARY 10

Personal Prayer

Praise God for the depth of his wisdom and knowledge, and for his unsearchable judgments. Thank God for guiding and directing your ways. Confess any resistance on your part to do his will. Commit yourself to acknowledging him in all your ways (Prov. 3:5-6). Ask God for the Spirit of wisdom and revelation, so that you may know him better and have the eyes of your heart enlightened, to know the hope to which you are called, the riches of his glorious inheritance (Eph. 1:17-18).

For Your Family and Friends

Pray that by God's grace, parents will be able to train their children in the ways of the Lord and that their children will always walk in these ways (Prov. 22:6).

For the Church

Pray for the Spirit of love in your church that believers may be one, even as the Father and Son are one, so that the world may believe that God sent Jesus Christ (Jn. 17:21).

For the Kingdom

Pray that measures honoring the sanctity of life will become law in the U.S. and Canada.

For the Unsaved

Pray that the Holy Spirit, who is sent to convict the world of guilt in regard to sin, righteousness, and judgment (Jn. 16:8), will work powerfully and effectively in the hearts and lives of unsaved persons you name.

JANUARY 11

Personal Prayer

Praise God for keeping his covenant promises to you. Give thanks that you have always been able to count on him in all circumstances. Confess any doubt you have had concerning God and his promises. Commit yourself to trusting the Lord and taking him at his word. Ask for his peace which transcends understanding to guard your heart and your mind in Jesus Christ.

For Your Family and Friends

Pray that family or personal financial problems may be eased and that each person may become a good steward of God-given financial resources.

For the Church

Pray that those who instruct within the church may be able to correctly handle the Word of truth (2 Tim. 2:15).

For the Kingdom

Pray for those who work in denominational publications that they may produce the educational material that will give strength to the church's educational ministries, lead many to Christ, and help all to be built up in the faith.

For the Unsaved

Name specific unsaved persons and pray that they may "repent and be baptized . . . in the name of Jesus Christ for the forgiveness of [their] sins. And [that they] will receive the gift of the Holy Spirit" (Acts 2:38).

Prayer Pointer

"Embark upon no enterprise you cannot submit to the test of prayer."
—ANONYMOUS

_____

_____

_____

_____

_____

JANUARY 12

Personal Prayer

Praise God for the beauty of his holiness (2 Chron. 20:21). Give thanks that he has removed the stain of sin from your life and made you holy. Confess any sin or unholiness that taints your life. Commit yourself to being holy, as God is holy (1 Pet. 1:16). Ask that you may be made holy through and through so that your spirit, soul, and body will be kept blameless (1 Thess. 5:23).

For Your Family and Friends

Pray for families undergoing severe marital strife, asking that God will rekindle a flame of love between husband and wife.

For the Church

Pray that God will give your church a vision for the mission task so that all will be motivated to pray and give faithfully.

For the Kingdom

Pray that laws against pornography will be enforced and new and more effective laws will be passed in Canada and the U.S. Pray for decency and morality in our countries.

For the Unsaved

Jesus said, "Whoever hears my word and believes him who sent me has eternal life" (Jn. 5:24). Pray that unsaved friends, neighbors, and associates will hear, believe, and be saved.

Prayer Pointer

"God eagerly awaits the chance to bless the person whose heart is turned toward him." —ANONYMOUS

_____

_____

_____

_____

_____

JANUARY 13

Personal Prayer

Praise Jesus Christ for his grace and beauty. Thank God for reproducing the beauty of Christ's character in you. Confess anything in your life which is displeasing to God. Commit yourself to pleasing him in every way. Ask God to help you live a life worthy of the Lord, to please him in everything you do, and to bear fruit in every good work (Col. 1:10).

For Your Family and Friends

Pray that each one of your family members and friends will develop a close personal relationship with the Lord and spend regular quiet times with him.

For the Church

Pray that members of your church will lovingly bear one another's burdens and so fulfill the law of Christ (Gal. 6:2).

For the Kingdom

Pray that all God's people will be able to stand against the principalities, powers, and the world rulers of darkness that seek to control the lives and destinies of people. Pray that they may put on the whole armor of God and may pray in the Spirit with all kinds of prayers and requests (Eph. 6:10-18).

For the Unsaved

God "commands all people everywhere to repent" (Acts 17:30). Pray that unsaved persons you know will come to the end of human efforts and excuses, and will turn away from sin unto God.

JANUARY 14

Personal Prayer

Praise the Lamb who is worthy "to receive power and wealth and wisdom and strength and honor and glory and praise" (Rev. 5:12). Thank God for the blood of the Lamb given for the complete remission of all your sin. Confess any self-centeredness which has taken your focus off God. Commit yourself to loving God with all your heart and soul and mind and strength, and your neighbor as yourself. Ask him to give you the kingdom and make you his priest that you may serve him and reign with him on earth.

For Your Family and Friends

Pray that sons and daughters who have wandered away from the faith may be restored.

For the Church

Pray that God will free you from the love of money and keep you from making it a god, showing you how to be content with what you have and how to lay up treasures in heaven.

For the Kingdom

Pray for your nation and its leaders that they may be enabled to rule according to God's good pleasure, to the hindrance of wickedness so that all may lead quiet and peaceable lives.

For the Unsaved

"Everyone who calls on the name of the Lord will be saved" (Acts 2:21). Pray that unsaved persons you know may call on the name of the Lord and be saved.

_____

_____

_____

_____

_____

JANUARY 15

Personal Prayer

Praise God as your rock, your fortress, your deliverer, the one in whom you take refuge. Thank God that he hears and answers prayer and showers you with unfailing kindness. Confess any unfaithfulness, impurity, or deceit. Commit yourself to courageously challenging the Lord's enemies as you are armed by his strength. Ask him to reach down and take hold of you, to arm you with strength, and to rescue you from evil powers.

For Your Family and Friends

Pray that family members and friends will be sensitive to the needs of others around them and will have a desire to help and care for them.

For the Church

Pray that your pastor will be used of the Lord to equip the saints for the work of ministry that your church may be built up. Pray that visitors to your worship services may be noticed, receive a warm welcome, and find worship meaningful.

For the Kingdom

Pray for agencies which assist established churches and newly planted churches to gather God's growing family. Pray for adequate funds, excellent resources, and effective leaders.

For the Unsaved

Pray that God will lay a burden on your heart for one or more unsaved persons he wants you to reach out to. He does not want anyone to perish (2 Pet. 3:9).

JANUARY 16

Personal Prayer

Praise the one who is King of kings and Lord of lords. Give thanks for everything in which you may find godly pleasure today: for work, food, books, music, and friends. Confess any pain you have unnecessarily brought into the lives of others. Commit yourself to doing to others today what you would have them do to you. Ask God to guide you in all your ways, to guard you against all that would harm you in body and soul, and to strengthen you in the face of temptation.

For Your Family and Friends

Pray that family members and friends will be protected from any temptation, such as sexual sin, love of money, desire for power, or overeating.

For the Church

Pray for your deacons, elders, and pastor. Ask God to give them wisdom and integrity and the filling of the Holy Spirit, that they may be mature in faith and may exercise their offices with prayer, patience, and humility.

For the Kingdom

Pray that officials in your city, state/ province, and nation will make decisions in accord with biblical justice and morality.

For the Unsaved

Pray that the seed of the gospel sown in the hearts of unbelievers may find good soil and produce a crop to the glory of God (Mt. 13:4-8).

JANUARY 17

Personal Prayer
Praise God as your beloved Father. Give thanks as a dear child for the undeserved love and grace you receive from him. Confess all the ways you have offended him. Commit yourself to trusting and obeying. Ask Christ to be with you always and to teach you to obey all things that he has commanded.

For Your Family and Friends
Pray for the ability to serve God in marriage and family life by reflecting his covenant love in lifelong loyalty, and by teaching his ways, so that children may know Jesus as their Lord and learn to use their gifts in a life of joyful service.

For the Church
Pray that your church may engage in and promote the work of evangelism so that those who are still sheep without a shepherd will experience your care, feel your love, and hear the good news through you.

For the Kingdom
Pray that God may help you be a good earthkeeper and caretaker, loving your neighbor, tending the creation, and using your skills in the unfolding and well-being of his world.

For the Unsaved
Pray that the Lord may open the hearts of unsaved persons to respond to the good news (Acts 16:14).

Prayer Pointer
"God's answers are wiser than our prayers." —ANONYMOUS

JANUARY 18

Personal Prayer

Praise the one who is able to do immeasurably more than all one can ask or imagine. Thank God for what he is doing in your life and in the church in response to prayer. Confess little asking and weak praying. Commit yourself to asking and expecting much in Jesus' name. Claim the promise that Christ will come to you and make his home in your heart if you love him and trust him.

For Your Family and Friends

Pray that your family may grow closer as children grow older and prepare to leave home. Ask the Lord to keep family and friendship ties strong and full of love across distances which separate.

For the Church

Pray for leaders, teachers, and committee personnel, that they may be qualified for and committed to their ministries. Ask that their ministries may make a difference in the lives of those they lead.

For the Kingdom

Pray that the countries currently banning the Bible may soon rescind these bans so that their people may have free access to the Bible.

For the Unsaved

God "commands all people everywhere to repent" (Acts 17:30). Pray specifically for unsaved persons you know, that they may repent and believe as God commands.

Prayer Pointer

"Prayer should be the key of the day and the lock of the night." —THOMAS FULLER

Personal Prayer

Praise him who is able to keep you from falling and to present you faultless before his presence with exceeding joy. Give thanks that God has preserved you through many physical and spiritual dangers. Confess a specific fault that you want God to remove. Commit yourself to courageous endurance in the way of Christ. Ask for undying hope in the Lord and a renewal of strength that you may soar on wings like an eagle, may run and not grow weary, may walk and not be faint (Isa. 40:31).

For Your Family and Friends

Pray that family members and friends of dating age may be wise in their dating choices and may be kept pure and spotless in their relationships. Ask God to give wisdom to each one in selecting a life partner.

For the Church

Ask the Lord to send the power of his Holy Spirit upon all the missionaries of your church and to give them the strength, courage, health, support, and spiritual gifts to be fruitful.

For the Kingdom

Pray that Christian colleges, Bible schools, and seminaries may effectively integrate the Christian faith into their curriculums as they prepare young men and women to serve as godly leaders.

For the Unsaved

Pray for specific unsaved persons that they may confess with their mouths, "Jesus is Lord" and believe in their hearts that God raised him from the dead (Rom. 10:9) and be saved.

JANUARY 20

Personal Prayer

Praise the righteous God whose face shines upon you (Psalm 4). Thank him for setting apart the godly for himself. Confess any unresolved anger that causes you to sin. Commit yourself to bringing to God gifts worthy of his name. Ask the Lord to surround you with his favor and spread his protection over you so that you may rejoice in him.

For Your Family and Friends

Pray that children may accept wise spiritual guidance from their parents and from spiritual mentors in the church.

For the Church

Pray that God will send holy angels to protect this flock from the attacks of Satan and his demons. Ask him to give your people supernatural strength to resist temptation.

For the Kingdom

Pray that the Spirit may thrust believers into worldwide mission, impelling young and old, men and women, to go next door and far away, into science and art, media and marketplace with the good news of God's grace.

For the Unsaved

Pray that by the power of the Holy Spirit unbelievers may "draw near to God with a sincere heart in full assurance of faith" (Heb. 10:22) so their hearts may be sprinkled and their guilty consciences cleansed.

JANUARY 21

Personal Prayer
God is light; in him there is no darkness at all. Praise God for the radiance of his presence. Give thanks that you can have fellowship with him and walk in the light. Confess any dark sin that you have not yet exposed to that light. Commit yourself to living by the light of God's truth (1 Jn. 1:5-7). Ask "that your love may abound more and more in knowledge and depth of insight, so that you may be able to discern what is best and may be pure and blameless until the day of Christ, filled with the fruit of righteousness . . ." (Phil. 1:9-11).

For Your Family and Friends
Pray for husbands that they will give spiritual leadership in their households and will love their wives as Christ loved the church.

For the Church
Pray that your church family may be so in love with the Lord, so wanting to please him, that they will see giving as a privilege and a joy, and will make tithing a way of life.

For the Kingdom
Pray that the kingdom of God will spread measurably, visibly, and irresistibly in all parts of the world. Ask that the kingdom of Satan be destroyed.

For the Unsaved
Pray that unsaved persons will receive "Christ Jesus as Lord, continue to live in him, rooted and built up in him, strengthened in faith . . . and overflowing with thankfulness" (Col. 2:6-7).

JANUARY 22

Personal Prayer

Magnify the Lord and exalt his name. Give thanks for the privilege of corporate worship. Confess any irreverent use of his name or wrong use of his day. Commit yourself to worshiping in Spirit and truth. Ask for the fruit of the Spirit in your life: love, joy, peace, patience, kindness, goodness, faithfulness, gentleness, and self-control (Gal. 5:22-23).

For Your Family and Friends

Pray for wives who will have the God-honoring beauty described in 1 Peter 3, who will love their husbands as the church loves Christ, and who will develop their gifts and skills for the sake of family and kingdom.

For the Church

Ask that believers' hearts may be prepared to hear from God and that pastors may faithfully proclaim the Word of God and relate it well to the needs of listeners. Pray that in worship God will receive the glory and the congregation will be edified.

For the Kingdom

Pray that the Lord of nations will bring peace and tranquility in this war-torn world as more and more believers unite in prayer for national renewal, spiritual awakening in the church, and the extension of God's kingdom worldwide.

For the Unsaved

Pray for specific unsaved persons that they may "want to know Christ and the power of his resurrection and the fellowship of sharing in his sufferings, becoming like him in his death, and so . . . attain to the resurrection from the dead" (Phil. 3:10-11).

JANUARY 23

Personal Prayer
Praise God, who is your refuge and strength (Psalm 46). Give thanks for his "ever present help in trouble" (v. 1). Confess any desire to live life apart from God. Commit yourself to being still and knowing that he is God. Ask him to prosper you and not harm you, to give you hope and a future (Jer. 29:11).

For Your Family and Friends
Pray that children and young people will choose godly companions and be protected from those who would lead them astray or wrongly influence their thinking.

For the Church
Pray that your pastor may have a fruitful ministry and that he may handle responsibilities with grace and patience. Ask that he may have a harmonious working relationship with other congregational leaders.

For the Kingdom
Pray for governments to do public justice and to protect the freedoms and rights of individuals, groups, and institutions.

For the Unsaved
Pray that you may "let your light shine before men, that they may see your good deeds and praise your Father in heaven" (Mt. 5:16). Offer to be used of God to reach certain individuals.

Prayer Pointer
"Prayer is the most vital force in world evangelism." —ANONYMOUS

JANUARY 24

Personal Prayer

Praise God as the blessed and only Ruler over all things (1 Tim. 6:15). Thank him for sustaining all things by his powerful Word and holding all things together. Confess any situation in which you have resisted God's rule in your life. Commit yourself to knowing and doing his will. Ask the Lord to put a hedge of protection around you and your loved ones.

For Your Family and Friends

Pray that the lives of children will be filled with growing love, true knowledge, and mature judgment so they will be able to choose what is best (Phil. 1:9-10).

For the Church

Pray that God will give your church members opportunities to witness to people and invite them to church (Col. 4:2-4).

For the Kingdom

Pray for nominal Christians who are caught in worldliness, lukewarmness, ignorance, indifference, and fruitlessness in their religious lives (2 Tim. 3:2-5). Pray that they may be awakened to the true realities of the Christian faith.

For the Unsaved

Pray that unsaved friends, relatives, and neighbors may come to know that "salvation is found in no one else [than Christ], for there is no other name under heaven given to men by which we must be saved" (Acts 4:12).

_____

_____

_____

_____

_____

JANUARY 25

Personal Prayer

Praise God that he is absolutely holy; that there is no sin in him at all. Thank him for making you holy through the blood of Jesus Christ. Confess any known sin that is contrary to God's will. Commit to his lordship in every area of life. Ask that in all you are facing, your faithful God will "not let you be tempted beyond what you can bear," but will always "provide a way out so that you can stand up under it" (1 Cor. 10:13).

For Your Family and Friends

Pray that families and friends experiencing financial problems will be strengthened in faith as they look to God for their "daily bread." Pray that they will seek his blessing and guidance in vocational and financial choices.

For the Church

Pray that children and young people of your church will commit their lives to Jesus Christ, make public profession of faith, and become fruitful members of the kingdom.

For the Kingdom

Pray for Christian schools and colleges, for wise board members, for supportive parents, and godly teachers. Ask God to help the church fulfill its duty of caring for and nurturing its children.

For the Unsaved

Pray that your Christian example may encourage others to seek the Lord. Ask that you will "always be prepared to give an answer to everyone who asks you to give the reason for the hope that you have" (1 Pet. 3:15).

JANUARY 26

Personal Prayer

Praise God that he is trustworthy. Give thanks that his unfailing love surrounds all who trust in him (Ps. 32:10). Confess any doubt you find in your heart. Commit yourself to knowing God better. Ask him to reveal himself to you through his Word and Spirit in the midst of life's circumstances.

For Your Family and Friends

Pray for parents who will create homes that are safe havens for the children, places where love is both tender and tough.

For the Church

Pray that your missionaries will have God's guidance regarding how to present the gospel in a different culture. Ask that they will know God's priorities in order to make the best use of their time.

For the Kingdom

Pray for laborers to be called into God's harvest field. Ask that hearts may be prepared to accept the gospel, and that the necessary tools, such as Bibles and Christian literature, may be readily available.

For the Unsaved

Pray that the barriers to salvation faced by unbelievers today may be demolished, that many may come into the kingdom.

Prayer Pointer

"Who rises from prayer a better man, his prayer is answered." —GEORGE MEREDITH

_____

_____

_____

_____

_____

JANUARY 27

Personal Prayer

Express your love and admiration for the Father, the Son, and the Holy Spirit. Thank the Father for his love, Christ for his grace, and the Holy Spirit for his fellowship. Confess any unresponsiveness to the Father's love, the Savior's grace, and the Holy Spirit's inner working. Commit yourself to loving God with all your heart, soul, mind, and strength. Ask that you may become a temple of the living God so that he will live in you, walk with you, and be your God (2 Cor. 6:16).

For Your Family and Friends

Pray that each family member and friend may develop a close walk with God and spend time with him each day to nurture this relationship.

For the Church

Pray for a congregation whose members are bound by love to each other and willing to say "I am sorry; please forgive me." Pray that the Spirit may mold your congregation into a loving, redemptive fellowship.

For the Kingdom

Pray for those in law enforcement that they may be recognized as God's servants working for the good of the community, "hold[ing] no terror for those who do right, but for those who do wrong" (Rom. 13:3).

For the Unsaved

Pray that the unsaved may realize that life is meaningless apart from God. Ask that they will seek true meaning in him.

_____

_____

_____

_____

_____

JANUARY 28

Personal Prayer

Praise God as the only true God who has revealed himself to you in his Word and through his Son. Give thanks for the Bible through which God reveals himself and his will for your life. Confess any failure to use and respond to that revealed Word. Commit yourself to meditating on the Word and allowing it to dwell richly in your heart (Col. 3:16). Ask that you may remain in Christ and his words in you, so that you can bear much fruit to the Father's glory (Jn. 15:7).

For Your Family and Friends

Pray that children may respect and obey their parents, and that parents may bring up their children in the training and instruction of the Lord (Eph. 6:4).

For the Church

Ask God to supply wisdom to those in charge of your congregational budgets so that dollars received in offerings will be wisely distributed in ways which recognize the Lord's priorities.

For the Kingdom

Pray that the church will be empowered to tell the good news to a world where millions are estranged from God. Ask that believers everywhere will proclaim the forgiveness of sins and new life for all who repent and believe.

For the Unsaved

Pray by name for unsaved friends and neighbors that they may know the love of God, may believe in his Son Jesus Christ, and will not perish but have everlasting life (Jn. 3:16).

_____

_____

_____

_____

_____

JANUARY 29

Personal Prayer
Praise God for the depth of his love, which is the very core of his being (1 Jn. 4:8-9). Thank God that he will never take his love from you or your family (Ps. 103:17). Confess any times during the last week when you gave little thought to God's great love for you. Commit yourself to beginning each day with the refreshment of God's love (Ps. 90:14). Ask that you "may have power . . . to grasp how wide and long and high and deep is the love of Christ, and to know this love that surpasses knowledge" (Eph. 3:17-19).

For Your Family and Friends
Pray that their experience of God's love through you will change their lives.

For the Church
Ask that visitors to your church will sense the love of God in your fellowship and be drawn to find more of it in God's family.

For the Kingdom
Pray for specific places in the world where violence, greed, and hatred are wounding many lives. Pray that this work of Satan will be defeated, overpowered by the love of God shown through Jesus and his church.

For the Unsaved
Pray that the unsaved persons you know will come to know God's love by hearing about the sacrifice of his only Son (1 Jn. 4:10).

JANUARY 30

Personal Prayer

Praise God as the source of every thing that is good, holy, just, and beautiful. Thank God for inviting you to remain in him, as a branch remains in the vine, so that you too can produce fruit that is good and holy (Jn. 15:7-8). Confess your failure to "remain in" Jesus, to find your fullness and your satisfaction in him. Be specific about the things that crowd out your desire to abide in him. Commit yourself to finding your fullness in Jesus during this day. Ask him to show you that apart from him you can do nothing (15:5).

For Your Family and Friends

Pray that parents will be so firmly rooted in Jesus that their children cannot miss seeing the fruit that they bear as his disciples.

For the Church

Pray that the spiritual leaders of your church will see their need to be abiding daily in Jesus and his Word, constantly in prayer, and completely dependent on him for their ministry.

For the Kingdom

Pray that Christians in positions of leadership—business, politics, medicine, teaching—may remain firmly attached to Christ and so bring glory to his name.

For the Unsaved

Make a list of the unsaved persons you know, and ask God to graft each one into the tree of life (Rom. 11:17).

Prayer Pointer

"Arguments never settle things, but prayer changes things." —ANONYMOUS

_____

_____

_____

_____

JANUARY 31

Personal Prayer

Praise God for his deep compassion for the poor, the suffering, the lonely (Isa. 58:5-7). Give thanks for the times when God has lifted you out of the pit of depression or loneliness or from the mire of circumstances (Ps. 40:2). Confess any times recently when your ears have been deaf to the cries of the poor in your area (Mt. 25:31-46). Commit yourself to becoming more aware of their needs. Ask God to show you his heart of compassion and how it can be revealed in your life (Isaiah 58).

For Your Family and Friends

Pray that those friends who are struggling with problems will receive from you the compassion and encouragement they need to go on.

For the Church

Pray that those involved in outreach ministries will offer comfort, compassion, and understanding for those who suffer from poverty, loneliness, abuse, guilt, and insecurity (2 Cor. 1:4).

For the Kingdom

Pray that oppressive governments may learn to respect the rights of all people and that true justice and mercy will prevail in courts and government decisions.

For the Unsaved

Pray that the unsaved persons on your list may experience God's love and compassion through the Christians they meet today.

_____

_____

_____

_____

_____

FEBRUARY 1

Personal Prayer

Praise God that "from him and through him and to him are all things" (Rom. 11:36). Thank God for being both your dwelling place and your destination. Confess times that you have tried to live independently of his authority. Commit yourself to offering your body "as [a] living sacrifice, holy and pleasing to God" (Rom. 12:1). Ask God to help you in "whatever you do, whether in word or deed, [to] do it all in the name of the Lord Jesus" (Col. 3:17).

For Your Family and Friends

Pray for children who struggle against authority, especially adolescents and teens, that they may find God's authority to be good and right in their lives.

For the Church

Pray for teachers who teach with both word and deed how to wholeheartedly love and serve the living God.

For the Kingdom

Pray for your local and regional public officials, that they may remain free from corruption and resist the temptation to misuse their authority.

For the Unsaved

Pray for all the unsaved persons in your city, that "at the name of Jesus every knee should bow, . . . and every tongue confess that Jesus Christ is Lord" (Phil. 2:10-11).

Prayer Pointer

"Prayer is hardest when it is hardest to pray." —ANONYMOUS

_____

_____

_____

_____

_____

FEBRUARY 2

Personal Prayer
Praise God, "the blessed and only Ruler, the King of kings and Lord of lords, who alone is immortal and who lives in unapproachable light" (1 Tim. 6:15-16). Thank him for being the light of the world. Confess any areas of your life that you may have been ashamed to bring into the light of God's truth. Commit yourself to living as a child of the light. Ask God to fill you with the fruit of light: all goodness, righteousness, and truth (Eph. 5:9).

For Your Family and Friends
Pray that any situations of family abuse may be brought into the light and healed.

For the Church
Pray that the missionaries your church supports may be like shining stars in dark places as they hold out the word of life (Phil. 2:15-16).

For the Kingdom
Pray along with thousands of other believers that God will send spiritual renewal to your country and community, pushing back apathy and materialism and setting hearts on fire for the gospel.

For the Unsaved
Pray that those who are sleeping in the darkness of their sins will wake and rise from their sleep of death, that Christ may shine upon them. Pray also that, as God's light in this world, you may make the most of every opportunity (Eph. 5:14-16).

FEBRUARY 3

Personal Prayer
Give glory to God as the Lord of peace. Thank Jesus that he himself is our peace, breaking down the barriers and the dividing walls of hostility (Eph. 2:14). Confess any areas where you are not at peace with another believer or group of Christians. Commit yourself to making every effort to live in peace with all people (Heb. 12:14). Ask God to help you bear with others and forgive whatever grievance you have against them, forgiving them as the Lord forgave you (Col. 3:13).

For Your Family and Friends
Pray for God's peace to be restored between husbands and wives where there is conflict and lack of forgiveness.

For the Church
Pray that the church may "make every effort to keep the unity of the Spirit through the bond of peace" (Eph. 4:3), realizing that as members of one body we are called to peace.

For the Kingdom
Pray for those who are called to settle disputes in our society—labor arbitrators, family counselors, court-appointed mediators, judges, juries—that they may discern the truth and restore goodwill and peace.

For the Unsaved
Pray that the restlessness and conflict in their lives will drive them to seek the peace of God, which transcends all understanding (Phil. 4:7).

_____

_____

_____

_____

_____

FEBRUARY 4

Personal Prayer
Praise God as the giver of every good and perfect gift (Jas. 1:5, 17). Give thanks for the indescribable gift of his only Son. Confess any times when you have taken God's gifts to you for granted. Commit yourself to searching Scripture for more knowledge of the "riches of God's grace that he lavished on us" (Eph. 1:7-8). Ask that your heart's thirst be quenched and your soul's hunger be satisfied in God as with the richest of foods (Psalm 63).

For Your Family and Friends
Pray that their private and family devotions be filled with thanksgiving, and that their hearts be moved to give to causes that help a needy world.

For the Church
Pray that your congregation may have faith that "you will be made rich in every way so that you can be generous on every occasion" (2 Cor. 9:11).

For the Kingdom
Pray for the agencies that show God's love to the needy in your community, that they not only may supply needs but also bring in overflowing expressions of thanks to God (9:12).

For the Unsaved
Pray that they might accept the gospel and be able to say, "How great is the love the Father has lavished on us, that we should be called children of God!" (1 Jn. 3:1).

_____

_____

_____

_____

_____

FEBRUARY 5

Personal Prayer
Praise the King for his powerful rule in this world, and that no plan of his can be thwarted (Job 42:2). Give thanks that this rule is evidenced around us and in us. Confess any doubts which you may have about God's kingly power. Commit yourself to being a living sacrifice, holy and pleasing, as your spiritual worship to God (Rom. 12:1). Ask that you would "never be lacking in zeal, but keep your spiritual fervor, serving the Lord" (12:11).

For Your Family and Friends
Pray that unconditional love will be demonstrated clearly and consistently in your family relationships and friendships. Ask the Lord to give you a fuller appreciation for those whom he has placed in your life.

For the Church
Pray that, as worshipers gather this week, they will be eager to exalt the Lord for his goodness and that their worship will move them to greater obedience.

For the Kingdom
Pray that, in a world filled with sin, "justice will roll on like a river, righteousness like a never-failing stream" (Amos 5:24).

For the Unsaved
Pray that unsaved persons whom you know will ask the reason for the hope that you have, and that you may be prepared to give an answer (1 Pet. 3:15).

Prayer Pointer
"Prayer is an end to isolation. It is living our daily life with someone; with him who alone can deliver us from solitude." —GEORGES LeFEVRE

FEBRUARY 6

Personal Prayer
Praise the saving God whose paths are beyond tracing out! (Rom. 11:33).
Give thanks for his continual, personal care for you. Confess any failure
to maintain a healthy relationship with the Lord. Commit yourself to disciplined, joyful Christian living, recognizing the tremendous blessing of
belonging to Jesus Christ. Ask that you will be "joyful in hope, patient in
affliction, faithful in prayer" (Rom. 12:12).

For Your Family and Friends
Pray that children will respect their parents as the God-given authority in
their lives, and that the counsel of senior family members and friends will
be honored.

For the Church
Pray that church leaders will resist Satan's schemes and will use their influence to lead the church to fulfill its mission of making disciples.

For the Kingdom
Pray that world leaders will have compassion and wisdom and the courage
to lead. Ask God to work in the hearts of these men and women, that they
might see him as their strength.

For the Unsaved
Pray that any personal difficulties experienced by unsaved persons around
you may be opportunities for them to come to know the grace that is found
in Jesus Christ.

FEBRUARY 7

Personal Prayer

Praise the heavenly Father, who has become your Father through Jesus Christ. Give thanks that in Jesus Christ you have been given a heavenly citizenship. Confess those habits which draw you from his love. Commit yourself to finding all that you desire in the Lord. Ask to be delivered from the power of the evil one.

For Your Family and Friends

Pray that family members and friends will reflect the lordship of Christ in their daily schedules, and that relationships will not be neglected.

For the Church

Pray that outreach will receive top priority in all the ministries of the church. Ask God to give his people a renewed vision to carry on the strategic mission of the church.

For the Kingdom

Pray that people who are gripped by the power of money may be freed. Ask God to show these individuals the value of heavenly treasure.

For the Unsaved

Jesus came, not for the healthy, but for the sick. Pray that unsaved persons whom you know will receive spiritual health by faith in Jesus Christ.

Prayer Pointer

"The right way to pray, then, is any way that allows us to communicate with God. For prayer is not a ritual; it is the soul's inherent response to a relationship with a loving Father." —COLLEEN TOWNSEND EVANS

FEBRUARY 8

Personal Prayer
Praise the God who cares even for the birds (Mt. 6:25-34). Give thanks that you can depend upon him completely to meet every need. Confess anything in your life which is rooted in pride and self-reliance. Commit yourself to not worrying about your life or about tomorrow. Ask the Father to help you to "seek first his kingdom and his righteousness . . ." (6:33).

For Your Family and Friends
Ask the compassionate Lord to remember single parents and their children.

For the Church
Pray that the truth will impress the people of your church in a way that causes them to be disciples who disciple others. Ask that words and lives will tell about Jesus.

For the Kingdom
Pray that the judges of the land will be ones who love justice and mercy.

For the Unsaved
Ask that unsaved persons around you will realize the folly of building their lives on foundations of sand. Pray that they will build on the rock, Jesus Christ.

_____

_____

_____

_____

_____

FEBRUARY 9

Personal Prayer

Praise the Maker of heaven and earth for the marvels of creation in this world. Thank the Lord that he never slumbers or sleeps and that he constantly watches over you. Confess those times in which you refuse God's help and resent his watching over you. Commit yourself to trusting fully in the Maker of heaven and earth. Ask that God himself will make you strong, firm, and steadfast (1 Pet. 4:13).

For Your Family and Friends

Pray that marriages in danger of breaking up will be healed and the pain of divorce avoided.

For the Church

Ask God to show churches how they can help to take the gospel to all nations. Pray that these churches will be motivated to do their part.

For the Kingdom

Ask God to encourage and support people whom you know with physical and mental limitations.

For the Unsaved

Pray that God will lead you to befriend an unsaved person. Ask God to use this relationship to bring that new friend to Jesus.

Prayer Pointer

"The first purpose of prayer is to know God." —CHARLES L. ALLEN

_____

_____

_____

_____

_____

FEBRUARY 10

Personal Prayer
Praise God that Jesus Christ is coming again to bring all things to perfection. Thank the Lord that you can anticipate dwelling with him in a new heaven and earth. Confess any attitudes or actions which are hindering the coming kingdom. Commit yourself to watching and praying, being ready for the coming of Christ. Ask that you may live in a way pleasing to God, so that he might say to you, "Well done, good and faithful servant" (Mt 25:21).

For Your Family and Friends
Pray that your family and friends will submit to one another out of reverence for Christ (Eph. 5:21).

For the Church
Ask God to make his people generous in giving their time and gifts for the benefit of others. Ask that the love of Christ will be evident in the care Christians give to each other.

For the Kingdom
Pray that those who suffer the effects of mental illness will find appropriate care. Remember also the families of these individuals.

For the Unsaved
Pray that the unsaved will see that "all have sinned and fall short of the glory of God" (Rom. 3:23), and find their justification in Christ.

_____

_____

_____

_____

_____

FEBRUARY 11

Personal Prayer
Praise God that he is completely trustworthy and that he has never failed anyone (Jn. 14:1-23). Thank God that Jesus Christ is preparing a place for you at this very moment. Confess any reluctance to trust God in everything. Commit yourself to living with your heart as Christ's home. Ask the Lord to do great things through you in the power of the ascended Lord.

For Your Family and Friends
Pray that you and your family and friends will not be ashamed of the gospel, which is God's power for salvation (Rom. 1:16).

For the Church
Pray that church members will view their finances as belonging to God and will give as the Lord has given to them.

For the Kingdom
Ask that our society will respect the value of human life at every stage of life. Pray especially for people who today are making decisions about the life of another.

For the Unsaved
Jesus said, "I am the way and the truth and the life. No one comes to the Father except through me" (Jn. 14:6). Pray that unsaved persons whom you know will accept this truth.

Prayer Pointer
"Trouble and perplexity drive me to prayer and prayer drives away perplexity and trouble." —PHILIPPE MELANCHTHON

_____

_____

_____

_____

_____

FEBRUARY 12

Personal Prayer
Praise God, the giver of wisdom and power (Dan. 2:20). Give thanks for opportunities to worship with others, to learn from God's wisdom, and to be touched by his presence. Confess attempts to survive through mere human wisdom and power. Commit yourself to carefully applying what God teaches you today. Ask God to empower you to live accordingly.

For Your Family and Friends
Pray that your household and friends will be ready to learn from God's wisdom and to be touched by his power.

For the Church
Pray that God's powerful presence will be sensed from the opening moments of worship this Sunday. Ask that all will be empowered to leave with the knowledge that God can work through their lives.

For the Kingdom
Pray that your company, culture, city, and country will submit to the wisdom of God. Ask God to help you to live openly for Jesus in every area of influence.

For the Unsaved
Pray for unsaved persons you know by name. Ask God to work through the power of his Holy Spirit to convict them of sin and lead them into his truth (Jn. 16:7-11). Ask God to use you to love them.

FEBRUARY 13

Personal Prayer

Praise God, the changer of times and seasons (Dan. 2:21), who is in control of all of history. Give thanks for this new day. Confess any misuse or waste of time. Commit yourself to taking hold of today's opportunities and to enjoying the special pleasures God provides during this season. Ask him to guide you to make wise and efficient use of your time.

For Your Family and Friends

Pray that God will give you wisdom to spend time with family and friends. Ask him to protect those special times together so that your relationships will flourish.

For the Church

Pray that your church leaders will be protected from overloaded schedules. Ask God to give them wisdom as they lead the church and care for their other concerns.

For the Kingdom

Pray that local and denominational leaders will sense God's timing in deciding when to move forward with new ministries or to make changes in existing ones.

For the Unsaved

Ask God to show an unsaved friend that "now is the time of God's favor, now is the day of salvation" (2 Cor. 6:2). Pray that he or she responds to God soon, while there is time.

Prayer Pointer

"When we say to people, 'I will pray for you,' we make a very important commitment. The sad thing is that this remark often remains nothing but a well-meant expression of concern." —Henri Nouwen

FEBRUARY 14

Personal Prayer

Praise God as the one who sets up leaders and deposes them (Dan. 2:21). Give thanks for your own opportunities to lead others. Confess any negligence or cowardice in leadership. Commit yourself to being a leader of integrity wherever God gives you influence. Ask God to grant you wisdom as you influence your children, friends, employees, and others.

For Your Family and Friends

Pray for God-honoring pacesetters among the peer groups of your children. Pray that your own influence on your family and friends will lead them closer to God.

For the Church

Pray that your church's outreach efforts will be guided by a clear vision of what God can do to gather and guide his family. Pray that you will have the courage to help your church minister to people beyond the church walls.

For the Kingdom

Pray for "all those in authority, that we may live peaceful and quiet lives in all godliness and holiness" (1 Tim. 2:2). Pray that leaders who uphold God's principles will be brought to power throughout the world so that the gospel will be unhindered.

For the Unsaved

Pray that God will use you to lead someone into a right relationship with him.

_____

_____

_____

_____

_____

FEBRUARY 15

Personal Prayer

Praise God because "he gives wisdom to the wise and knowledge to the discerning. He reveals deep and hidden things" (Dan. 2:21-22). Thank God for revealing himself to you in his written Word. Confess any lack of interest or discipline in regularly reading and meditating on God's Word. Commit yourself to a steady and balanced spiritual diet. Ask God to be your teacher, leading you to knowledge and wisdom.

For Your Family and Friends

Pray that your family and friends will grow not only in knowing about God but also in knowing God himself.

For the Church

Pray that the people who conduct your church's education ministry will diligently prepare lessons and lovingly involve themselves with their class members. Pray that both adults and children will continue to learn and grow.

For the Kingdom

Thank God for the people writing and editing church education materials. Ask that these materials will be tools to help believers apply God's Word to daily decisions.

For the Unsaved

Pray that God will use you to lead unsaved people out of the darkness of ignorance and rebellion into the light of his truth.

Prayer Pointer

"The prime need of the church is not men of money nor men of brains, but men of prayer." —E. M. BOUNDS

FEBRUARY 16

Personal Prayer

Praise the most high God, whose kingdom is eternal and who is sovereign over all the earth (Dan. 4:2-3, 17). Thank God for being your Lord, as well as your Savior. Confess any pockets of resistance to his rule in your life. Commit your full and lifelong allegiance to the Lord. Ask him to use you in extending his rule.

For Your Family and Friends

Pray that your family will be God's loyal subjects in his kingdom. Pray that "the footprints that we leave will lead them to believe, and the lives we live inspire them to obey."

For the Church

Ask God to develop a global vision in you and your church. Pray specifically for missionaries and their families whom you know.

For the Kingdom

Thank God for those who are called to serve as missionaries in other countries. Ask him to help them learn the languages and customs and to serve effectively as his ambassadors in lands foreign to them.

For the Unsaved

Pray that people in other countries who hear the message of the gospel presented by strangers will be led into an intimate love of God.

_____

_____

_____

_____

_____

FEBRUARY 17

Personal Prayer

Praise God, the one who rescues and saves (Dan. 4:27). Give thanks for specific ways he is caring for you right now. Confess any areas in which you are worrying instead of praying and accepting his loving care (Phil. 4:6-7). Commit a concern to God, thanking him for his care for you. Ask him to help you believe in his willingness to handle it.

For Your Family and Friends

Pray that your family and friends may be rooted and established in love and may have "power, together with all the saints, to grasp how wide and long and high and deep is the love of Christ, and to know this love that surpasses knowledge—that [they] may be filled to the measure of all the fullness of God" (Eph. 3:18-19).

For the Church

Pray that your church will be a fellowship which experiences the signs and wonders of God's loving care. Pray for those especially in need of care or friendship right now, and offer yourself to God as his caregiving child.

For the Kingdom

Pray for relief workers extending care in the name of Jesus Christ to those suffering from recent disasters. Pray that the care is given openly in Jesus' name.

For the Unsaved

Pray for at least three unsaved people you know. Ask God to use you in finding and enfolding them into his growing family.

FEBRUARY 18

Personal Prayer

Praise God, the ultimate owner of all, who gives and takes away the privilege of managing those resources (Daniel 4). Thank God for specific resources he has put under your care. Confess any attempts to own (rather than manage) "your" money. Commit yourself to being a faithful steward who puts God's kingdom and righteousness first (Mt. 6:33). Ask him to teach you the secret of being content in any and every situation (Phil. 4:12).

For Your Family and Friends

Pray that God will give you, your family, and your friends the daily provisions you need (Mt. 6:11). Ask also that you all will excel in the grace of giving (2 Cor. 8:7).

For the Church

Pray that believers will be diligent and loving in returning the first portion of their income to God. Ask that needed church resources will be provided and handled with utmost integrity.

For the Kingdom

Pray that God's name will be honored in Christian ministries by their prudent management of resources.

For the Unsaved

Pray that the unsaved will notice the generous and enthusiastic support of gospel ministries throughout the world by God's people and be attracted to him.

_____

_____

_____

_____

_____

FEBRUARY 19

Personal Prayer

Praise God for his holiness and righteousness. Thank him for promising to work all things together for good. Confess any coldness of heart. Commit yourself to becoming more and more conformed to the image of Christ (Rom. 8:29). Ask God to renew your love for him as it was when you first believed.

For Your Family and Friends

Pray that the future spouses of your children and unmarried friends may be persons who are godly, humble, and obedient to God. Ask God to honor himself in these marriages.

For the Church

Pray for your pastor and family today. Ask that God would use your pastor to convey his message to the church with power and anointing. Pray that your church will respond positively to the pulpit ministry with heartfelt praise and worship of God.

For the Kingdom

Lift up oppressed peoples who are open to the gospel. Ask God to prepare their hearts, to keep them from false religions, and to cause them to discern and reject false doctrine.

For the Unsaved

Ask God to lay on your heart those for whom he desires you to pray. Request the Holy Spirit to show you how to pray for each person.

Prayer Pointer

"Productive prayer requires earnestness, not eloquence." —ANONYMOUS

_____

_____

_____

_____

FEBRUARY 20

Personal Prayer

Praise Jesus for being "the same yesterday and today and forever" (Heb. 13:8). Thank him for always being with you regardless of your circumstances. Confess your weakness and inability to escape certain temptations. Commit your way to the Lord's total control. Ask for his help today to overcome sin in your life.

For Your Family and Friends

Ask the Lord to give harmony and peace to your family and friends. Pray that each person will respect and honor others, following God's plan for relationships in the family (Eph. 5:22-6:4).

For the Church

Pray that church leaders will be conscientious, seeking God's will and not their own. Ask that they will have a servant's heart in ministry and work in harmony and unity with all.

For the Kingdom

Pray that believers will be strengthened to recognize God's voice and reject the enemy's lies and tricks "in order that Satan may not outwit us" (2 Cor. 2:11).

For the Unsaved

Ask God to disturb the hearts of the unsaved so they find no rest or satisfaction in anything apart from him (Eccl. 1:2; 2:17). Pray that the Holy Spirit will bring strong conviction of sin to them.

FEBRUARY 21

Personal Prayer

Praise God for his limitless power. Thank the Spirit for being "in you" and for being "greater than the one who is in the world" (1 Jn. 4:4). Confess moments when you have limited God's power because of doubts or unbelief. Commit yourself to living in the presence and power of God every day. Ask him to make you more aware of his presence and protection daily and not to take it for granted.

For Your Family and Friends

Ask God to help children choose their friends wisely. Pray that young people will not give into the "evil desires" of this world (2 Tim. 2:22).

For the Church

Pray that each member of your church will have a strong burden for unsaved people they know. Ask that they will have the courage to speak when God gives them the opportunities.

For the Kingdom

Pray that believers worldwide will be strengthened for the spiritual battles they face. Ask that they will "put on the full armor of God so that [they] can take [their] stand against the devil's schemes" (Eph. 6:10-18).

For the Unsaved

Ask God to provide answers for unsaved persons you know who have serious questions about the claims of Christ. Pray that God will use you to provide some answers.

_____

_____

_____

_____

_____

FEBRUARY 22

Personal Prayer

Praise God for his abundant mercy. Thank him for not punishing you as your sins have deserved (Ezra 9:13). Confess any secret sins which hold you back from full fellowship with God. Commit yourself to turning away from sin by the power of the Holy Spirit and living completely for God's glory. Ask God to restore the joy of his salvation and to grant you a willing spirit (Ps. 51:12).

For Your Family and Friends

Ask that your family and friends will hunger and thirst for God, walk closely with him always, and take time for prayer and Bible reading.

For the Church

Ask God to inspire teachers and group leaders as they prepare Bible lessons this week. Pray that they will be able to communicate clearly and faithfully.

For the Kingdom

Pray for your elected and appointed public servants. Ask that they will initiate and enact laws based on godly principles (Prov. 14:34).

For the Unsaved

Ask the Lord to create a hunger and thirst for him and his Word in the lives of unsaved persons you know. Pray that you will be sensitive to their struggles and questions.

FEBRUARY 23

Personal Prayer

Rejoice in God's majesty, glory, and might. Thank God that in all things he works for the good of those who love him (Rom. 8:28). Confess any fear, worry, or anxiety you may be feeling about your present circumstances. Commit your day to God and rest in his good planning for your life (Prov. 3:5-6). Ask for his peace to remain with you throughout your day.

For Your Family and Friends

Ask God to convict and bring back any family member or friend who has strayed from him.

For the Church

Ask God to help each member see the fields that are ready for harvest and to respond accordingly. Pray for the physical, emotional, and spiritual health of all the missionaries your church supports.

For the Kingdom

Pray that believers everywhere will walk in truth and unity. Ask the Holy Spirit to draw them closer to each other.

For the Unsaved

Pray that the Holy Spirit will show self-righteous people the truth and comfort of salvation by grace alone (Eph. 2:8-9).

Prayer Pointer

"I have been driven many times to my knees by the overwhelming conviction that I had nowhere else to go." —ABRAHAM LINCOLN

FEBRUARY 24

Personal Prayer

Praise God for his controlling presence everywhere. Give thanks that no circumstance in life—even death itself—is beyond his loving control. Confess your desire to act according to your own timetable rather than God's. Commit yourself to drawing closer to God in every way and waiting patiently for him. Ask for the ability to live by faith and not by sight (2 Cor. 5:7).

For Your Family and Friends

Request that a hedge of protection be placed around each family member and friend to fend off the enemy's attacks.

For the Church

Ask that members will have the humility and gentleness to consider others better than themselves. Pray that believers will not only look out for their own interests, but also for the interests of others (Phil. 2:3-4).

For the Kingdom

Ask God to bless the training of Christian workers who desire to take the gospel into cultures which are unlike their own. Pray that the Spirit will remove any doubt or fear from them and their families as they prepare to serve as mission workers.

For the Unsaved

Name the name of one unsaved person whom you know. Ask God to bring that person to salvation. Pray that you may be used to lead that person to Jesus and then commit yourself to obedience.

_____

_____

_____

_____

_____

FEBRUARY 25

Personal Prayer

Praise God for caring intimately about you. Thank God for choosing you to help fulfill his plans. Confess any self-centeredness or preoccupation with your desires and needs rather than those of God and others. Commit yourself to walking under the Spirit's control, trusting him with the circumstances of life (Ps. 31:15). Ask for more sensitivity to the needs of others.

For Your Family and Friends

Ask God to meet the needs of family members and friends who are experiencing a financial, physical, or emotional crisis.

For the Church

Pray for the prosperity of the members of your congregation. Pray especially for those on fixed incomes that they will have sufficient means to live. Ask God's blessing on the deacons of your church as they manage the temporal resources of your congregation.

For the Kingdom

Ask for urgency and boldness for believers worldwide. Pray that they will never grow deaf to God's call to the harvest fields.

For the Unsaved

Pray for persons who have decided to follow false religions. Ask God to open their hearts and minds to Jesus Christ, who is the way, the truth, and the life (Jn. 14:6).

Prayer Pointer

"We ought not to tolerate for a minute the ghastly and grievous thought that God will not answer prayer. History, as manifested in Christ Jesus, demands it."
—CHARLES H. SPURGEON

_____

_____

_____

FEBRUARY 26

Personal Prayer

Praise God as the one who can wash every part of your life clean from the stain of sin. Thank him for offering his only Son as a sacrifice for you (Jn. 3:16). Confess those times when you have listened to Satan's accusations of guilt even after confessing your sin to God. Commit yourself to receiving God's forgiveness and acceptance of you with a free and joyful heart. Ask the Lord to help you see yourself through his eyes—clean, holy, and dearly loved (Eph. 1:3-8).

For Your Family and Friends

Pray that those in your circle of relatives or friends who have not yet found cleansing for their sin may do so this year.

For the Church

Pray that the spirit of worship in your congregation is not hindered by some members' refusal to forgive others or themselves (Eph. 4:32).

For the Kingdom

Pray that those involved in fighting, racial conflict, or persecution may find God's forgiveness and cleansing and offer it to their enemies.

For the Unsaved

Pray that your love and forgiveness for your critics and opponents will attract them to the same God that you love and serve (Lk. 6:27-29, 35-36).

Personal Prayer

Give praise to God as the Spirit of wisdom and understanding, the Spirit of counsel and of knowledge (Isa. 11:2). Thank God for freely giving wisdom to all who ask and who trust him to answer (Jas. 1:5). Confess those times in the past week or month when you have relied on human wisdom rather than seeking God's wisdom. Commit yourself to seeking God's wisdom at all costs (Prov. 2:1-6). Ask God to show you how his wisdom is different from the world's (Jas. 3:13-18).

For Your Family and Friends

Pray that God will give your young people the discernment and ability to choose the way of wisdom over foolishness (Prov. 2:12-15).

For the Church

Pray that your church's leaders will be filled with wisdom as they make both public and private decisions, so that their whole lives will glorify God.

For the Kingdom

Pray for wisdom for all political leaders whose decisions will affect the lives of thousands or millions.

For the Unsaved

Pray that God will use you to share with an unsaved friend "the Scriptures which are able to make you wise for salvation" (2 Tim. 3:15).

Prayer Pointer

"Prayer requires more of the heart than of the tongue." —ADAM CLARKE

FEBRUARY 28

Personal Prayer

Worship God with reverence and awe as a consuming fire blazing with holiness (Heb. 12:28-29). Give thanks for his plan to refine your faith through trials and tests (Jas. 1:2-4). Confess any times this week when you have not seen God's purpose for you in these trials (Mal. 3:2-4). Commit yourself to submitting to God's testing in your life. Ask God to strengthen you with his power (Eph. 6:10-11).

For Your Family and Friends

Pray for those who are undergoing severe testing, that God may show them his purpose and strengthen them in their weakness (Heb. 12:7-13).

For the Church

Pray for those who work in your church's outreach programs, that they may help unsaved people to see God's love and purposes through the trials they face in their lives.

For the Kingdom

Pray that Christians in leadership positions around the world will not fall under testing but be strengthened. Their witness is crucial!

For the Unsaved

Pray that God will lead you to pray this week with an unsaved person who struggles with trials in his or her life.

MARCH 1

Personal Prayer

Praise God as the creator of all life, including your own (Isa. 45:18). Give thanks for his splendor, seen in all his mighty creation (Psalm 148). Confess to God those times when you have forgotten that all of your life and this world is a creation of God. Commit yourself to seeing your life as God's workmanship, created in Christ Jesus (Eph. 2:10). Ask God to show you the good works that he has prepared in advance for you to do.

For Your Family and Friends

Pray that parents will raise their children as the handiwork of God and encourage their children's creativity as image-bearers of the Creator.

For the Church

Pray that those who educate in the church will be able to teach children that they have a new self, which is being renewed in knowledge in the image of their Creator (Col. 3:10).

For the Kingdom

Pray for the public and private schools in your area, that they may nurture rather than stunt children's awareness of God, the Creator.

For the Unsaved

Pray that people may once again worship and serve the Creator rather than the things that God created (Rom. 1:25).

Prayer Pointer

"Teach us to pray that we may cause
The enemy to flee,
That we his evil power may bind,
His prisoners to free." —WATCHMAN NEE

Personal Prayer
Glorify the Almighty God, who has the power to defeat your accuser and deceiver, Satan (Rev. 12:7-10). Thank God that his immeasurable power is at work within you (Eph. 3:20). Confess those times when you have tried to battle against Satan in your own strength. Commit yourself to living in God's all-surpassing power (2 Cor. 4:7). Ask God to help you see how his power can be made perfect in your weakness (2 Cor. 12:9).

For Your Family and Friends
Pray that Christian families may be given the power to withstand Satan's attacks on their homes and relationships.

For the Church
Pray for your foreign missionaries, that they may be given divine power to demolish arguments and take people's thoughts captive for Christ (2 Cor. 10:4-5).

For the Kingdom
Pray for those countries that are clearly under Satan's power, marked by cruelty, injustice, and horrible poverty. Ask God to bring his light into the darkness.

For the Unsaved
Pray that, through you, Jesus might turn people from the power of Satan to God (Acts 26:18).

MARCH 3

Personal Prayer

Praise God, whose kindness toward you will last forever and ever. Thank God for loving you with an everlasting love and drawing you with lovingkindness (Jer. 31:3). Confess any ways in which you have not reflected that kindness to others. Commit yourself to considering God's kindness to you (Rom. 11:22). Ask God to clothe you with compassion, kindness, and humility (Col. 3:12).

For Your Family and Friends

Pray for a prevailing spirit of kindness between husbands and wives, parents and children.

For the Church

Pray that your neighborhood may see the kindness, compassion, and forgiveness of God in the way the members of your congregation treat each other and outsiders.

For the Kingdom

Pray that the poor, the mentally ill, the lonely, and the abused may be treated with great kindness and respect in the places where they live and by the people who work to serve them.

For the Unsaved

Pray that you might have an opportunity this week to tell someone of the many kindnesses of the Lord to you (Isa. 63:7).

MARCH 4

Personal Prayer

Praise God, whose incomparable riches are revealed in Christ Jesus (Eph. 2:7). Give thanks for your inheritance that can never perish, spoil, or fade—kept in heaven for you (1 Pet. 1:4). Confess those times when you have valued material things over your inheritance in Jesus Christ. Commit yourself to appreciating daily your inheritance from God (Ps. 16:6). Ask the Holy Spirit to teach you more about what you have received through faith in Christ.

For Your Family and Friends

Pray that parents may be wise enough to pass on a spiritual inheritance to their children—faith in Christ—and to retell the stories of faith from grandparents and older members of the church.

For the Church

Pray that your church's giving may be generous in response to neighborhood needs, knowing that as you give, it will be given you (Lk. 6:38).

For the Kingdom

Pray for the poor who trust in the Lord to meet their needs, that God will be their rich inheritance and their provider.

For the Unsaved

Pray that unsaved persons also may come to share in the inheritance of the saints in the kingdom of light (Col. 1:12).

Prayer Pointer

"Without prayer no work is well done."—ANONYMOUS

MARCH 5

Personal Prayer
Praise God for being the Creator and Lord of the Sabbath. Give thanks for a weekly "day of rest and gladness." Confess any lack of commitment to the holiness of the Christian Sabbath (Ex. 20:8-11). Commit yourself to seeking Jesus' honor in all your Sabbath activities. Ask God to make it a day of true joy and light for you and your loved ones.

For Your Family and Friends
Pray that your loved ones will experience physical and emotional rest from the cares and concerns of daily life.

For the Church
As your church gathers to worship and fellowship, pray that your pastor will be empowered by the Holy Spirit as he brings God's Word to you.

For the Kingdom
Ask God to bring about the day when his people in every nation will "live in peaceful dwelling places . . . in undisturbed places of rest" (Isa. 32:18).

For the Unsaved
Pray that multitudes of unbelievers will hear and obey Jesus' invitation to "come to me, all you who are weary and burdened, and I will give you rest" (Mt. 11:28).

Prayer Pointer
"Prayer is the language of a man burdened with a sense of need." —E. M. BOUNDS

_____

_____

_____

_____

_____

MARCH 6

Personal Prayer

Praise God, who is majestic in holiness (Ex. 15:11). Give thanks for the privilege of sharing in his holiness (Heb. 12:10). Confess any impure thoughts or actions that remained unconfessed. Commit yourself anew to living the holy life that God has called you to live (1 Thess. 4:7). Ask God to impress upon you the vision of Isaiah: "Holy, holy, holy is the LORD Almighty; the whole earth is full of his glory" (Isa. 6:3).

For Your Family and Friends

Pray that your loved ones will be drawn closer to God as they see your example of holy living.

For the Church

Ask that your church leaders may exhibit holiness as they carry out their responsibilities in your congregation, in their personal lives, and in their work. Pray that their holiness will be based on the holiness of God, rather than on the expectations of others.

For the Kingdom

Holiness in life is mocked by much of our modern culture. Pray that this attribute of God will become an abiding characteristic of his kingdom here on earth.

For the Unsaved

Pray that men and women, boys and girls around the world may turn from sin and seek the Lord—for "without holiness no one will see the Lord" (Heb. 12:14).

_____

_____

_____

_____

_____

MARCH 7

Personal Prayer

Praise God, who fills you with rich spiritual food (Isa. 55:2). Thank God for not allowing you to go hungry for spiritual nourishment. Confess any craving you may have for things which are not spiritually satisfying (55:2). Commit yourself to daily feeding on Jesus, the living bread (Jn. 6:51). Ask God to instill in you a hunger for the Word of Life.

For Your Family and Friends

Pray that any of your loved ones who are physically or spiritually malnourished will receive the food that they need.

For the Church

Pray that those involved in outreach from your congregation will be empowered to offer "the bread of God . . . who comes down from heaven and gives life to the world" (Jn. 6:33).

For the Kingdom

Pray for Christian agencies of mercy who take nourishing food and clean water to starving nations on the African continent. Ask that they may also take the gospel message.

For the Unsaved

Pray for any persons you know who are dying spiritually. Pray for opportunities to invite them to the sumptuous wedding banquet of the king (Mt. 22:2-10).

Prayer Pointer

"Prayerless pews make powerless pulpits." —ANONYMOUS

MARCH 8

Personal Prayer
Praise the Rock—the one whose works are perfect and whose ways are just (Deut. 32:4). Thank him for being the God of truth. Confess any times that you have believed the lies of Satan and acted accordingly. Commit yourself to speaking only the truth in every situation (Eph. 4:25). Ask God to help you be a truthful person in whom he would delight (Ps. 12:2).

For Your Family and Friends
Ask that your loved ones will discover the preciousness of God's truth (Prov. 23:23).

For the Church
Pray that the truth of God's Word will be the solid foundation of the educational programs in your congregation.

For the Kingdom
Reflect on Jn. 8:44. Pray against the influence of Satan—"the father of lies"—as he attempts to subvert the spread of the gospel throughout the earth. Ask that his lies will be exposed in every arena of life.

For the Unsaved
Jesus said, "I am the way and the truth and the life" (Jn. 14:6). Pray that unsaved persons you know will submit themselves to this Savior and begin to live in the light of his teachings.

Personal Prayer

Praise God for being perfectly just in all his works. Thank him for loving righteousness and justice (Ps. 33:5). Confess any ungodly bias you harbor toward any people. Commit yourself to viewing others with a loving, Christlike attitude. Ask God to help you value justice more highly in all relationships of life.

For Your Family and Friends

Pray that the members of your family will treat each other with mutual love and respect.

For the Church

Ask God to give wisdom and discernment to missionaries in other countries who must suffer injustices and slander for the sake of the gospel. Ask that they will have patience with and love for persons who treat them unfairly.

For the Kingdom

Pray for the uprooting of governments which oppress their citizens and withhold justice from them. Ask that justice will "roll on like a river, righteousness like a never-failing stream" (Amos 5:24) in countries held in the grip of lawlessness.

For the Unsaved

Pray that those who are seeking for God will be drawn to the one who does not show favoritism, but "blesses all who call on him" (Rom. 10:12).

Prayer Pointer

"He who prays as he ought, will endeavor to live as he prays." —JOHN OWEN

_____

_____

_____

_____

_____

MARCH 10

Personal Prayer

Praise God for being a welcoming Father. Thank him for preparing an eternal home for all who believe (Jn. 14:2). Confess any unwillingness to show Christian hospitality to others (1 Pet. 4:9). Commit yourself to the practice of hospitality (Rom. 12:13). Ask God to help you separate Christian hospitality from self-absorbed "entertaining."

For Your Family and Friends

Pray for opportunities to use your home or apartment as a tool for ministering the welcoming love of Christ to unsaved loved ones.

For the Church

Pray that the members of your congregation will excel in showing mutual care and intentional acts of love toward each other and to outsiders. Ask God to move your church out of its "comfort zone" when it comes to showing hospitality.

For the Kingdom

Pray that the practice of hospitality might be a significant factor in breaking down walls of misunderstanding and distrust which divide Christians today.

For the Unsaved

Pray that your example of godly, welcoming hospitality might be a first step for some unsaved persons to come to Jesus.

MARCH 11

Personal Prayer

Praise God, the giver of all good gifts (Mt. 7:11). Thank him for the greatest gift of all: his Son, Jesus Christ, our Savior (Lk. 22:19). Confess any lack of thankfulness for all of God's gifts to you. Commit yourself to giving your time, talents, and resources for the gospel. Ask God to grant you a heart of generosity (Lk. 6:38).

For Your Family and Friends

Children and parents are a rich blessing from the Lord. Give thanks for your children, grandchildren, and parents. Pray that your friends, too, will recognize and appreciate the gift of family.

For the Church

Pray that the members of your church will be faithful in managing their personal resources and cheerful in bringing their tithes and offerings to the Lord (2 Cor. 9:7).

For the Kingdom

Pray that all Christian ministries will be blessed with overflowing abundance. Ask God to give wisdom and integrity in the handling of their financial resources.

For the Unsaved

Pray by name for one unsaved friend or loved one. Ask God to open this person's heart to receive the indescribable gift of salvation through faith alone (2 Cor. 9:15; Eph. 2:8-9).

MARCH 12

Personal Prayer

Using Psalm 145, praise the King whose greatness goes beyond your comprehension (145:1, 3). Give thanks for the opportunity to worship him. Confess any unwillingness or negligence in daily worship (145:2). Commit yourself to meditating on his works and proclaiming his great deeds daily (145:3-7). Ask God to lead you in worship that brings him joy.

For Your Family and Friends

Pray for God to open hearts and minds of specific family members to his greatness. Ask God's Spirit to help you tell the stories of his greatness to your children or the children of friends (145:4).

For the Church

Ask God to prompt the saints in your church to join in praising him for his grace, compassion, and patience (145:8-10). Pray that such praise will convince many to follow the Lord (145:11-13).

For the Kingdom

Pray that people around the world will lift their eyes to God (145:13-15). Ask God to show his greatness by continuing to provide for all his creatures (145:16).

For the Unsaved

Ask God to show himself to specific friends in such ways that they are impressed by his great acts of love and call upon him in truth rather than continuing toward destruction (145:17-20). Pray that your faithful praise will attract them to worshipful lives of praise (145:21).

_____

_____

_____

_____

_____

MARCH 13

Personal Prayer

Praise our God, who is unfailing in love and great in compassion (Ps. 51:1-2). Give thanks for the forgiveness of all your past, present, and future sins through Jesus' death 2,000 years ago! Confess that your sin has been against God himself (51:3-5). Commit to the full integrity of having God's truth and wisdom in the inner recesses of your heart (51:6). Ask God for full cleansing, purity, joy, and gladness (51:7-9).

For Your Family and Friends

Pray for a pure and steady heart for each of your household members and friends (51:10). Ask God for a willing spirit to stay in the joy of his Spirit (51:11-12).

For the Church

Pray for the integrity and understanding of your church's leaders. Ask God to give them effectiveness in equipping you to lead people to God's forgiveness and righteousness (51:13-14).

For the Kingdom

Pray that God will raise up religious and political leaders who understand God's desire for right relationships with him rather than mere lip service or token gestures (51:16-17). Ask God to lead his kingdom into true repentance and revival.

For the Unsaved

Pray for God's Spirit to open opportunities for witnessing to a friend. Ask him to lead you and your contacts into a life that brings delight to him (51:18-19).

MARCH 14

Personal Prayer

Read Psalm 24 and praise God as the King of glory, the Lord strong and mighty, the Lord mighty in battle, the Lord almighty! Give thanks for God's power poured into your life and ministries. Confess any attempts to live and minister by your power instead of the power of the Spirit. Commit yourself to being a channel of his powerful love. Ask God to give you clean hands, a pure heart, integrity of soul and honest speech (24:4), so his power can flow through you unhindered.

For Your Family and Friends

Pray that your family and friends will seek God's face (24:3) and be allowed into his presence through Christ. Ask God to work with power on a particular need in your home.

For the Church

Pray that God will powerfully prompt your church to reach out. Ask God to make those outreach efforts effective, bringing many into fellowship with him and his people.

For the Kingdom

Pray that God will strengthen church planters and developers and their core groups. Ask God to make all churches in your denomination effective in their outreach efforts.

For the Unsaved

Pray that God will bring a powerful revival to your nation. Ask him to bring his almighty, King-of-glory presence into your neighborhood through your own example and words.

MARCH 15

Personal Prayer

Read Psalm 139 and praise the all-knowing one who perfectly knows you in every action, thought, and word (139:1, 4). Thank God for the comforting knowledge that he is with you wherever you go (139:5-6). Confess any attempt to flee his all-knowing presence (139:7-12). Commit yourself to learning more about these wonderful human bodies he has made (139:13-16). Ask him to give you a love for knowing his thoughts (139:17-18), an informed hatred for those he hates (139:19-22), and an "open-book" relationship with him (139:23-24).

For Your Family and Friends

Pray that God will give those you know and love a love for knowing him. Ask that they be filled with a conscious desire to think God's thoughts after him (139:17-18).

For the Church

Pray by name for your church's Bible study leaders, Sunday school teachers, and others. Ask God to help them prepare sensitively and thoroughly.

For the Kingdom

Pray that your nation will repent of willful ignorance of God's thoughts and ways. Ask that the beauty and purpose of human life be accepted and promoted (139:12-16).

For the Unsaved

Pray by name for unsaved friends. Ask God to lead you in helping them to truly know him (139:23-24).

_____

_____

_____

_____

_____

MARCH 16

Personal Prayer

Read Psalm 108 and praise the Lord, whose love is higher than the heavens and whose faithfulness reaches to the skies. Give thanks for specific acts of faithfulness to you so far this week. Confess any unfaithfulness which has robbed God of his glory. Commit yourself to praising God among the nations (108:3). Ask him to show you the nations in our cities and around the globe.

For Your Family and Friends

Pray especially for any family members or friends living in another country. Ask God to also use them in showing his glory over all the earth (108:5).

For the Church

Pray for a more visible unity in his church throughout the world, giving the world a credible witness to his love (John 17:20ff). Ask God to focus your eyes more on oneness than differences.

For the Kingdom

Pray that God will be exalted "above the heavens" and have his "glory be over all the earth" (Ps. 108:5) through broadcast missions and on-site missionaries.

For the Unsaved

Pray that everyone will see clearly that human strength cannot win the battle for peoples' hearts (108:12-13). Ask God to gain the victory over spiritual enemies that bind the unsaved.

_____

_____

_____

_____

MARCH 17

Personal Prayer

Praise the Lord, who made and cares for heaven and earth, the sea, and everything in them (Ps. 146:1-6). Give thanks for his personal care for you. Confess instances of putting ultimate trust "in mortal men, who cannot save" (146:3). Commit yourself to putting your hope in the Lord your God. Ask God to help you hand your cares to him through daily prayer.

For Your Family and Friends

Pray that your children (or those of your friends) will learn to present their concerns to God. Ask God to help you authentically model such prayer.

For the Church

Pray that your local church grows as a loving people who genuinely administer God's care. Ask for great wisdom for the deacons and the leaders of care/fellowship committees or groups.

For the Kingdom

Pray that God will continually prompt his people to join him in caring for those oppressed or otherwise in need (146:7-10). Ask God to grant corporate and individual wisdom, persistence, and love in seeking to extend his kingdom.

For the Unsaved

Pray that the witness of God's people will be consistent in word and deed. Ask God to guide you in helping specific people in your neighborhood to put their trust in the caring God.

MARCH 18

Personal Prayer
Praise God as "the Mighty One, God, the Lord" who owns "every animal of the forest . . . the cattle on a thousand hills . . . the creatures of the field . . . the world . . . and all that is in it" (Ps. 50:1, 10-12). Give thanks for the blessings God has put under your care. Confess any irresponsible decisions you have made with his resources. Commit to being a wise and faithful manager of all he gives to you. Ask him to prompt you to wise stewardship from a spirit of thankfulness (50:14-15).

For Your Family and Friends
Pray for God's special treasure of loving relationships. Ask his help in managing these with great care and joy.

For the Church
Pray that your church's members will care for one another in love. Ask God to prompt them to loving generosity with his treasures.

For the Kingdom
Pray for God's blessing on all relief agencies which help people exercise appropriate dominion (Gen. 1:28-30). Ask God to enable you to see and respond to the needs of these aid-givers.

For the Unsaved
Pray that the unsaved will more responsibly care for this planet as they observe the stewardship of God's people.

Prayer Pointer
"Prayer is first and foremost an act of love." —BRENNAN MANNING

MARCH 19

Personal Prayer

Praise the wonderful God who causes mountains and hills to burst into song and all the trees of the fields to clap their hands (Isa. 55:12). Give thanks that the Lord "comforts his people and [has] compassion on his afflicted ones" (Isa. 49:13). Confess any lack of joy which you may have and admit to God your failures to receive his joy. Commit yourself to considering all of life as pure joy, whatever the circumstance, since Jesus Christ is alive and victorious over all. Ask the Lord to restore to you the joy of his salvation (Ps. 51:12), so that you may be a prime exhibit of Christ's life-changing power.

For Your Family and Friends

Pray that your family and friends may have Christian joy. Ask God to help them to discipline themselves in the Christian faith and grow together in genuine love.

For the Church

When your church gathers to worship, ask that members will have a taste of the joyful assembly that is heaven.

For the Kingdom

Pray that relief agencies may operate efficiently and make a lasting difference in the lives of those who are assisted.

For the Unsaved

Ask the Spirit to cause non-Christians whom you know (be specific) to seek out real joy in Jesus.

Prayer Pointer

"Christ actually means prayer to be the great power by which his church should do its work." —ANONYMOUS

_____

_____

_____

MARCH 20

Personal Prayer
Praise the Lord, who is your strength, your rock, your fortress and your deliverer (Ps. 18:1-2). Give thanks that "the weakness of God is stronger than man's strength" (1 Cor. 1:25). Confess your desire to rely upon your own strength. Commit yourself to doing everything through him who gives you strength (Phil. 4:13). Ask God to cause you to serve him with the strength that he provides, so that in all things God may be praised through Jesus Christ (1 Pet. 4:11).

For Your Family and Friends
Ask God to remove habits which destroy and limit relationships among your family and friends, and to replace these with habits which are life-giving and Spirit-led.

For the Church
Pray that your church leaders will be persons of spiritual power and that they will carry "weapons of righteousness" (2 Cor. 6:7) with which to battle the enemy.

For the Kingdom
Ask God to watch over the powerless of the world—the sick, the poor, the orphaned—that his strength would be sufficient to help them endure.

For the Unsaved
The gospel is the power of God for the salvation of everyone who believes (Rom. 1:16). Ask the Lord to apply this power to individuals whom you know are without it.

_____

_____

_____

_____

_____

MARCH 21

Personal Prayer

Praise the One who sits upon his throne, supreme in power and authority. Give thanks that the Almighty is your Father in Jesus Christ. Confess your own hardness of heart and disobedience against God's authority over you. Commit yourself to God so that you "do not let sin reign in your mortal body so that you obey its evil desires" (Rom. 6:12). Ask God to help you endure, so that you may reign with Christ (2 Tim. 2:12).

For Your Family and Friends

Pray that the relationships among your family and friends will be spiritually honest and productive. Pray that Jesus Christ will be a frequent and comfortable topic of conversation.

For the Church

Ask the King of the Church to reveal to your church its opportunities to lead lost persons to Jesus Christ. Pray that church members will be enthusiastic about this task.

For the Kingdom

Pray that ancient hostilities among peoples in various parts of the world will be eased so that life may be spared.

For the Unsaved

At the name of Jesus, every knee will bow and every tongue confess that Jesus Christ is Lord (Phil. 2:10-11). Pray that your unsaved friends will bend their knees to Jesus now and confess him as Lord.

Prayer Pointer

"Prayer moves the hand that moves the world." —JOHN AIKMAN WALLACE

MARCH 22

Personal Prayer

Praise God that he graciously chooses people to belong to him! Give thanks "that in all things God works for the good of those who love him, who have been called according to his purpose" (Rom. 8:28). Confess to the Father any doubts or objections you may have about how he works things out. Commit yourself to the one who chose you in Christ before the creation of the world to be holy and blameless in his sight (Eph. 1:4). Ask that "he who began a good work in you will carry it on to completion until the day of Christ Jesus" (Phil. 1:6).

For Your Family and Friends

Entrust all your loved ones, including all their troubles, to the marvelous care of God. Ask him to work his purpose in their lives.

For the Church

Pray that the educational ministry of the church will lead young and old to dedicate their lives to Jesus Christ.

For the Kingdom

Pray that governmental officials may not be tempted by power or money. Ask God that those who have fallen to these temptations may be changed or removed from their positions.

For the Unsaved

Ask the Holy Spirit to bring new life to particular unsaved persons whom you know. Pray that you may be used in this task.

_____

_____

_____

_____

_____

MARCH 23

Personal Prayer

Praise God that he is the creator of prayer. Give thanks because he gives you an audience with himself whenever you choose to pray. Confess any misuse or neglect of prayer. Commit yourself to making prayer a priority in your life. Ask God to lead you to "approach the throne of grace with confidence, so that [you] may receive mercy and find grace to help [you] in time of need" (Heb. 4:16).

For Your Family and Friends

Ask God to draw your family and friends closer to him and each other through prayer. Pray that their prayers would be "powerful and effective" (Jas. 5:16).

For the Church

Pray that missionaries will be encouraged in their efforts to communicate the good news to those of another culture. Pray that the words will be understandable and relevant.

For the Kingdom

Pray for the rights of Christians to be protected as they speak out for Jesus Christ. Remember especially Christian brothers and sisters who are being severely persecuted for their faith.

For the Unsaved

The Holy Spirit convicts the world of guilt in regard to sin, righteousness, and judgment (Jn. 16:8). Pray that your non-Christian acquaintances will be so convicted, repent, and claim the forgiveness of Jesus Christ.

_____

_____

_____

_____

_____

MARCH 24

Personal Prayer
Praise God because he is the encourager and comforter of his people. Give thanks that God loved you and by his grace gave you eternal encouragement and good hope (2 Thess. 2:16). Ask forgiveness for all those times when fear and anxiety replace the courage that God gives. Commit yourself to seeking God's encouragement to face every obstacle in your life. Ask God to encourage your heart and strengthen you in every good deed and word (2:17).

For Your Family and Friends
Pray that God will help your family and friends to do all their work and play in an excellent, God-glorifying way.

For the Church
Ask God to lead your church to care about welcoming newcomers and including them in the life of the church. Pray that no one be neglected in this important ministry.

For the Kingdom
Pray for special encouragement for teachers as they educate. Pray that parents will be supportive of teachers who seek what is best for students.

For the Unsaved
"There is now no condemnation for those who are in Christ Jesus" (Rom. 8:1). Ask that specific persons whom you know will be free from condemnation as they come to be "in Christ Jesus."

Prayer Pointer
"I have so much to do [today] that I shall spend the first three hours in prayer."
—MARTIN LUTHER

MARCH 25

Personal Prayer

Praise God for seeking and saving the lost. Give thanks that Jesus is "the good shepherd [who] lays down his life for the sheep" (Jn. 10:11). Confess those instances and ways in which you ignore the voice of your Shepherd. Commit yourself to learning to be content whatever the circumstances (Phil. 4:11). Ask God to give you the fullness of life which comes with following the Savior.

For Your Family and Friends

Pray that your family and friends will learn to appreciate and respect each other, and that any divisions will be mended.

For the Church

Ask God to teach Christians to ask not "how little?" but rather "how much?" when they make decisions about giving finances. Pray that Christ's great gift of himself will lead Christians to give liberally.

For the Kingdom

Pray for those who serve in law enforcement, that the stress of their jobs will not be too much for them to bear. Ask God to give them special strength to do their jobs well.

For the Unsaved

Pray that non-Christians whom you know will be sensitive to hear the voice of the Good Shepherd and desire to be part of his flock.

_____

_____

_____

_____

_____

MARCH 26

Personal Prayer

Praise God, who is perfect in beauty and holiness (Ps. 50:2). Thank him for making everything beautiful in its time (Eccl. 3:11), including your own life. Confess those times during this past week when your words or actions did not reflect to others the beauty of Christ. Commit yourself to being transformed into his likeness (2 Cor. 3:18). Ask God daily to change the ugliness of sin in your life to his loveliness.

For Your Family and Friends

Pray that your own family will reflect God's beauty in your relationships, so that others may be drawn to God through you.

For the Church

Pray that the spirit of worship may fall upon all who enter your church's sanctuary on Sunday, that they may desire "to gaze upon the beauty of the LORD and to seek him in his temple" (Ps. 27:4).

For the Kingdom

Pray for those in ministry in your denomination, that they may not get so caught up with administrative details that they forget to seek and reflect the Lord's beauty to everyone.

For the Unsaved

Ask God to spread the fragrance of the knowledge of God through you to the people you meet this week (2 Cor. 2:14-16).

_____

_____

_____

_____

_____

Personal Prayer

Praise Jesus as your King and husband, the bridegroom of the church (Eph. 5:25-27). Give thanks for his power to wash you and make you clean and holy, radiant and without stain or wrinkle. Confess any impure thoughts you may have had this week. Commit yourself to purifying yourself "from everything that contaminates body and spirit, perfecting holiness out of reverence for God" (2 Cor. 7:1). Ask God to help you think about whatever is true, noble, right, pure, lovely, and admirable (Phil. 4:8).

For Your Family and Friends

Pray that the young people you know will not be drawn into sexual relationships outside of marriage. Ask God to give them the grace to resist peer pressure.

For the Church

Pray for pastors who work with couples experiencing marital problems. Ask God to give them the wisdom to counsel effectively and the strength to bear this heavy burden.

For the Kingdom

Pray for sexual purity in all Christian leaders. This is an area where Satan works overtime to discredit the gospel.

For the Unsaved

Ask Jesus to help you invite others to his wedding banquet (Lk. 14:15-23).

Prayer Pointer

"They who have steeped their soul in prayer
Can every anguish calmly bear." —RICHARD M. MILNES

_____

_____

_____

_____

MARCH 28

Personal Prayer

Express your praise to God as the compassionate Father (Ps. 103:13). Thank him for desiring only good things for his children, including you (Lk. 11:11-13). Confess those times when you have not wanted what God wanted for you or others. Commit yourself to seeking first God's desire—his kingdom and his righteousness (Mt. 6:33). Ask God to "fill you with the knowledge of his will through all spiritual wisdom and understanding" (Col. 1:9).

For Your Family and Friends

Pray that God will give guidance to single persons as they seek to know what God has in store for their future (1 Cor. 7:32-35).

For the Church

Pray that God will place his own desire to reach the lost into the hearts of those who work in your church's outreach ministries. Plead for renewal and a new sense of God's power in evangelism.

For the Kingdom

Pray for Christians living in oppressive conditions, that God's desire for spreading his Word may be so strong in their hearts that they speak the Word boldly, without fear.

For the Unsaved

Pray that your own heart may be set on fire with God's passion to bring all people into his family.

Personal Prayer

Praise God as the Creator who makes all things new (Rev. 21:5). Give thanks for his power to bring even the most deadened souls to life in Jesus—including your own (Eph. 2:1-5). Confess those times when you have lost faith in God's power to renew and restore. Commit yourself to renewing your mind every day in prayer and in reading God's Word. Ask God to teach you what it means that you are now God's workmanship, created in Christ Jesus to do good works (2:10).

For Your Family and Friends

Pray for marriages that are floundering, that God's power may heal, renew, and restore love and forgiveness to dying relationships.

For the Church

Pray that church education teachers may be effective in renewing the minds of children and adults, so that they may resist conforming to the pattern of this world (Rom. 12:2).

For the Kingdom

Pray that those prayer warriors who intercede daily for politicians and governments around the world will never lose faith in God's power to renew and restore.

For the Unsaved

Pray that those who are outside of God's family may be made new creations in Christ (2 Cor. 5:17).

_____

_____

_____

_____

MARCH 30

Personal Prayer

Give praise to Jesus, the Alpha and the Omega, the First and the Last, the Beginning and the End (Rev. 22:13). Thank him for his promise, "Yes, I am coming soon" (22:12). Confess those periods of time when you have lost sight of the hope of his coming. Commit yourself to waiting each day for "the blessed hope—the glorious appearing of our great God and Savior, Jesus Christ" (Titus 2:13). Ask God to renew in you the hope that "when he appears, we shall be like him, for we shall see him as he is" (1 Jn. 3:2).

For Your Family and Friends

Pray that Christian families may not be consumed with materialism but may long "for a better country—a heavenly one" (Heb. 11:13-16).

For the Church

Pray for world missions, so that "this gospel of the kingdom will be preached in the whole world as a testimony to all nations, and then the end will come" (Mt. 24:14).

For the Kingdom

Pray for social justice agencies in your area, that God's kingdom may be advanced through their work.

For the Unsaved

Ask God to open the eyes of your unsaved friends so that they may see the spiritual kingdom that lies behind the physical realm.

_____

_____

_____

_____

_____

MARCH 31

Personal Prayer

Praise God as Comforter, Immanuel ("God with us"), Paraclete ("one who stands alongside"). Give thanks for his promise: "I . . . have called you in righteousness; I will take hold of your hand" (Isa. 42:6). Confess those times when you have doubted that God's hand has been in front of and behind you, guarding your life (Ps. 139:5). Commit the times of your life into God's hands (Ps. 31:14-15). Ask him to show you how close he is to you.

For Your Family and Friends

Ask God to make his presence known to family members or friends who are going through difficult times (Isa. 43:1-2).

For the Church

Pray that your deacons may be God's hands of compassion and God's presence to those who are struggling, frightened, or lonely.

For the Kingdom

Pray for missionaries who work in Muslim countries, that through them God may "open eyes that are blind, . . . free captives from prison, and . . . release from the dungeon those who sit in darkness" (Isa. 42:7).

For the Unsaved

Ask God to make you his hands of compassion in the life of one unsaved person this week.

Prayer Pointer

"A person must recognize his need for God before he can request divine aid and give God due thanks." —ANONYMOUS

_____

_____

_____

_____

_____

APRIL 1

Personal Prayer
Glorify God as measureless, incomparable, infinite, and generous Giver. Give thanks that his resources are bottomless (Col. 1:15-17). Confess those times when you have not asked for what you have needed, or have asked with the wrong motives (Jas. 4:2-3). Commit yourself to relying on God's resources rather than on your own. Ask God to help you see how rich is the inheritance and how mighty the power that he has given you (Eph. 1:18-19).

For Your Family and Friends
Pray that parents may teach their children how to give cheerfully and generously to God, responding with compassion to needs in the lives of others (2 Cor. 9:7).

For the Church
Pray that church leaders will look beyond apparent financial limitations to claim by faith God's abundant provisions for their ministries (9:8-11).

For the Kingdom
Ask God to provide for the needs of the poor in your area through your own generous giving of time and money.

For the Unsaved
Pray that the church's outpouring of gifts in times of disaster and need may move the unsaved to praise God and commit their lives to him (2 Cor. 9:13).

APRIL 2

Personal Prayer
Praise God for being a great and awesome God (Deut. 7:21). Thank him for bending down low in order to bring salvation and faith to you. Confess times when you've thought God was small and powerless. Commit yourself to worshiping God with "reverence and awe" (Heb. 12:28). Ask for a true sense of awe as you meet God in the sanctuary (Ps. 68:35).

For Your Family and Friends
Pray that the worship experience of your family might be "awesome" because it is centered on an awesome God.

For the Church
Pray that visitors to your church will be struck by the awesomeness of God as they join in worship with you.

For the Kingdom
The psalmist says to God: "How awesome are your deeds! . . . All the earth bows down to you" (Ps. 66:3-4). Pray that God's awesome power might be clearly evident throughout his kingdom worldwide.

For the Unsaved
Ask that the spiritual eyes of the unsaved will be opened so that they will be able to recognize and appreciate God's awesome power and majesty.

Prayer Pointer
"Do not pray by heart, but with the heart." —ANONYMOUS

APRIL 3

Personal Prayer
Praise God for individuals whom he has called to be your spiritual guides. Thank God for establishing order and authority in his church. Confess any lack of appreciation for the responsibility God has given to your pastor, elders, and deacons. Commit yourself to regularly upholding your spiritual leaders in prayer. Ask God to grant you a willingness to follow their leadership.

For Your Family and Friends
Pray that God's design for roles and relationships in your family may be preserved and enhanced. Pray that spiritual leadership in the home may be loving and faithful.

For the Church
Pray by name for your pastor(s), elders, and deacons. "They keep watch over you as men who must give account." Ask that "their work will be a joy, not a burden" (Heb. 13:17).

For the Kingdom
Pray for Christians who serve God in business, government, education, industry, and other fields of labor. Pray that their witness will be clear. Ask that they will not sacrifice spiritual principles as they carry out their tasks for the Lord.

For the Unsaved
Ask God to open the eyes of leaders in your church to the spiritual plight of the unsaved. Pray that they will be active in sharing their faith and so model a lifestyle of evangelism for others to follow.

APRIL 4

Personal Prayer

Praise God, who is light and in whom there is no darkness at all (1 Jn. 1:5). Thank the Lord for being your light and your salvation (Ps. 27:1). Confess any times you have willingly hidden the light of Christ from others. Commit yourself anew to living as a child of the light (Eph. 5:8). Ask—humbly—that you will become increasingly blameless and pure and that God will make you shine like a star in the universe (Phil. 2:15).

For Your Family and Friends

Pray for any family members or friends who are still walking in spiritual darkness. Ask that the light of the world will dawn on them.

For the Church

Pray that the outreach ministries in your church and denomination will drive back spiritual darkness. Pray for a spirit of urgency as real needs are met and lives are changed by the power of Jesus.

For the Kingdom

How big is your vision of the kingdom of God? Share Isaiah's exciting vision: "Nations will come to your light, and kings to the brightness of your dawn" (Isa. 60:3). Ask God to cause "nations" and "kings" to come to Jesus Christ today.

For the Unsaved

Name two or three people who are walking in spiritual darkness. Pray that the Holy Spirit will open their eyes so that they might have the light of life (Jn. 8:12).

APRIL 5

Personal Prayer
Praise God for the wonderful gift of language. Thank him for communicating with you in words and ways which you can understand. Confess those times when you have used words to harm or dishearten another person (Prov. 12:25; 15:1). Commit yourself to keeping your tongue in check at all times (Jas. 3:3-12). Ask God to enable you to overcome the evil which an untamed tongue so quickly breeds in one's life.

For Your Family and Friends
Pray for opportunities to build up and encourage any friends whose spirits may be sagging. Pray that the tongue will be an instrument of peace and not strife in your family life.

For the Church
Uphold those who teach Christian doctrine in your congregation. Pray that they will be careful to teach the truth. Ask that they might communicate spiritual truths in an engaging and effective manner.

For the Kingdom
Pray for ministries and organizations which are translating the Bible into written languages for the first time ever. Ask God to prosper the translation and distribution of his Word.

For the Unsaved
What a wonder that Jesus is the Word made flesh (Jn. 1:1-2, 14). Pray that many who hear of him will repent and believe.

Prayer Pointer
"The more we pray, the more our horizons expand and the more we come to expect from a supernatural, miracle-working God." —ANONYMOUS

Personal Prayer

Praise God, the one whose name is great among the nations (Mal. 1:11). Give thanks that the good news is being preached in so many countries today and that it has been proclaimed to you, too. Confess anything in your life which hinders your own witness to the saving grace of Christ. Commit yourself to regular prayer support of missionaries whom you know. Ask God to open doors for their ministries.

For Your Family and Friends

Your family can be a missionary family right in your neighborhood! Ask for opportunities for your family to be a witness among your neighbors and friends. (And then be ready when God answers!)

For the Church

Pray for the work of missionaries whom you know in other countries. Ask God to keep them safe from political or religious oppression. Pray that their marriages and family life will be strong.

For the Kingdom

Jesus instructed his followers to "go and make disciples of all nations" (Mt. 28:19). Pray that God will bring about the day when "all nations" have the opportunity to hear and believe the gospel.

For the Unsaved

As you think of unsaved friends, ask God to "open their eyes and turn them from . . . the power of Satan to God, so that they may receive forgiveness of sins and a place among those who are sanctified by faith in [Jesus]" (Acts 26:18).

_____

_____

_____

_____

_____

APRIL 7

Personal Prayer
Praise the Lord for being your shepherd (Psalm 23). Give thanks for those refreshing times when you experience "green pastures" and "quiet waters." Confess any dissatisfaction concerning God's care for you. Commit yourself to faithfully following the Good Shepherd in every area of your life. Ask God to "strengthen and protect you from the evil one" (2 Thess. 3:3).

For Your Family and Friends
Pray that members of your family would have genuine love and concern for each other. Ask especially that your children will reflect Jesus' love as they interact with each other.

For the Church
Pray that your congregation might be known as a loving and caring church. Intercede for those who plan special opportunities for fellowship within the body.

For the Kingdom
Pray for agencies and organizations which provide care in the name of Jesus for the elderly, for those with mental or physical handicaps, and for the ill. Ask God to meet their needs.

For the Unsaved
Ask the Good Shepherd to touch the lives of those who have not yet put their trust in him. Pray that they may experience his loving and redeeming care.

APRIL 8

Personal Prayer
Praise God for the liberality of his love. Give thanks for the ways that he has blessed you. Confess any attempts you have made to meet your needs or the needs of others in your own strength. Commit yourself to a lifestyle of generosity as you handle your personal finances and assets. Ask God to keep your motives pure as you have opportunity to help others (Mt. 6:1).

For Your Family and Friends
Ask God to meet the needs of your family or friends who are experiencing a lack of physical necessities.

For the Church
Pray that the deacons of your church will be persons of integrity and compassion. Intercede for your church treasurer and financial officers as they handle the Lord's finances.

For the Kingdom
Ask God to "throw open the floodgates of heaven and pour out [his] blessing (Mal. 3:10) upon churches, agencies, and organizations which minister in the name of Christ throughout the world.

For the Unsaved
Ask that unsaved persons you know will realize that there is nothing so valuable in all the world as a saving relationship with Jesus Christ. Pray that they will yield to the promptings of the Holy Spirit and give their lives to Christ.

_____

_____

_____

_____

_____

APRIL 9

Personal Prayer

Praise God that he is a provider, meeting "all your needs according to his glorious riches in Christ Jesus" (Phil. 4:19). Thank God that you do not need to believe in luck, chance, fate or fortune. Confess any times in which you have believed in yourself as your provider. Commit yourself to not being "anxious about anything, but in everything, by prayer and petition, with thanksgiving, present your requests to God" (4:6). Ask that God's peace, which transcends all understanding, will guard your heart and mind in Christ Jesus (4:7).

For Your Family and Friends

Ask that those you hold dear will have their minds fixed on whatever is true, noble, right, pure, lovely, admirable, excellent, or praiseworthy (4:8).

For the Church

Ask that God's name will be made great in your private and corporate worship.

For the Kingdom

Pray for those who are suffering from mental illness. Ask that they will find relief and support, and be restored to wholeness.

For the Unsaved

Pray that specific non-Christians whom you know will be struck by the futility of living without God and will seek out a relationship with Jesus Christ.

APRIL 10

Personal Prayer

Adore the merciful God who has given you "new birth into a living hope through the resurrection of Jesus Christ from the dead" (1 Pet. 1:3). Give thanks that you have "an inheritance that can never perish, spoil or fade—kept in heaven for you" (1:4). Seek God's forgiveness as you confess times when you fail to maintain your hope. Commit yourself to seeing trials as opportunities in which your faith "may be proved genuine and may result in praise, glory and honor when Jesus Christ is revealed" (1:7). Ask God to fill you "with an inexpressible and glorious joy" (1:8-9).

For Your Family and Friends

Pray that your family and friends will be given extra patience, wisdom, and strength as they deal with adversities. Ask that these challenges will mature their faith.

For the Church

Pray that your church leaders will be beautiful examples of Christian maturity.

For the Kingdom

Pray that Christians will be diligent stewards of the earth's resources.

For the Unsaved

The Lord says, "Though your sins are like scarlet, they shall be as white as snow" (Isa. 1:18). Pray that unsaved persons will understand that God desires to forgive and that they will seek that forgiveness.

_____

_____

_____

_____

APRIL 11

Personal Prayer
Praise God for his love (1 Jn. 4:16). Give thanks that "we know what love is: Jesus Christ laid down his life for us" (1 Jn. 3:16). Confess those times when you fail to love others. Commit yourself to laying down your life for your brothers and sisters in Christ (3:16). Ask God to drive all fear away with perfect love (1 Jn. 4:18).

For Your Family and Friends
Give thanks to the Father for the family members and friends that he has given you, and ask him to help you love them deeply.

For the Church
Pray that your church will be seen as a valuable asset in your community, and that its love will be so real and apparent that non-Christians will seek it out.

For the Kingdom
Ask God to expose the foolishness and treachery of the kingdom of darkness. Pray that the forces of the kingdom of God, in politics, education, science, media, business, entertainment, church, etc., will be united and focused in their efforts.

For the Unsaved
"God is light; in him there is no darkness at all" (1 Jn. 1:5). Ask God to cause specific non-Christians you know to desire light instead of darkness.

Prayer Pointer
"If we cannot recognize the value of simply being alone with God, without doing anything, we gouge the heart out of Christianity." —BRENNAN MANNING

APRIL 12

Personal Prayer

Praise God for the fact that he has revealed himself to mere mortals. Give thanks that the Lord has spoken plainly about himself and his will in his Word, which is a lamp to your feet and a light for your path (Ps. 119:105). Confess any failures in seeking the teaching, rebuking, correcting, and training in righteousness that come from the inspired Scriptures (2 Tim. 3:16). Commit yourself to being "thoroughly equipped for every good work" (3:17). Ask God to do good works through you.

For Your Family and Friends

Pray that God removes any distractions to wholesome love among your family and friends. Ask that all ungodly priorities and self-interests will be wiped away so that love can abound.

For the Church

Thank God for faithful teachers in the church. Pray that they will be encouraged by the Spirit to communicate life-changing truths.

For the Kingdom

Pray for those nations (name them) in which war has caused great human hardship and many casualties. Ask God to bring peace-loving, stable governments to power in these places.

For the Unsaved

Pray that unsaved persons whom you know will have an interest in studying the Bible, and that they will meet the Author as they do so.

_____

_____

_____

_____

_____

APRIL 13

Personal Prayer
Praise God for being the dwelling place for his saints in all generations (Ps. 90:1). Thank him that before the mountains were born or he had brought forth the earth and the world, from everlasting to everlasting he is God (90:2). Confess your rebellion against God's greatness. Commit yourself to numbering your days rightly, so that you may gain a heart of wisdom (90:12). Ask the Lord to have his favor rest upon you and to establish the work of your hands (90:17).

For Your Family and Friends
Pray that God moves your family and friends to live with dependence upon him and with a wholesome awareness of their own mortality.

For the Church
Pray that the Lord will supply wisdom and perseverance to your church's missionaries (name them) and that they will be blessed with encouraging results in their work.

For the Kingdom
Ask God to give wisdom to those in the justice system who are making decisions about guilt and innocence, that the guilty may be punished properly and the innocent be freed quickly.

For the Unsaved
"Let [the wicked] turn to the LORD, and he will have mercy on him . . ." (Isa. 55:7). Pray that unsaved ones close to you (name them) would turn and seek the mercy of God.

_____

_____

_____

_____

_____

APRIL 14

Personal Prayer

Praise God that he cares about this world. Thank Christ that he calls the church "his" and that he has promised to build it (Mt. 16:18). Confess your own failures in using your time, talents, and tithe as God desires. Commit yourself to being an energetic, ability-using, enthusiastic part of the body in which Christ has placed you. Ask that, as a part of the church, you will live the fact that you belong to all the others (Rom. 12:5).

For Your Family and Friends

Pray that the marriages of your family and friends will be strong, and that spouses will invest time in building and maintaining God-pleasing marriages.

For the Church

Ask God that your congregation will tirelessly live out the love that it has been given in Jesus Christ. Pray that the character and depth of this love will cause non-Christians in your community to want it for themselves.

For the Kingdom

Ask God to cause a woman who is planning the abortion of her baby to change her mind. Pray that abortion clinics will close for lack of business.

For the Unsaved

Ask God to bring you in contact with a non-Christian and allow you the opportunity to tell what God has done for you.

Prayer Pointer

"Prayer is essentially man standing before his God in wonder, awe, and humility; man, made in the image of God, responding to his maker." —GEORGE APPLETON

APRIL 15

Personal Prayer

Praise God that you know who he is because you have Jesus Christ, "the image of the invisible God" (Col. 1:15). Give thanks that "God was pleased to have all his fullness dwell in [Christ], and through him to reconcile to himself all things . . . by making peace through his blood" (1:19-20). Confess the instances when you spurn the reconciliation that God has accomplished. Commit yourself to continuing in your faith, "established and firm, not moved from the hope held out in the gospel" (1:23). Ask that Christ will have first place in every part of your life, and that nothing else will rival him.

For Your Family and Friends

Pray that those who are wandering away from God will be drawn back, and that they will have a contagious faith.

For the Church

Ask God to change not only what people in your church give, but also how they give. Pray that the uncheerful will become what God loves—cheerful givers (2 Cor. 9:7).

For the Kingdom

As teenagers are bombarded by the lies of "safe sex," ask God to lead them to save their virginity for marriage.

For the Unsaved

Pray that "Christ-less" individuals on your street or in your community will begin to feel a spiritual hunger for the Lord.

APRIL 16

Personal Prayer

Praise the God of Israel, who comes in glory to meet with his people. Thank God for coming to consume the darkness and to make what is purified radiate with his glory (Ezek. 43:1-5). Confess any wickedness that hinders the brightness of his presence. Commit to letting God's glory shine upon you in worship. Ask God to shine through you to others.

For Your Family and Friends

Pray that those close to you will go into God's presence in spirit and in the light of his truth.

For the Church

Pray that, as those at your church look at God's glory, his brightness may be reflected in their faces. Ask God to change them from "glory to glory" (2 Cor. 3:18).

For the Kingdom

Pray that Jesus, the light of the world, will shine through his people and fill the land with the Father's glory. Ask God to mirror his glory to the world through his people.

For the Unsaved

Pray that the Holy Spirit will cause the glory of God to blaze in you, setting your heart on fire for the lost. Ask that God will send forth his Word, bringing his light to lives swamped in darkness.

Prayer Pointer

"Pray not for lighter burdens but for stronger backs." —THEODORE ROOSEVELT

APRIL 17

Personal Prayer

Praise God as your Sovereign Lord (Ezek. 2:5). Give thanks for the true prophets God has placed in your life (2:3). Confess times when you have spent more time critiquing the Lord's spokespersons than listening to his Word through them. Commit to listening to the Word he gives you today. Ask God to help you respond appropriately to what he says.

For Your Family and Friends

Pray that the children have hearts open to God's Word from their earliest years. Ask God to help them keep their ways pure by living according to his Word (Ps. 119:9).

For the Church

Pray that your pastor will present God's message courageously, whether it is accepted or not (Ezek. 2:3-7). Ask God to help all your church's leaders to consistently follow God's Word themselves (2:8).

For the Kingdom

Pray that the civil leaders of your country and community will humbly submit to God's ways. Ask God to use you in clearly and sensitively speaking out to dissuade fellow citizens from evil (3:16-21).

For the Unsaved

Pray to be empowered and emboldened to speak to the unsaved so that you will not be guilty of their blood (3:18-19). Ask God to make your words and lifestyle effective.

APRIL 18

Personal Prayer
Praise God for his world-sized love (Jn. 3:16)! Thank God for loving you before you ever began to love him (Rom. 5:8). Confess times of turning away from the Lord, acknowledging that such betrayal of his love is spiritual prostitution (Ezekiel 16). Commit yourself again to faithfulness in loving God. Ask him to help you live with purity of love toward him.

For Your Family and Friends
Pray that your household will more and more consistently live in God's love. Ask that his love be reflected from your household to your neighborhood.

For the Church
Pray for the Bible studies and other small groups of your church. Ask God to work his kind of intimacy into the lives of each person involved with these groups.

For the Kingdom
Pray that the world will be drawn to Christ through the magnetic love of his church. Ask that the public witness of the church be protected from angry zealots who act with merely human methods.

For the Unsaved
Pray that the purity of your life will draw your contacts from relationships of abuse and despair to the love of God. Ask God's Spirit to convict of sin and convince of righteousness (Jn. 16:8).

Prayer Pointer
"Seven days without prayer makes one weak." —ALLEN E. BARTLETT

APRIL 19

Personal Prayer
Praise God as the all-knowing one. Thank God for caring enough for you to teach you his ways and warn you when you stray. Confess times of willful ignorance of his ways. Commit to listening and following God's directions. Ask him to provide faithful teachers and examples for you.

For Your Family and Friends
Pray that you will be diligent in teaching those under your care. Ask God to help you be an excellent model for your children (or for the children of your friends).

For the Church
Pray that the teachers of the church will be "watchmen" who faithfully relay God's Word to his people (Ezekiel 33). Ask God to prompt them to diligence.

For the Kingdom
Pray that believers will speak boldly to their countrymen about the essential nature of righteous living (Ezek. 33:12-20). Ask God to soften their hearts to hear, repent, and follow him.

For the Unsaved
Thank God that he does not take pleasure in the death of the wicked. Pray for him to work powerfully through you to call people to turn from the foolish ways leading to death to the life-producing ways of his wisdom (33:11).

APRIL 20

Personal Prayer

Praise God as the sovereign Lord (Ezek. 17:22-24) who deserves the praise of all the people-groups of the world! Thank him for making himself known to you. Confess any smallness of your vision of God and his mission in this world. Commit yourself to a world-sized vision. Ask him to show you some specific way to serve him.

For Your Family and Friends

Pray that someone you love will be led by God to be an "on the scene" world missionary. Ask God to thoroughly prepare that person from an early age.

For the Church

Pray that the church will become a "splendid cedar" in which "birds of every kind will nest" (17:23). Ask God to provide through the church an abundance of wisdom, personnel, and financial resources for entering open doors for mission.

For the Kingdom

Pray that the kingdom of the world will soon become the kingdom of our Lord and of his Christ (Rev. 11:15). Ask God to prompt you to pray regularly for his reign to spread.

For the Unsaved

Pray for international students on the campuses of your country. Ask God to reach many of them so that they will go back to their homelands as his ambassadors.

APRIL 21

Personal Prayer
Praise the sovereign Lord who cares for his sheep (Ezek. 34:11). Thank the Lord for shepherding you, caring for you in his rich pasture (34:14). Confess times of wandering away from the side of the Good Shepherd. Commit yourself to rejoicing in the bounty he provides for you. Ask God to help you be a blessing with the blessings you've been given.

For Your Family and Friends
Pray that those closest to you will always remain close to God. Ask God to nurture them to wholeness in his care (34:11-16).

For the Church
Pray that your church's caregiving and fellowship efforts will be led by faithful shepherds who care for the flock (34:1-10). Ask God to give them compassionate diligence to strengthen the weak, heal the sick, and bind up the injured (34:4).

For the Kingdom
Pray that God's covenant of peace will soon be experienced in fullness, when we will fully know that the sovereign Lord is our God and we are his people (34:25-31).

For the Unsaved
Pray that God will search for the lost and bring back the strays, bringing wholeness to them (34:16). Ask him to seek an unsaved or straying friend through you.

APRIL 22

Personal Prayer
Praise God for his powerful actions on your behalf. Thank God for saving you and bringing you into the richness of life with him. Confess attitudes of self-reliance and independence from God. Commit yourself to remembering that all he has placed in your hands is still his. Ask God to give you a giving spirit.

For Your Family and Friends
Pray that children and young Christians will learn patterns of joyful giving early in their walk with God. Ask God to lead them into this joy through your example.

For the Church
Pray that your church's members and regular attendees will be faithful and insightful in giving. Ask that God will open the doors to his ministry resources stored in our bank accounts.

For the Kingdom
Pray that your church will rejoice in its opportunities to be part of spreading God's kingdom throughout the world. Ask God to bring excellent results to the work of relief agencies.

For the Unsaved
Pray that God will show himself holy through his people in the sight of the nations (Ezek. 39:27).

Prayer Pointer
"In the morning, prayer is the key that opens to us the treasures of God's mercies and blessings; in the evening, it is the key that shuts us up under his protection and safeguard." —ANONYMOUS

APRIL 23

Personal Prayer
Praise God for his jealousy toward you (Zech. 8:1-3; Ex. 20:5-6) that roots out rivals for your love or unfaithfulness on your part. Thank God for such love that will not let you go. Confess times at which you have not given God your undivided love and allegiance. Commit yourself to being exclusively devoted to him. Ask God to give you an undivided heart and life for him.

For Your Family and Friends
Pray that your family will willingly demonstrate undivided love for God with open enthusiasm and deep commitment. Ask God to surround your household with an intimate sense of his presence.

For the Church
Pray for your church to be filled with the fires of first-love devotion (Rev. 2:4-5). Ask that your corporate worship will serve to deepen this love.

For the Kingdom
Pray that the Father will convince the world of his love through the unity of Christians with God and one another (Jn. 17:20-23). Ask that barriers to unity be removed.

For the Unsaved
Pray that God's Spirit will convince your neighbors or coworkers that his love is for them. Ask him to use you in the process, showing you specific ways to put love into action.

APRIL 24

Personal Prayer

Praise God, the one mightier than all the officials of all the nations. Give thanks that he is interested in the substance of justice and mercy rather than mere outward forms (Zechariah 7). Confess times during which your walk with God doesn't go much deeper than formality. Commit yourself to a life-style of justice, mercy, and compassion (Zech. 7:9). Ask God to regularly prompt you to loving faithfulness in such a life.

For Your Family and Friends

Pray that your children will develop a sensitivity toward the needs and concerns of others. Ask God to help you model such concern in relationships and contexts where you exercise authority.

For the Church

Pray that your church's leaders will not be sidetracked by mere adherence to forms or accepted patterns. Ask God to fill them with courage to effectively lead you into his justice, mercy, and compassion.

For the Kingdom

Pray that your government officials will adopt God's priorities as their own. Ask God to help them restrain oppression of widows, the fatherless, the aliens, and the poor (7:10).

For the Unsaved

Pray that the practical displays of God-honoring justice, mercy, and compassion will be combined with a clear call to repent and believe. Ask God to draw specific unsaved people you know into his holiness.

APRIL 25

Personal Prayer
Praise God for his great mercy. Thank God for forgiving you and bringing you back after failure and rebellion (Zech. 8:7-8). Confess times of presuming on his patience and mercy. Commit yourself to consistent obedience from a heart of gratitude for God's forgiveness. Ask him to forgive your debts as you have forgiven your debtors, and to lead you not into temptation but to deliver you from evil.

For Your Family and Friends
Pray that your family will forgive one another for past sins, including abuse of any kind. Ask God to bring restoration and wholeness into your household and friendships.

For the Church
Pray that your church will have eyes to see those who need to be brought back into the fold after failure. Ask God's Spirit to convince all to be sensitive and forgiving rather than judgmental and begrudging.

For the Kingdom
Pray that God will inspire you in all relationships and professional involvements to be a peacemaker and restorer. Ask him for the humble courage such work requires.

For the Unsaved
Pray that the unsaved in your network of relationships will be won to the Prince of Peace by seeing fallen Christians restored. Ask God to show them his healing through the mending of your own life.

APRIL 26

Personal Prayer

Praise God as the God of truth. Thank him for replacing the facades of your life with the substantive realities of his truth. Confess any time you've rejected difficult aspects of that truth for the appealing glitter of Satan's lies. Commit yourself to honesty with God, other people, and yourself. Ask God to lead you into fuller and fuller application of his truth to your lifestyle.

For Your Family and Friends

Pray that your children and those of your friends will be taught the truth about God and his world in their schools. Ask God to give special insight to all Christian teachers.

For the Church

Pray for the education departments of your local church and your denomination. Ask him to speak through them so consistently that the church becomes known as the City of Truth (Zech. 8:3).

For the Kingdom

Pray that God's people will speak the truth to each other in all avenues of life, render true and sound judgment in the courts, and keep their word (8:16-17).

For the Unsaved

Pray that such truth-oriented living will break through the lies the Deceiver has used with unsaved neighbors. Ask God to speak his truth in love to one of them through you today.

_____

_____

_____

_____

_____

APRIL 27

Personal Prayer
Praise the Lord Almighty, who allows city dwellers around the world to seek him (Zech. 8:20ff). Thank God for letting you find him. Confess times you have become indifferent and inattentive to his presence. Commit yourself to ongoing communion with him throughout the day. Ask God to regularly fill you with the joy of his salvation (Ps. 51:7-12).

For Your Family and Friends
Pray that God will always be the main guest of your home. Ask him to save each member of your circle of family and friends.

For the Church
Pray for your denomination's mission agency(ies) and any missionaries your church helps to support. Ask God to give you a special way to encourage your missionary(ies) today.

For the Kingdom
Pray that God will move the hearts of national leaders throughout the world to provide open doors for the spread of God's salvation. Ask that the kingdom of this world will become the kingdom of our Lord and of his Christ (Rev. 11:15) very soon!

For the Unsaved
Pray for eyes to see the different groups needing to be evangelized, including groups in cities near you. Ask God to send forth reapers, and to send you to your unsaved acquaintances.

Prayer Pointer
"A vital prayer life in your church leadership is one of the most important indications of your congregation's spiritual life." —ANONYMOUS

APRIL 28

Personal Prayer

Praise God for the fullness of life he brings, from blessings of old age to a community filled with playing boys and girls (Zech. 8:4-5). Give thanks for your own physical and spiritual life. Confess any ways in which you regularly waste moments of your life. Commit yourself to diligent self-control. Ask the Holy Spirit to produce this part of his fruit (Gal. 5:23) in you.

For Your Family and Friends

Pray that the impact of your life will greatly enhance the lives of those close to you. Ask God to help you be consistently pro-life.

For the Church

Pray for your church's deacons and any fellowship-enhancing committee or care-giving groups in your congregation. Ask God to show you specific ways to encourage others.

For the Kingdom

Pray for those agencies showing love in the name of Jesus Christ. Ask God to hold back disasters and other developments which rob people of the fullness of life.

For the Unsaved

Pray for someone you know who is going through especially difficult times without the comfort of God. Ask God to use you in drawing that person to himself.

Prayer Pointer

"O, do not pray for easy lives. Pray to be stronger men. Do not pray for tasks equal to your powers. Pray for powers equal to your tasks." —PHILLIPS BROOKS

APRIL 29

Personal Prayer

Praise God, who is the one who can withhold daily necessities or provide for his obedient people (Zech. 8:12-13). Give thanks for abundant crops, necessary moisture, productivity in industry, and other ways in which God provides an abundance of "daily bread." Confess times you have blocked his blessings through disobedience. Commit yourself to trusting and obeying God. Ask God to make you a wide-open channel of his blessings to the world.

For Your Family and Friends

Thank God for daily opportunities to be a blessing in your household. Ask him to give you a generous spirit.

For the Church

Pray that the financial needs of your local church will be abundantly met. Ask God for a devotion that prompts his people to urgently plead for the privilege of sharing (2 Cor. 8:4).

For the Kingdom

Pray that people will be convinced of the folly of living for this world's toys. Ask God to give his people the selfless perspective to seek first God's kingdom and righteousness.

For the Unsaved

Pray that the unsaved around you will see such a difference in your God-honoring values that they will leave materialistic life-styles to take up their cross and follow Jesus. Ask God to continue the fulfillment of his promise to Abraham through you (Gen. 12:2-3).

APRIL 30

Personal Prayer
Praise God for his faithfulness in calling you into fellowship with his Son, Jesus Christ (1 Cor. 1:9). Thank God for the privilege of being his adopted child. Confess those times when you've foolishly acted like an orphan rather than as one of God's own children. Commit yourself to strengthening the fellowship you enjoy with Christ and with other Christians. Ask God to reveal to you anything that might hinder your fellowship with Christ.

For Your Family and Friends
Pray for a close and loving bond to grow between the members of your immediate family. Ask that this bond will be rooted only in Christ Jesus.

For the Church
Ask that the truth of Jesus' promise to be present "where two or three come together in my name" will be very evident in your congregational worship. Pray for the outpouring of God's Spirit in your prayers and praise.

For the Kingdom
Ask God to thwart Satan's efforts to build barriers between Christians, especially believers from differing ethnic backgrounds. Pray for a spirit of love and respect for brothers and sisters of all ethnic backgrounds. Thank God for such a colorful mosaic of believers in his church worldwide!

For the Unsaved
Ask God to draw more and more people from all cultures into his fellowship.

MAY 1

Personal Prayer

Praise God for his holiness (Ex. 15:11). Thank him for calling you to live a life of holiness through the power of the Holy Spirit. Confess contentment with areas of your life that do not reflect God's holiness. Commit yourself to avoiding anything that "contaminates body and spirit" (2 Cor. 7:1). Ask God to give you a daily desire to obey his command to "be holy, because I am holy" (Lev. 11:45).

For Your Family and Friends
Pray for the teens in your family or among your friends. Ask God to protect them from all the "contaminants" offered by our modern culture.

For the Church
Thank God for the leaders in your congregation. Ask that they would be committed to personal holiness. Pray also for their marriages and families.

For the Kingdom
Pray that God would be glorified throughout his kingdom as it spreads around the world. Ask for renewal to sweep the churches of the West. Thank God for great harvests in the former Soviet Union, in Asia, and in South America.

For the Unsaved
Ask God to open the eyes and hearts of unsaved friends. Pray for an opportunity this week to share the good news with at least one other person.

Personal Prayer

Praise God for communicating with you in his inspired Word. Thank him for providing a "lamp to [your] feet and a light to [your] path" (Ps. 119:105). Confess any doubts you've harbored concerning the authority of God's Word in your life. Commit yourself to treasuring the words of God more than daily bread (Job 23:12). Ask God to feed you spiritually as you look to his Word for guidance throughout this week.

For Your Family and Friends

Think of one specific family. Pray that this family would set aside time every day for family devotions and prayer. Ask God to make this practice a blessing in their family life.

For the Church

Thank God for the outreach ministries of your congregation. Pray for the work of your deacons. Pray for the ministries of mercy which they perform on your behalf.

For the Kingdom

Pray for Bible publishers and distribution agencies, such as the Gideons, who make the Word of God readily available to millions of people. Ask that God will prosper their work and witness.

For the Unsaved

Ask that unsaved people you know will discover the irresistible sweetness of God's Word (Ps. 119:103) and be drawn to Christ through it.

Prayer Pointer

"The answer of our prayers is secured by the fact that in rejecting them God would in a certain sense deny his own nature." —JOHN CALVIN

MAY 3

Personal Prayer

God sends his teaching like rain and his words like the dew (Deut. 32:2). Praise God for being your teacher (Ps. 71:17). Thank God for the privilege of receiving his instruction through his Word. Confess any lack of attention you've paid to God's teaching. Commit yourself to listening closely to what God has to say to you. Ask God to reveal himself more clearly through his Word each day.

For Your Family and Friends

Pray for the parents in Christian families close to you. Ask God to help them to be excellent teachers and role models for their children.

For the Church

Pray for the teachers and helpers in your church school program. Thank God for their dedication and hard work. Pray also for adult education classes and teachers.

For the Kingdom

Thank God for the work of Christians who are helping to refocus the educational system in the former Soviet Union. Pray for Russian teachers who now have much greater freedom to present biblical truths in the classroom.

For the Unsaved

Ask that God will shower the blessings of salvation on unsaved people in your community as they learn of Christ.

MAY 4

Personal Prayer

Praise God, whose name is great among the nations (Mal. 1:11). Give thanks that the gospel has reached around the world and into your heart. Confess any sin that has hindered you from gaining a clear vision of God's work in the world. Commit yourself to God's plan for the gospel to be preached in the whole world (Mt. 24:14). Ask God to use you in that plan.

For Your Family and Friends

Pray for the children and teens among your family and friends. Ask that the gospel of the kingdom will take root among them at an early age.

For the Church

Boldly intercede for the work of gospel missions worldwide. Pray by name for world missionaries whom your church supports. Ask God to protect them and prosper their work.

For the Kingdom

Thank God that one day "all the ends of the earth will remember and turn to the LORD, and all the families of the nations will bow down before him" (Ps. 22:27). Ask that that special day will arrive soon.

For the Unsaved

Ask God to burden your heart with the plight of one unsaved person you know. Pray for that person by name. Ask that God's global mission will touch that one soul and spark new life in Christ.

MAY 5

Personal Prayer

Praise God for his great love and mercy shown to you (Eph 2:4). Give thanks that nothing can separate you from the love of Jesus (Rom. 8:35). Confess any lack of love which you have shown to God or to another person. Commit yourself to loving God with your whole being (Deut. 6:5). Ask God to prune your life so that the spiritual fruit of love will grow large and appetizing to others.

For Your Family and Friends

Ask God to root out all hatred, jealousies, anger, and bitterness that may have sprouted up in your family life. Pray for love to grow in every relationship.

For the Church

How do the members of your church show love to one another and to their neighbors? Pray for fellowship and caregiving programs in your congregation.

For the Kingdom

Ask God to bring an end to civil wars, urban violence, racial bigotry, economic injustice, and every other sin that scars nations and neighborhoods. Pray for love to reign instead of hate.

For the Unsaved

It was Jesus' love for sinners that sent him to the cross. Pray for an opportunity to share that kind of sacrificial love with another person (Jn. 15:9).

Prayer Pointer

"Beyond the preoccupation we all have with our needs, the rock-bottom reality of prayer is the sharing of experience." —MICHAEL CARD

_____

_____

_____

_____

_____

MAY 6

Personal Prayer

Praise God, who is the source of all wealth and prosperity on earth (1 Chron. 29:12). Give thanks for all the material blessings God has given to you. Confess any occasions when you have tried to "store up for yourself treasures on earth" (Mt. 6:19). Commit yourself to remembering that wealth and possessions, and the ability to enjoy them, are a gift from God (Eccl. 5:19). Ask him to open your eyes to new opportunities to use your possessions for the benefit of others.

For Your Family and Friends

Pray for family members or friends who have difficulty managing their household finances. Ask God to provide the help they need to be better managers.

For the Church

Pray for the deacons of your church. Thank God for their integrity and honesty as they handle the financial resources of your congregation. Pray also that your congregation will be a church of cheerful givers.

For the Kingdom

Ask God to raise up people to contribute generously to the ministries of the church worldwide. Pray that real needs will be met without undue strain. Pray also that contributions will be used wisely.

For the Unsaved

Pray Eph. 1:18 for any unsaved person you know, asking especially that his or her spiritual eyes will be opened to see the eternal treasure of life in Christ.

Personal Prayer

Glorify God as the beginning and end of all things, the Alpha and the Omega. Give thanks for his love for you—a love that has kept you in mind since the beginning of the world and will continue to hold you when this world has passed away. Confess those times when you have seen yourself and your needs as the beginning and end of your existence. Commit yourself to giving God the highest place in your life and heart. Ask God to reveal his glory to you so that you cannot help but praise him with your whole heart.

For Your Family and Friends

Pray for the children in your family and congregation, that they may receive a blessing and a sense of God's love and presence in worship.

For the Church

Pray for worship leaders in your congregation, that they may see the Alpha and the Omega, the Living One whose "face was like the sun shining in all its brilliance" (Rev. 1:16-18) and lead the people in praise of the Lord.

For the Kingdom

Pray that worship services all over the world will glorify the name and power of Jesus rather than promote lesser things.

For the Unsaved

Ask God to reveal his glory and power to any unbelievers who attend worship services in your community, so that they begin to worship him.

MAY 8

Personal Prayer

Praise your Father as the God of gods and the Lord of kings and a revealer of mysteries (Dan. 2:47). Give thanks for the mystery of salvation through Christ, which has been revealed to you through God's Word and Spirit (Eph. 3:3-6). Confess that there are times when you do not rely on his wisdom and insight in your daily struggles. Commit yourself to spending more time in God's Word and prayer, seeking to understand the mystery of your life in Christ. Ask God to fill you with a spirit of wisdom and revelation (Eph. 1:17).

For Your Family and Friends

Pray for those you know whose minds have been blinded by the gods of this age, unable to see the light of the gospel of the glory of Christ (2 Cor. 4:4).

For the Church

Ask God that the leaders in your congregation may be especially gifted with wisdom as they lead your members through the challenges that you face in your neighborhood, outreach, and nurturing programs.

For the Kingdom

Pray especially for Christian leaders in strife-torn areas, that they may have the wisdom to speak God's Word in difficult situations and bring truth and love where there is hatred and division.

For the Unsaved

Pray for one family on your street who does not attend church. Ask God to give you the opportunity to speak to them within the next few weeks.

MAY 9

Personal Prayer
Praise God as a rock of refuge, as a shelter, as a safe dwelling place (Ps. 31:3, 20). Give thanks that you have been rescued from forces in this world that would have overwhelmed your soul. Confess those times when you have paid little attention to the safety and refuge he offers. Commit yourself to remaining under the shadow of his protection. Ask God to shelter you this day.

For Your Family and Friends
Ask God to be a shelter and protection to single-parent families. Pray that the children of divorced parents will especially feel God's loving presence.

For the Church
Pray that your congregation may offer the security of God, our rock, to those in your neighborhood who live in fear of death, poverty, crime, sickness, or loneliness.

For the Kingdom
Pray that God will be especially close to those Christians around the world who are imprisoned or persecuted for their faith. Ask that they may sense your prayers around them like a shelter and a cloak of protection.

For the Unsaved
Pray for those in nursing homes who are dying without the assurance of God's love to welcome them home. Ask God to send people to tell them about Jesus, the rock of our salvation.

Prayer Pointer
"The first stage of prayer is not an activity of mind but a passive mode of receiving. Like slipping into a tub of hot water, I let God's love seep in, saturate, permeate every part of my being." —BRENNAN MANNING

MAY 10

Personal Prayer

Give praise to the one who said, "I am . . . the truth" (Jn. 14:6). Thank God for rescuing you from the darkness of Satan's deceit and placing you in the kingdom of his marvelous light (1 Pet. 2:9). Repent of those times that you have been uncomfortable with the light of God's truth and have preferred twisting the truth to suit your purposes. Commit yourself to walking in the light of God's truth with your whole heart. Ask God to make you willing to do that, no matter the cost to your pride or reputation.

For Your Family and Friends

Ask God to build truthful relationships between parents and children. Pray that God will restore trust and love so that children can be honest about their feelings and problems.

For the Church

Pray that your church's education classes will help those who struggle with Satan's deceit in their lives to come to know the truth in Christ.

For the Kingdom

Pray that those in government, especially judges and lawmakers, will make their decisions in the light of God's truth. Ask that they not be influenced by Satan's claim that there is no God and no standard of truth.

For the Unsaved

Ask God to use your example of honesty and truthfulness this week to move someone's heart to see the reality of God.

_____

_____

_____

_____

_____

MAY 11

Personal Prayer

Praise the Lamb of God, who was beaten and crucified for the sins of the world. Thank him for taking your place, your punishment, your sins on himself. Confess the sins that have been on your conscience this past week, knowing that God will deal gently with you (Heb. 4:14-16). Commit yourself to living for Christ, not for the empty way of life that his blood redeemed you from (1 Pet. 1:18-19). Ask Jesus to help you understand the depth of the love that sent him to the cross for you.

For Your Family and Friends

Pray that the Christian singles you know may be kept free from immorality and may give their full energy and time to the Lord's work (1 Cor. 7:32-35).

For the Church

Pray for the children and young people in your congregation that God is already preparing to become missionaries. Ask God to use you to encourage them and to set an example for them by your interest and support of world missions.

For the Kingdom

Intercede for specific missionaries that you know, asking God to protect them from evil, provide for all their financial needs, and encourage them by giving a good response to their message.

For the Unsaved

Pray especially for the millions of Muslims around the world, that God will break through their darkness and help them find freedom and forgiveness in Christ's blood.

MAY 12

Personal Prayer

Praise the Father who has compassion on his children. Thank him for forgiving all your sins, healing all your diseases, redeeming your life from the pit, crowning you with love and compassion, and satisfying your desires with good things (Psalm 103). Confess those periods in your day when you are unaware of God's faithful, watching, loving presence beside you and within you. Commit yourself to watching for signs of his love and tenderness toward you. Ask him to draw you closer to himself.

For Your Friends and Family

Pray for families where you suspect abuse, that God will provide healing, protection, and love for those who suffer.

For the Church

Pray that the oil of God's love will be like a sweet scent in all the activities of your church's fellowship this week. Ask God to let you share his love in a specific way with at least one other church member this week.

For the Kingdom

Pray for "those who are least in the kingdom of heaven"—the poor, sick, lonely, outcast, struggling, grieving—that they may find the Father's love in a warm church fellowship.

For the Unsaved

Pray that through your loving concern this week, one person may be brought closer to the kingdom of God.

MAY 13

Personal Prayer

Praise the Creator of the stars, the sun, the sky, the earth, and all life in this vast creation. Thank him for having created you and providing for all your needs. Confess the doubts you've had that God could supply your needs from the storehouse of his abundance. Commit yourself to a way of giving that is as generous and loving as your Father's. Ask God to continue to supply all your needs.

For Your Family and Friends

Ask God to meet the needs of families who struggle to make ends meet financially. Pray that their eyes will be turned to the Lord and to his ability to provide.

For the Church

Pray that believers will be moved to honor God by bringing him the full tithes from their earnings. Ask that they will depend on God to "throw open the floodgates of heaven and pour out so much blessing that [they] will not have room enough for it" (Mal. 3:10).

For the Kingdom

Ask God to help all believers make him Lord of their finances as well as every other area of life. Pray for wisdom in financial dealings, in spending, in investing, and in giving for all Christians.

For the Unsaved

Pray that as people receive financial and material assistance from churches, they will see God's love for them and turn to him for salvation.

_____

_____

_____

_____

_____

MAY 14

Personal Prayer

Praise the Lamb, Jesus Christ, who with his blood "purchased men for God from every tribe and language and people and nation" (Rev. 5:9). Thank the Lord that he covenanted with Abraham long ago and that you have the blessing of being part of God's own people. Confess any tendencies that you have to judge people by color, ethnicity, or background. Commit yourself to showing no favoritism, just as God shows none (Acts 10:34). Ask that you will do your part in the kingdom of priests who serve God (Rev. 5:10).

For Your Family and Friends

Give thanks for the gifts, abilities, and perspectives of those whom God has given to you, and ask his blessing upon them.

For the Church

Pray that the worshipers of your own church body will have a sense of the church as it gathers in many places throughout your community and the world. Pray that you and your fellow believers will not be cliquish or divisive.

For the Kingdom

Ask that the power of racism in our society will be broken, and that Christians will lead the way in this.

For the Unsaved

Pray that specific non-Christians around you will understand that God looks upon the heart, and that they will seek to have their hearts made right through Christ.

_____

_____

_____

_____

_____

MAY 15

Personal Prayer

Praise the Lord God Almighty, whose deeds are great and marvelous. Thank God for the opportunity to become godly, and that "godliness has value for all things, holding promise for both the present life and the life to come" (1 Tim. 4:8). Confess your lack of the devotion to God which results in a life pleasing to him. Commit yourself to a life of compassion, kindness, humility, gentleness and patience (Col. 3:12). Ask that the grace of God will teach you "to say 'No' to ungodliness and worldly passions, and to live [a] self-controlled, upright and godly [life] in this present age" (Titus 2:12).

For Your Family and Friends

Pray that your family and friends will make godliness a priority, and that your own godliness will be a real encouragement to them.

For the Church

Pray that your church leaders will be uncompromising examples of godliness for your congregation. Ask that they will receive consistent support from the congregation.

For the Kingdom

Pray for "kings and all those in authority, that we may live peaceful and quiet lives in all godliness and holiness" (1 Tim. 2:2).

For the Unsaved

Pray that Jesus will become the Lord of the non-Christians around you.

_____

_____

_____

_____

MAY 16

Personal Prayer

Praise the Lord, your Savior and your God. Thank God for the hope that he gives to you and for the fact that he never forgets you. Confess all the desires which you have that crowd out your desire for God himself. Commit your soul to panting after God "as the deer pants for streams of water" (Ps. 42:1). Ask that you will "delight yourself in the LORD and [that he will give] you the desires of your heart" (Ps. 37:4).

For Your Family and Friends

Ask God to cause your friends and family to have a deep thirst for him, and to allow nothing else to quench that thirst.

For the Church

Pray that your church's efforts to reach others for Christ will be driven by a deep desire for people to experience what you have experienced in Christ.

For the Kingdom

Pray that your local and regional government leaders will come to know Christ and give him glory by making decisions according to his will. Pray for strength for Christians in government.

For the Unsaved

Jesus said, "Whoever drinks the water I give him will never thirst" (Jn. 4:14). Pray that three unsaved persons you know will drink the living water from Jesus.

Prayer Pointer

"Do not work so hard for Christ that you have no strength to pray, for prayer requires strength." —J. HUDSON TAYLOR

MAY 17

Personal Prayer

Praise God as the master even of the grave. Thank the Father that "Christ has indeed been raised from the dead, the firstfruits of those who have fallen asleep" (1 Cor. 15:20). Confess your failure to place your life and death fully in the hands of the risen Christ. Commit yourself to standing firm in the victory which Christ has achieved over sin and death and hell. Ask that you will "know that your labor in the Lord is not in vain" (15:58), and so work with extra fervor.

For Your Family and Friends

Pray that your family and friends will be energetic in their living for Christ. Give special thanks for those who already do this.

For the Church

Pray that the people of your congregation will become well-grounded in the basics of the Scriptures, and that they will faithfully live their beliefs.

For the Kingdom

Give thanks for your local law enforcement, fire protection, and emergency personnel, and ask God's blessing on their work.

For the Unsaved

Ask that several non-Christians (name them) will come to believe, and so, at the return of Christ, "bear the likeness of the man from heaven" (15:49).

Personal Prayer

Praise God as your faithful Creator and Re-creator in Christ. Give thanks that you can "participate in the sufferings of Christ, so that you may be overjoyed when his glory is revealed" (1 Pet. 4:13). Confess the times in which you have shirked responsibility by failing to speak or act for Christ. Commit yourself to living up to the weighty name "Christian." Ask that you will never "repay evil with evil or insult with insult" (1 Pet. 3:9).

For Your Family and Friends

Ask that your family and friends will not be ashamed of their faith, but will openly share what God has done for them.

For the Church

Thank the Lord for missionaries, and pray that he will be glorified by people being won for Christ through their work. Ask for patience for those workers.

For the Kingdom

Pray for people who are experiencing the effects of natural disasters. Pray that they will feel the closeness of God even in the turmoil, and that relief will be offered to them in Jesus' name.

For the Unsaved

Pray that unsaved persons whom you know will hear of and understand God's judgment and love, and respond by trusting in Christ alone.

Prayer Pointer

"I have to hurry all day to get time to pray." —MARTIN LUTHER

MAY 19

Personal Prayer

Praise the Lord, "the compassionate and gracious God, slow to anger, abounding in love and faithfulness" (Ex. 34:6). Thank God that you have been forgiven of all your sins because of Jesus' work for you. Confess in detail your sins, asking for a greater awareness of sin in your life. Commit yourself to putting on "the new self, created to be like God in true righteousness and holiness" (Eph. 4:24). Ask "to be made new in the attitude of your [mind]" (Eph. 4:23).

For Your Family and Friends

Pray that all your family and friends will daily seek God's gracious forgiveness and will live fitting Christian lives.

For the Church

Pray that no animosities or rivalries will be at home in your congregation, and that your congregation will experience peace and wholeness. Ask that you and your fellow Christians will prize the healthy relationships which you have with each other.

For the Kingdom

Pray for your local educational systems—staff, administration, board, students, and parents. Ask that they will honor God by what they do. Pray that anything which does not meet with God's approval will be rooted out.

For the Unsaved

Ask that acquaintances who do not know Jesus will become conscious of sin and seek his forgiveness.

Personal Prayer

Praise God as the constant and loving provider for all your needs. Give thanks to the Lord that his grace is sufficient for you (2 Cor. 12:9). Confess any times you have questioned the Lord's dealing with you and others. Commit yourself to "be content whatever the circumstances" (Phil. 4:11). Ask that daily you may confidently say, "I can do everything through him who gives me strength" (Phil. 4:13).

For Your Family and Friends

Pray that your friends and family members will base their attitudes and actions on their status in Christ and not their status in the world.

For the Church

Ask that contentment and dependence upon God will be expressed in your congregation's giving. Pray that Christians will understand giving as a prime part of their worship life.

For the Kingdom

Pray that Christians will not relinquish their ministry to governmental agencies and programs. Ask that Christians will work together to meet needs locally and worldwide and thereby be a visible expression of the power of Jesus Christ.

For the Unsaved

Pray that specific "Christ-less" individuals whom you know will be discontented with life without Christ, and seek life in him. Ask for the privilege of being involved in their conversion.

MAY 21

Personal Prayer

Praise God as the one from whom all things have come; praise him as the one to whom you are going when you are called home. Thank God that your relationship with him extends beyond this life. Confess the times when your focus has been only on physical needs, not God's eternal purpose for you (Mt. 6:33). Commit yourself to seeking God's will for you and to hearing the voice of his Spirit through the preaching of the Word. Ask God to reveal himself to you in his splendor and glory.

For Your Family and Friends

Pray that as your family members and friends worship, God may "give [them] the Spirit of wisdom and revelation, so that [they] may know him better" (Eph. 1:17).

For the Church

Pray that people in your congregation may worship with more of a desire to praise the living God than to be pleased or entertained.

For the Kingdom

Pray for those preachers in other countries who must serve eight or ten churches at a time. Ask God to give them strength and to provide lay leaders who can minister in their absence.

For the Unsaved

Ask God to put in the hearts of unsaved friends a hunger for him and for the warmth of fellowship in a local church.

_____

_____

_____

_____

_____

MAY 22

Personal Prayer

Praise God as the great and powerful Creator who has no equal on earth or in the spiritual realm. Give thanks for the vast, eternal reaches of God's knowledge and wisdom. Confess those times when you have not trusted in God's leading. Commit yourself to spending more of your prayer time meditating on the depth of his knowledge and understanding. Ask God to daily make you aware of his power, his wisdom, and his great love for you.

For Your Family and Friends

Pray that the families in your congregation will make a special point of seeking God's will together daily in prayer.

For the Church

Pray that your pastor and elders will spend increasingly more time in prayer for God's guidance in the direction of the church, relying on the Spirit's leading and the instruction of God's Word (Acts 6:4).

For the Kingdom

Pray that those who have been called by God to intercede for Christian leaders and ministers will be faithful in this vital means of supporting the kingdom of God and its leaders (2 Thess. 3:1).

For the Unsaved

Pray for unsaved people you know who are struggling to find direction and meaning for their lives. Ask God to use you to speak to them with a wisdom they cannot resist (1 Cor. 1:23-25).

MAY 23

Personal Prayer

Praise God as the provider and sustainer of all things (Ps. 145:15-16). Give thanks for the tenderness and the care that the Lord gives to the creatures that he has made (145:8-9). Confess those times this past week when you have forgotten to look on other people or other parts of God's world with the same love that is in God's heart. Commit yourself to treating others with the same compassion as God does. Ask God to fill your heart with his care, concern, and tenderness.

For Your Family and Friends

Pray for families in which the parents are too busy to really listen and respond to their children's needs. Ask God to help them set their priorities in line with his will for their families.

For the Church

Pray for the deacons who work in your area or community, asking God's Spirit to charge their work with energy, compassion, and love for those who come seeking their help.

For the Kingdom

Pray for specific missionaries that your church supports, that God will enable them to identify more closely with the people and cultures they serve. Pray for understanding and encouragement in the face of cultural differences.

For the Unsaved

Pray for those you know who are not only outside of the family of God but also outside of your own cultural "family." Ask for an opportunity to talk with such a person this week, sharing God's love and concern for him or her.

_____

_____

_____

_____

_____

Personal Prayer

Praise God as the Rock, your stronghold and fortress (Ps. 144:1-2). Thank him for being a solid foundation on which to stand spiritually, so that nothing can shake you (Mt. 7:24-25). Confess those times in your life when you have stepped off the rock solid foundation of God's Word and relied on your own understanding. Commit yourself to building your life on Christ's teachings. Ask God to help you plant your feet firmly in his Word each day.

For Your Family and Friends

Pray for the devotional times of the families that you know, that regular times of prayer and Bible reading will help bond family members to each other and to God. Pray that your single friends may find a group of spiritual brothers and sisters to do this with as well.

For the Church

Pray for those who teach adult and children's education classes in your church, that they may find the time for new learning themselves, for new growth in their spiritual lives.

For the Kingdom

Pray for those who write educational books and materials for the Church, that they may be moved by God's Spirit to touch on the needs of their readers and to write clearly the truths of Scripture.

For the Unsaved

Ask God to bring your unsaved friends into a knowledge of the truth, so that they can rest their feet on the solid rock of Christ's offer of complete salvation for them.

MAY 25

Personal Prayer

Give praise to God as the Comforter, who feels deeply for those who have been mistreated and abandoned (Isa. 49:13). Thank him for calling many believers into compassionate ministries for the sake of those who are suffering. Confess those times when you may have withheld comfort from others who needed it. Commit yourself to receiving God's encouragement and grace each morning and allowing that to flow through you to others. Ask God to fill you with the knowledge of his love, so that you may be filled with all the fullness of God (Eph. 3:19).

For Your Family and Friends

Pray that families in your church will open their homes to others who do not have a loving family to turn to.

For the Church

Pray for those in your church's neighborhood who have no family or friends to turn to. Ask that God will touch their lives through your calls, visits, and expressions of concern.

For the Kingdom

Pray for the efforts of disaster relief teams from churches all over the world. Ask God to make their compassion and commitment a shining light to people who have been struck by famine, storm, earthquake, or poverty.

For the Unsaved

Ask God to show himself to the unsaved who live on your street as a God who saves, as one who daily bears our burdens (Ps. 68:19-20).

MAY 26

Personal Prayer

Praise God as the eternal and triune God—the mystery of God in three persons of Father, Son, and Holy Spirit. Thank him for promising to make all believers one, just as the three persons of God are one (Jn. 17:20-23). Confess any tendency in your conversations or thoughts to work against this oneness of mind and purpose in the church. Commit yourself to working toward the unity of believers that is beautiful in God's sight (Psalm 133). Ask God to make you more sensitive to his will and purpose in this area.

For Your Family and Friends

Pray for those who are experiencing alienation from their families for the sake of their faith in God and their desire to follow Jesus (Lk. 12:52-53).

For the Church

Pray that less important issues and controversies not be allowed to prevent the church from "being like-minded, having the same love, being one in spirit and purpose" (Phil. 2:2).

For the Kingdom

Pray that Satan not be able to break the unity and fellowship of missionaries from different denominations and cultural backgrounds as they minister together in their common fields.

For the Unsaved

Pray that many outside the church will be convicted of the truth of the gospel when they see the unity and love that prevails in your church fellowship (Jn. 17:23).

Personal Prayer

Glorify the Son of God as one who is worthy to receive all power, wealth, wisdom, strength, honor, glory, and praise (Rev. 5:12). Thank him for having given up all this to die on a cross in your place. Confess any times when you have put your own interests above those of God and others. Commit yourself to being a faithful disciple of Jesus, finding your life by losing it for him and the gospel (Mk. 8:35). Ask Jesus to help you understand what it means to deny yourself, take up your cross, and follow him.

For Your Family and Friends

Pray that family and friends will be kept from a materialistic lifestyle that serves money rather than God (Lk. 16:13).

For the Church

Pray that believers will consider God's priorities as they set their budgets and plan their giving this week.

For the Kingdom

Pray that the money collected from tithes and offerings around the world will be used for the very best purposes, according to God's plan (2 Cor. 9:12).

For the Unsaved

Ask God to show your unsaved friends the emptiness of their pursuit for possessions and security (Lk. 12:15).

Prayer Pointer

"The greater our empathy and the more closely we identify through compassion with those for whom we pray, the more perfect is our communion with the merciful God." —ANTHONY BLOOM

_____

_____

_____

_____

MAY 28

Personal Prayer
Praise your Father in heaven (Mt. 6:9). Thank him for including you as a son or daughter in his family. Confess moments when you've acted like an orphan, turning your back on God's fatherly love. Commit yourself to deeper fellowship with your Father. Ask him to reveal his abiding love in your life through his Word and Spirit.

For Your Family and Friends
Intercede for children in your family or community who are growing up without a mom or dad in the home. Pray for single parents whom you know.

For the Church
As you gather for worship with your brothers and sisters, ask the Father to quell any jealousies or sibling rivalries that would mar your church's worship and fellowship (Eph. 4:2).

For the Kingdom
Pray for war-torn areas of the world where parents and children are suffering deprivation, separation, and death. Ask the Father to bring peace on earth.

For the Unsaved
Think of one friend or coworker who has not experienced God's fatherly love in a redeeming way. Pray for an opportunity this week to speak to that person of the hope that you have (Eph. 2:12; 1 Pet. 3:15).

Prayer Pointer
"God's chief gift to those who seek him is himself." —E. B. PUSEY

MAY 29

Personal Prayer
Praise the name of God (Mt. 6:9). Thank God for revealing his name to you through his Word and Spirit (Ex. 3:15). Confess times when you have misused the name of God in word or deed. Commit yourself to living in a way which hallows God's name. Ask God to glorify his majestic name in all the earth (Ps. 8:1).

For Your Family and Friends
If you have believing relatives and friends, thank God for calling them by his name into his family. Pray for their spiritual well-being. Intercede also for those who do not yet know Jesus.

For the Church
Pray for the pastor, elders, deacons, and other leaders in your congregation. Ask that their walk with the Lord will be vibrant and alive.

For the Kingdom
Pray for Christians working in public service. Ask that they will have the courage to hallow the name of God without compromise in their daily work.

For the Unsaved
Ask God to bless the work of missionaries who preach the gospel in unfamiliar surroundings. Pray that they will be encouraged by Joel's prophecy that "everyone who calls on the name of the LORD will be saved" (Joel 2:32).

MAY 30

Personal Prayer

Praise King Jesus, who today rules and reigns over his kingdom (Mt. 6:10). Thank him for including you as a citizen of his earthly and heavenly realm. Confess any disloyalty you've felt as one of Christ's much-beloved subjects. Commit yourself to serving as an agent of peace in God's kingdom. Ask that all of Satan's attempts to overthrow this divine government will come to nothing.

For Your Family and Friends

Pray that God will protect your family from the realities of the kingdom of darkness and the power of Satan.

For the Church

Ask God to prosper the outreach ministries of your congregation. Pray that the lost and hurting in your community may be found and brought to Christ.

For the Kingdom

Thank God that his kingdom has no end (Dan. 7:27) and that it extends to every corner of the map (Ps. 103:19). Pray for revival in countries where the church is weak and has lost its way.

For the Unsaved

Pray that those who are not yet citizens of the kingdom of heaven will be drawn by the irresistible power of the Holy Spirit. Ask that you might be used to bring them in.

Prayer Pointer

"Prayer is the most difficult and costly activity of the Christian." —ALAN WALKER

MAY 31

Personal Prayer

Praise your Father for his perfect will (Mt. 6:10). Give thanks that nothing occurs in life that God does not cause to happen. Confess those times when you've doubted that his will was best for you. Commit yourself to living by Ps. 40:8: "I desire to do your will, O my God." Ask that God's perfect will may be accomplished in your life.

For Your Family and Friends

Intercede for teens in your family who face strong temptations from many sides. Ask God to protect them from making unwise decisions (1 Thess. 4:3-5).

For the Church

Ask God to bless the work of your Sunday school teachers and assistants. Pray also for the children and adults who attend your church's educational programs. Pray that the hearts of the children and youth will be turned toward God.

For the Kingdom

Take a global perspective. Pray for God's will to be done on earth even as it is in heaven. Ask that Satan's dark dominion will be exposed by the pure light of the gospel.

For the Unsaved

Ask God to make his will known to unsaved persons whom you know. Pray that they might find freedom from the bondage of sin. Ask God to show you how you can help them find Christ.

JUNE 1

Personal Prayer

Praise the God who supplies all your needs. Give thanks for the many material blessings you enjoy in this life. Confess any dissatisfaction or jealousy you have felt about God's provision for you. Commit yourself to living a truly thankful life. Ask God to give you today your daily bread (Mt. 6:11).

For Your Family and Friends

Pray for those who lack the necessities of life. Ask God to provide for specific needs of which you are aware.

For the Church

Thank God for world missionaries supported by your church. Pray for them by name. Ask God's blessing as they share the Bread of Life in other countries.

For the Kingdom

Picture in your mind scenes of starvation and pain in such places as Somalia, Bosnia, and Romania. Ask God to put an end to fighting and bloodshed. Pray that he will open his hand of spiritual and material blessings on the people of these nations.

For the Unsaved

Pray for new churches which God is using to reach unsaved people all across North America. Pray for their pastors and leaders. Ask for effective outreach into communities and neighborhoods.

Prayer Pointer

"God can pick sense out of a confused prayer." —RICHARD SIBBES

_____

_____

_____

_____

_____

JUNE 2

Personal Prayer

Praise God for the forgiveness of sins. Give thanks for God's marvelous promise that "if we confess our sins, he is faithful and just and will forgive us our sins and purify us from all unrighteousness" (1 Jn. 1:9). Confess your sins to God. Commit yourself to living in the joyous assurance that your sins are, indeed, forgiven (Ps. 103:3). Ask God to help you sincerely forgive others who have wronged you (Mt. 6:12).

For Your Family and Friends

Every family experiences the effects of sin. Pray that forgiveness will be a common practice in your home and that family members will be quick to forgive offenses both small and large because of Christ.

For the Church

Thank God for those in your congregation who reach out to the disadvantaged. Pray for those who are afflicted in body and soul and for those who care for them.

For the Kingdom

Ask God to ease the tension of racial conflict in our cities and on some campuses. Pray for repentance and forgiveness to heal neighborhoods and communities. Ask God to protect and empower believers who are working for reconciliation.

For the Unsaved

Name one unsaved person you know. Pray that he or she will "repent and be baptized . . . in the name of Jesus Christ" so that his or her sins may be forgiven (Acts 2:38).

JUNE 3

Personal Prayer

Praise God, who is your rock, your fortress, and your deliverer (2 Sam. 22:2). Thank God for delivering you from your sins and for promising to keep you safe from harm even into old age (Isa. 46:4). Confess times when you've played with temptation and not sought God's way out. Commit yourself to living a holy and godly life. Ask God to deliver you from the evil one day by day (Mt. 6:13).

For Your Family and Friends

Pray that Satan will not be able to gain a foothold in the relationships of your family. Ask God to keep the evil of divorce far from your home. Pray for strong marriages among your family and friends.

For the Church

Ask God to pour out his blessing upon the members of your congregation as they give their tithes and offerings each week. Thank God for the opportunity you have to give to his work. Intercede for your deacons.

For the Kingdom

Pray for Christian ministries which help persons with AIDS. Ask God to give them wisdom and grace to reach out to hurting people who have little hope without a cure. Pray for successful AIDS research.

For the Unsaved

God is a God who rescues and saves (Dan. 6:27). Pray that God will rescue and save persons you know who do not yet believe. Ask that they will find God to be the rock, fortress, and deliverer they've been looking for all along.

JUNE 4

Personal Prayer
Praise God as the one who loves you like no one else can. Thank him for loving you "with an everlasting love," drawing you to himself "with loving kindness" (Jer. 31:3). Confess times of presuming upon his love. Commit yourself to reflecting God's love as his image-bearer. Ask him to love others through you, knowing that you can do all things through Christ (Phil. 4:13).

For Your Family and Friends
Pray that God's love will be at least as fully evident in your home as in other relationships. Ask him to regularly prompt you to love your family and friends in ways they can identify.

For the Church
Pray that worship services around the world today will be beautiful reflections of God's love back to him. Ask God to make love a key characteristic of your own congregation.

For the Kingdom
Pray that love for God's ways will prompt you to love mercy (Mic. 6:8) in your societal involvements. Ask God to overcome hatred, violence, and prejudice in your area.

For the Unsaved
Pray that God's people will have so much love for one another that all those around will know they are Jesus' disciples (Jn. 13:35). Ask God to draw the observers to himself through that love.

JUNE 5

Personal Prayer

Praise the one whose control covers even the details of your life (Mt. 6:25-34). Thank God for knowing about your daily needs. Confess any worry. Commit to taking hold of areas where you are to be in charge in your life with the clear knowledge of being "second in command" under God. Ask him for the Spirit's fruit of self-control.

For Your Family and Friends

Pray that God will work self-control into your private life. Ask him to help you be self-controlled with family members and with private disciplines such as eating habits, TV watching, reading materials, time usage, and exercise patterns.

For the Church

Pray that leaders of high-profile ministries and local churches will be men and women of great integrity. Ask God to help them control themselves in temptation, frustration, and other difficulties.

For the Kingdom

Pray that your local, regional, and national government leaders will exercise self-control in fiscal matters as well as other issues of justice. Ask God to strategically place his people in positions of control.

For the Unsaved

Pray that the lack of self-control by some Christians will not effectively barricade non-Christians' receptivity to the good news. Ask the sovereign God to break through barriers to save a particular person in your neighborhood.

JUNE 6

Personal Prayer
Praise your faithful God! Give thanks for God's faithfulness to you even when you are unfaithful to him (2 Tim. 2:11-13). Spend a few minutes asking God to help you think through your life and confessing any unfaithfulness he brings to your attention. Commit yourself as God's image-bearer to reflecting his faithfulness in your own.

For Your Family and Friends
Pray that you and those close to you will be fully faithful—as spouses to marriage vows and as parents to baptismal vows. Ask God to show you how you can encourage such faithfulness.

For the Church
Pray that Christians will be faithful to use individual and corporate outreach opportunities. Ask for the vision to see opportunities and the loving determination to follow through.

For the Kingdom
Pray for opportunities to engage in civic responsibilities. Ask God to help you be effective in service.

For the Unsaved
Pray that faithfulness to one another will draw those who are in the pain of broken marriage vows. Ask God to bring healing and new faithfulness to them through evidences of his healing and faithfulness in your own life.

Prayer Pointer
"We only have to consider the lives of biblical personalities to realize that almost everything they did of kingdom significance followed the exercise of serious prayer." —GORDON MacDONALD

JUNE 7

Personal Prayer

Praise God for being sovereign, all-powerful, just, and gentle—all at the same time! Thank him for dealing gently with you in your faults. Confess times of lashing out at others. Commit yourself to reflecting the gentleness of God to those around you, and ask God to produce that part of his Spirit's fruit in abundance in you.

For Your Family and Friends

Pray that you will be consistently gentle with those closest to you. Ask God to help you avoid reactionary responses to family members with habits that annoy you.

For the Church

Pray that gentleness will be a noticeable characteristic of your local church. Ask that those teaching children and new or broken believers be given a special measure of gentleness as they lead.

For the Kingdom

Pray that Christians who differ with one another will present a positive example to the world of how to gently disagree in love. Ask God to present that example also through you in your own conflict situations.

For the Unsaved

Pray that your gentleness will be evident to all (Phil. 4:5). Ask God to use such a witness in the process of saving those near you who are watching your actions.

Prayer Pointer

"No answer to prayer is an indication of our merit; every answer to prayer is an indication of God's mercy." —JOHN BLANCHARD

JUNE 8

Personal Prayer
Praise God for the joy and peace he brought to the world through Jesus! Thank him for bringing joy and peace to your own life. Ask God to show you any ways you inhibit the joy or peace of others. Confess those ways, as well as any anxiety. Commit yourself to rejoicing continually, handing anxieties to God, and living in the peace which he then gives (Phil. 4:9).

For Your Family and Friends
Pray that you might serve as a peace-maker for those close to you. Ask God to make your home a "safe place," especially for a family member or friend presently in great turmoil.

For the Church
Pray that your local church will be authentically known as a joyful and peaceful people. Ask God to work through world mission efforts to spread true joy and peace to the farthest parts of the earth.

For the Kingdom
Pray that world missionaries working in the midst of spiritual darkness and brokenness will be shining lights of joy and peaceful bearers of God's peace. Ask God to protect them from depression and violence.

For the Unsaved
Pray that the joy and peace of Jesus will draw an unsaved acquaintance to him through you. Ask God to continually produce these parts of the Spirit's fruit in you.

JUNE 9

Personal Prayer

Praise God that he is patient with you, "not wanting anyone to perish, but everyone to come to repentance" (2 Pet. 3:9). Thank God for his patience with you in aspects of life you are slow to let him change. Confess times of presuming upon his patience, and commit yourself to ready and diligent responses to his leading. Ask God to help you, as his image-bearer, to reflect his patience.

For Your Family and Friends

Pray that you and your network of family and friends will remember God's standard: "Love is patient" (1 Cor. 13:4). Ask him to help all of you move that from thought to practice.

For the Church

Pray that all members of your local church will be patient with one another as they minister in the midst of their weaknesses. Ask that fellowship not be broken by impatience or critical spirits.

For the Kingdom

Pray that such patience will also reach out to care for those who are indigent. Ask that patience and wisdom be mixed together to truly assist rather than enable irresponsibility.

For the Unsaved

Pray that you will especially exercise the Spirit's fruit of patience with those who spew their anger at you. Ask God to use that patient love to help them "come to repentance" (2 Pet. 3:9).

Personal Prayer

Praise God that he is kind and good. Give thanks for specific ways you have experienced that since the beginning of this week. Confess times when you have not been a clear and consistent image-bearer of these characteristics of your God. Commit to reflecting him with such quality that others will praise God for his kindness and goodness shown to them through you. Ask God to produce this part of his Holy Spirit's fruit in you.

For Your Family and Friends

Pray that family members and friends will be kind and good to each other in private as well as in public. Ask God to help them hate what is evil and cling to what is good (Rom. 12:9).

For the Church

Pray that good people in your church will bring good things out of the good stored up in their hearts (Lk. 6:45). Ask God to help members extend this to their financial stewardship.

For the Kingdom

Pray that God's people will honor him by being kind to the needy (Prov. 14:31). Ask God to use those efforts to spread his kingly influence.

For the Unsaved

Pray that God will draw an unsaved person you know to himself with his loving kindness (Jer. 31:3). Ask God to draw that person through his goodness and kindness in you.

_____

_____

_____

_____

_____

JUNE 11

Personal Prayer

Praise God that he is great and greatly to be praised (Ps. 48:1). Give thanks for psalms and hymns that remind us to praise God every day in every activity with which we are involved. Confess your shortcomings in praising God too seldom or too generally. Commit yourself to thanking God for two things every day which you often take for granted. Ask him to help you be a more thanks-living person, joyfully serving him (1 Thess. 5:18).

For Your Family and Friends

Pray that your life may be an example of thanks-living so that family and friends may also give thanks in all things.

For the Church

Pray that your worship this day as well as throughout the week will "extol the LORD at all times, his praise will always be on [your] lips" (Ps. 34:1-2).

For the Kingdom

Pray that thanks-living on the part of every Christian will result in the lessening of racial tension, resolve conflict between peoples and nations, and make even "enemies live at peace with [you]" (Prov. 16:7).

For the Unsaved

Pray for salvation for many seekers as a result of your thanks-living.

Prayer Pointer

"The one concern of the devil is to keep Christians from praying. He fears nothing from prayerless studies, prayerless work, and prayerless religion. He laughs at our toil, mocks at our wisdom, but trembles when we pray."
—SAMUEL CHADWICK

_____

_____

_____

_____

JUNE 12

Personal Prayer

Praise Jesus for his mighty victory over temptation in his confrontation with Satan in the desert (Mt. 4:1-11). Thank God for his promise that you are never tempted beyond what you can handle (1 Cor. 10:13). Confess the many times you have yielded to temptation, not claiming God's power to "resist the devil" (Jas. 4:7). Commit yourself to God that you may overcome evil with good (Prov. 3:7-8). Ask him to assure you that you will overcome all the power of the enemy because of his ultimate victory over Satan at the cross.

For Your Family and Friends

Pray that your family and friends may celebrate your victory over temptation—then feel God's special power for them to be overcomers as well.

For the Church

Pray that the leaders of your church may be real examples of victory over temptation and help others to that end as well.

For the Kingdom

Pray that those in our armed forces will be given extra strength in the face of strong temptation.

For the Unsaved

Pray that you, with the power of God, might use an opportunity today to help an unsaved friend have victory over temptation (Col. 4:5-6).

JUNE 13

Personal Prayer

Praise God for his unsearchable riches in Christ, riches with which nothing can compare (Rom. 11:33-36; Eph. 3:8-12). Thank him for allowing you to share in these riches because of your relationship to Jesus Christ (Col. 2:2-3). Confess your failure to appreciate God's riches and the many times you've looked to what the world calls riches for your happiness. Commit yourself to finding your security in Christ alone. Ask God to help you fully appreciate his riches in Jesus, giving him the glory.

For Your Family and Friends

Pray for opportunities to show God's riches in Christ by some specific act of giving today (Lk. 12:21).

For the Church

Finances are such a big concern in most churches—pray that your church will move forward in faith with outreach ministries it believes God will bless without asking the question "What will it cost?"

For the Kingdom

Pray that the church will give willingly to combat the forces of evil which promote abortion, murder, starvation, etc.

For the Unsaved

Pray that funds will be readily available to further evangelism throughout the world, through such means as church planting, media, local church, crusades, literature, etc.

_____

_____

_____

_____

_____

JUNE 14

Personal Prayer

Praise God for his love for children who often are full of insight (Mk. 10:14-16). Thank God that he teaches you to have a childlike faith (Mt. 11:25). Confess how often you make things so complicated and act so independently of him. Commit yourself to giving out the simple gospel message, "Believe in the Lord Jesus Christ and you will be saved" (Acts 16:31). Ask God to help you recognize every opportunity to have a childlike faith, and not to be childish (Mt. 18:4).

For Your Family and Friends

Pray for all your dear ones to experience that childlike faith, not trying to impress others but to truly be as little children whom Jesus so readily welcomed (Mt. 19:14).

For the Church

Pray that your church will be involved in presenting the gospel simply and sweetly, through the preaching of the Word and the teaching ministry offered for children and adults.

For the Kingdom

Pray that Christians all over the world may "tell the good news" in a childlike way and be ready to welcome all who respond as little children, eager to know more.

For the Unsaved

Pray that your simple acts of love for another will lead you to an opportunity to share the gospel with an unsaved person today.

JUNE 15

Personal Prayer

Praise God that he is greater than all gods—and does what pleases him (Ps. 135:5-6). Give thanks that God has "set apart the godly for himself; . . . [and] hears [you] when [you] call" (Ps. 4:3). Confess your difficulty in accepting that what the Lord does is always good for you or will work out for good (Jer.29:11-14; Rom. 8:28). Commit yourself to spending time with God daily, reading his Word, and claiming these promises for your life. Ask God to keep you faithful as you seek to grow in him.

For Your Family and Friends

Pray for your family and friends to trust God for the wisdom and victory he has available for all as they recognize his greatness (Prov. 2:6-7).

For the Church

Pray that God's greatness will be shown as your church willingly and joyfully supports a specific world missionary with encouragement, prayer, and finances.

For the Kingdom

Pray that God's plan and purpose will not be hindered by threats of Satan and his hosts as God does not want "anyone to perish, but everyone to come to repentance" (2 Pet. 3:9).

For the Unsaved

Pray that the unsaved will recognize the opportune time which God gives them to repent.

_____

_____

_____

_____

_____

JUNE 16

Personal Prayer

Praise God that he wants you to have the full measure of his joy in you as he prayed to his Father in Jn. 17:13. Thank God for filling your heart with joy (Ps. 4:7). Confess any inability to feel "the joy of the LORD is your strength" (Neh. 8:10) due to some situation that may trouble you right now. Commit yourself to reading Paul's letter to the Philippians to inspire you toward greater joy. Ask God to help you be joyful in every situation and to do everything without complaining or arguing (Phil. 2:14).

For Your Family and Friends

Pray that your family and friends may see your joy in the Lord in all situations and likewise be joyful.

For the Church

Pray that God will use you as well as other caregivers in your church to joyfully serve those with special needs today.

For the Kingdom

Pray that God will break down the barriers of hatred within and between nations that cause calamities and problems, by loving and joyful acts which cannot be resisted or denied.

For the Unsaved

Pray that God will use your joy in him to attract your unsaved friends and neighbors and lead you to being a joyful witness for him always (1 Pet. 3:15).

Prayer Pointer

"Prayer is incredibly simple. God answers prayer because his children ask."
—RICHARD FOSTER

JUNE 17

Personal Prayer

Praise God for his wisdom—for your being in Christ Jesus who has become for you wisdom from God! (1 Cor. 1:30, 2:7). Thank God that you may have the full riches of complete understanding to know the mystery of God, namely Christ (Col. 2:2). Confess your lack of understanding. Commit yourself to being wise in the things of God, who makes the wisdom of the world look like foolishness (1 Cor. 1:19-20). Ask God to keep you from being a "wise guy" and to help you lead others to biblical wisdom.

For Your Family and Friends

Pray that God will help you avoid a "holier than thou" attitude with your family and friends (1 Cor. 4:5).

For the Church

Pray for God to give your church and its leaders a real heart for ministry and wisdom to use the resources given in the name of Christ.

For the Kingdom

Pray that Christians will cooperate to resolve many of the issues that separate, rather than unite, neighbors, communities, nations, and peoples, in the love of Jesus.

For the Unsaved

Pray for wisdom to show a specific act of kindness today to an unsaved neighbor.

_____

_____

_____

_____

_____

JUNE 18

Personal Prayer
Praise God as the one to whom you have given your entire life. Thank him for desiring to be Lord of everything that you have and are, and for asking nothing less. Confess those parts of your life that you still hold back from God's complete authority. Commit yourself to laying these areas before God throughout the day, looking for his help in surrendering them completely. Ask God to help you be completely devoted to him and his will (Col. 3:17).

For Your Family and Friends
Pray that God will help young adults that you know become willing to give their lives completely for him and the gospel.

For the Church
Ask that your church's worship be made uplifting not only by music and preaching but also by the sacrificial lives of members who have served Christ during the week (Rom. 12:1).

For the Kingdom
Pray that throughout the world, worship will lift up the name of Jesus and defeat the forces of Satan.

For the Unsaved
Pray that the unsaved who visit church services in your city this week will be struck with the genuineness of believers' worship and the power of the Word in their lives (1 Cor. 14:24-25).

_____

_____

_____

_____

JUNE 19

Personal Prayer
Give praise to the one who has created love, the one who is the very heart and nature of love (1 Jn. 4:16). Thank God for his love for you—a deeply personal love that will never let you go (Rom. 8:38-39). Confess those times when you have been unable to receive and return God's love for you this past week. Commit yourself to meditating daily on God's strong love for you. Ask him to fill you with the knowledge of his love, so that you may be filled with the fullness of God (Eph. 3:17-19).

For Your Family and Friends
Pray for those marriages where love is failing, that God will miraculously restore the ability to forgive, to cherish, and to receive each other with affection.

For the Church
Pray that your congregation will be so saturated and overwhelmed with a sense of God's love that you will reach out to your neighborhood with a love that is unmistakably Christlike.

For the Kingdom
Ask God for leaders who embody love in every way, putting aside ambition and pride to serve others (Phil. 2:3).

For the Unsaved
Pray that Christ will show his love through you to one unsaved person today.

Prayer Pointer
"God shapes the world by prayer. Prayers are deathless. They outlive the lives of those who utter them." —E. M. BOUNDS

_____

_____

_____

_____

_____

JUNE 20

Personal Prayer

Praise God as the high and lofty One who lives forever, who lives in a high and holy place, but also with those who are contrite and lowly in spirit (Isa. 57:15). Thank him for choosing the lowliness of the cross to show his power and wisdom to the world (1 Cor. 1:20-25). Confess any resistance on your part to sharing in the humility of the gospel. Commit yourself to laying your pride daily before the feet of Christ. Ask Jesus to help you empty yourself in service to God, as he did (Philippians 2).

For Your Family and Friends

Pray against any rifts between family members that you know of, that the spirit of pride may be defeated and relationships be restored in a spirit of humility and love.

For the Church

Ask that your church's outreach ministries be done in a spirit of humility that sees the beauty of Jesus in everyone who is served (Mt. 25:34-40).

For the Kingdom

Pray that the leaders of your country will be given the humility to seek wisdom and strength from God for their tasks.

For the Unsaved

Ask God to break down the spiritual blindness of unsaved friends, enabling them to see the power and wisdom of the cross.

_____

_____

_____

_____

_____

JUNE 21

Personal Prayer
Give glory and honor to God as one whose wisdom and knowledge are too vast and deep ever to be grasped by the human mind. Thank the Father for having revealed himself in human, finite form in his Son, Jesus (Jn. 14:7). Confess the times during this week when you have failed to look to Jesus for help in understanding the Father's heart and mind. Commit yourself daily to prayer for this understanding (Eph. 1:17). Ask God to open the eyes of your heart as you look to Jesus and study his life and words in the gospels.

For Your Family and Friends
Commit your immediate family members to the wisdom of God, remembering that God's ways are past understanding and claiming that God will work all things for their good (Rom. 8:28).

For the Church
Pray that your church education teachers will not limit God's Word to simple formulas but will also teach children awe at the splendor, glory, and unsearchable wisdom of God in Jesus.

For the Kingdom
Pray for those who speak of God's Word on the radio and television, that they may clearly present the wisdom of the cross to those whose minds are darkened (1 Cor. 2:11-14).

For the Unsaved
Ask for wisdom in explaining the cross of Christ to an unsaved friend or acquaintance this week.

_____

_____

_____

_____

_____

JUNE 22

Personal Prayer

Magnify God as the one whose Word will outlive this world (Isa. 40:8). Thank Jesus that he is coming again to establish a new heavens and earth, at an hour that the Father has set (Mt. 24:30-31, 36). Confess those times when you let this perspective slip out of your daily life and prayers. Commit yourself daily to setting your hope and expectation on Jesus' coming again. Ask God to show you what you must do in the time that you have left (24:45-51).

For Your Family and Friends

Pray for the homes you know that are nominally Christian, that God would set their hearts on fire and may show them the urgency of his kingdom work.

For the Church

Pray that the members of your congregation would join with other churches in your neighborhood as they see how large the harvest is and how many workers are still needed to reach the unsaved around you (Mt. 9:37-38).

For the Kingdom

Ask God's Spirit to give clear leading to those who are considering his call to world missions. Examine your heart also to see what God may be asking of you in this area.

For the Unsaved

Ask God to show you the urgency of the gospel message and to give you the opportunity to share it with someone today.

_____

_____

_____

_____

JUNE 23

Personal Prayer
Praise God as one who is perfect in power and judgment but also perfect in mercy and kindness. Give thanks for God's mercy to you (Eph. 2:4-5). Confess your inability to show mercy as completely and graciously as your Father does. Commit yourself to living with a greater awareness of God's mercy and kindness in your life (Eph. 1:7-8). Ask God to extend this grace to others who have irritated or hurt you.

For Your Family and Friends
Ask God to give you the power to extend forgiveness and mercy to family members or acquaintances with whom you have a broken relationship.

For the Church
Pray that those in your church who struggle with guilt and an inability to forgive will be changed by an awareness of God's great and free mercy toward them in Jesus. Pray for wisdom for your pastor, elders, and others who counsel these people.

For the Kingdom
Ask God to make his church worldwide a shining example of people who extend mercy and kindness even to their enemies (Mt. 5:44-45).

For the Unsaved
Intercede for your unsaved friends and acquaintances, that God would put in their hearts a hunger for his mercy and forgiveness.

Prayer Pointer
"All who have walked with God have viewed prayer as the main business of their lives." —DELMA JACKSON

_____

_____

_____

_____

JUNE 24

Personal Prayer

Glorify God as the all-sufficient one, who through his limitless power fills everything in every way (Eph. 1:23). Thank God for giving you his Spirit to meet all your needs as you do his will. Confess those times you have sought fulfillment in ways which did not honor God. Commit your needs to him (Phil. 4:19). Ask God for a greater awareness of his power to help you grow spiritually (2 Pet. 1:3-8).

For Your Family and Friends

Pray for friends who struggle with material or spiritual poverty. Ask God to help them understand that he can meet both areas of need with his riches in Christ.

For the Church

Intercede for your deacons in their work of mercy, that they will be moved to pray daily for God's provision, recognizing him as the source of their funds and their desire to help others.

For the Kingdom

Ask that God will use you and others in your congregation to answer the desperate pleas for help and funds from kingdom ministries (2 Cor. 9:10-14).

For the Unsaved

Pray that no nation, city, or person will go without hearing the gospel simply because there was not enough money given to support evangelists and preachers.

JUNE 25

Personal Prayer

Praise God for his quietness, restoration, and strength (Ps. 23:2-3). Give thanks that God will give you that quiet time to reflect on his restoring power and quietness (Ps. 46:10). Confess your failure to be still before the Lord so he can speak to you. Commit yourself to a daily time of worship and adoration of God. Ask God for assurance that in quietness and trust is your strength (Isa. 30:15).

For Your Family and Friends

Pray that your family and friends would "rejoice in the Lord always" (Phil. 4:4) as they realize that God quiets us with his love (Zeph. 3:17).

For the Church

Pray that the church will not be silent, but will spread the Word of God in mighty ways today, even as Jesus told the Pharisees in Lk. 19:40 that "if they keep quiet, the stones will cry out."

For the Kingdom

Pray that God's kingdom will prosper as his servants lead the way in having "the unfading beauty of a gentle and quiet spirit, which is of great worth in God's sight" (1 Pet. 3:4).

For the Unsaved

Pray that your quietness before God will result in winning the "respect of outsiders" (1 Thess. 4:11-12) so that they will see Jesus in you.

JUNE 26

Personal Prayer

Praise God for his leadership over the redeemed because of his unfailing love and strength (Ex. 15:11, 13). Give thanks for leaders who speak the Word of God to you (Heb. 13:7). Confess your lack of recognizing God's leadership through others that he brings into your life and your failure to support them with your prayers (1 Tim. 2:1-2). Commit yourself to following God's leadership as he brings you into a land "flowing with milk and honey" (Num. 14:8). Ask God to help you be a good leader in bringing others to him.

For Your Family and Friends

Pray that your family members and friends may accept the leadership you offer, leading many to righteousness and shining like the stars as stated in Dan. 12:3.

For the Church

Pray for church leaders to depend on God for skills that will be recognized by others and used for God's glory.

For the Kingdom

Pray that all would obey their leaders and submit to their authority (Heb. 13:17) so their work will be a joy.

For the Unsaved

Ask that all Christians will "walk the walk" and not just "talk the talk" that will lead others to salvation in Jesus.

Prayer Pointer

"The power of the promise 'Ask, and it will be given you' lies in the loving relationship between us as children and God as our Father." —MAXIE DUNNAM

_____

_____

_____

_____

JUNE 27

Personal Prayer

Praise God for his strength and confidence, enduring from everlasting to everlasting (1 Chron. 29:10-11). Give thanks that God is your strength and confidence and that he will never fail you or forsake you (1 Chron. 28:20). Confess to the Lord your failure to rely completely upon him and his Word (Isa. 41:10). Commit yourself to being strong and doing the work God has for you without complaining (Phil. 2:14). Ask God to forgive you for not depending on him and that you may wait on the Lord and be confident of his love (Jeremiah 31:3).

For Your Family and Friends

Pray that your family and friends would also claim the strength and peace that God gives to his people (Ps. 29:11).

For the Church

Pray that your church will be strong in preparing its membership to grow in their daily walk and work for him as parents, teachers, workers, etc.

For the Kingdom

Pray that God's kingdom will prosper as we all move forward in his strength and confidence—not on our own!

For the Unsaved

Pray that your unsaved friends and neighbors will benefit from your confidence in God as you speak to them about it—and come to know God personally as a result (1 Pet. 3:15).

_____

_____

_____

_____

_____

JUNE 28

Personal Prayer

Praise God for being the great healer who gives real peace and security for you to enjoy (Jer. 33:6). Give thanks for the many miraculous healings that show God's power at work. Confess your failure to appreciate the health God gives you and your complaining when things aren't going well (Ps. 139:23). Commit yourself to praising God each day for a healthy body, for legs and arms, fingers and toes, eyes and ears—a body that functions so beautifully. Ask him for guidance in blessing him at all times even if these body parts aren't always working right (Ps. 34:1).

For Your Family and Friends

Pray for family members and friends who are not experiencing good health. Praise him for accepting your prayers (Ps. 6:9).

For the Church

Pray for your church to be very compassionate and able to minister to those who do not experience good health, have disabilities, or have met with serious accident.

For the Kingdom

Pray for God's kingdom to advance in meaningful ways as you seek new means to reach out to the "sin-sick" people of the world (Mt. 9:13).

For the Unsaved

Pray for the unsaved to see that "it is not the healthy who need a doctor but the sick" (9:12)—to see their "sick" condition and come to Jesus' open arms of love.

JUNE 29

Personal Prayer

Praise God that he is in control of every storm (Mk. 4:35-39). Thank him that he does not want anyone to perish but to have everlasting life in him (2 Pet. 3:9). Confess to God your wrong response to the stormy, unexpected events in your life that leave you feeling panicky and fretful. Commit every stormy situation, as well as every good one, to God as he cares for you, restores you, and makes you strong (1 Pet. 5:7, 10). Ask God to calm any anxiety or fear that you are experiencing.

For Your Family and Friends

Pray for your family and friends to experience real calm in their lives, to be carefree and not afraid, to stand firm in the Lord as Isaiah was reminded in Isa. 7:4, 9.

For the Church

Pray for the needs, fears, and storms encountered in the daily lives of missionary families.

For the Kingdom

Pray that God's kingdom will prosper as Christians spread the words of Ps. 107:29, "[God] stills the storms to a whisper . . . he guide[s] them to their desired haven. Let them give thanks to the LORD for his unfailing love."

For the Unsaved

Pray for troubled unbelievers to find victory over stormy lives in the calm that only Jesus can give.

_____

_____

_____

_____

_____

JUNE 30

Personal Prayer
Praise God for his plans, from all eternity, done in perfect faithfulness (Isa. 25:1) which will come to pass as he purposes (Isa. 14:24). Thank God for his plans for you—to prosper you and not to harm you, to give you hope and a future (Jer. 29:11). Confess to him your failure to learn contentment in every situation as Paul did (Phil. 4:11). Commit yourself to fearing the Lord, which leads to life, and thus rest content, untouched by trouble (Prov. 19:23). Ask God for real contentment in what you have (Heb. 13:5), remembering that he will never fail you nor forsake you.

For Your Family and Friends
Pray that your family and friends will obey and serve the Lord and thus spend their years in contentment (Job 36:11).

For the Church
Pray that your church will experience real contentment, that internal problems will be resolved so real caregiving will be ongoing!

For the Kingdom
Pray that God will challenge you to be involved in some kingdom endeavor close to home such as an assistance ministry. Ask God to give you real satisfaction in helping others.

For the Unsaved
Pray that your contentment in a difficult situation God has placed you in may result in the salvation of an unsaved friend.

Prayer Pointer
"Men May spurn our appeals, reject our message, oppose our arguments, despise our persons, but they are helpless against our prayers." —SIDLOW BAXTER

JULY 1

Personal Prayer

Praise God for being the God of all creation (Gen. 1:31). Thank God for the variety in his creation, in plants and animals, and especially in people (Rom. 12:4-6). Confess to him your lack of appreciation for so many of the things he has done and made (1 Tim. 4:4-5). Commit each day to the Lord, showing special appreciation for one thing in nature that you've not noticed in the past. Ask God to help you be more observant as you are involved in your daily activities, praising him abundantly (Ps. 135).

For Your Family and Friends

Pray that your appreciation of little things will help your family and friends be more appreciative of the beauty of God's creation (Psalm 148).

For the Church

Pray that your church leaders may take a greater stand in teaching everyone to respect and take care of God's beautiful creation.

For the Kingdom

Pray that you may be concerned about your environment and make a difference in the pollution problems that face our world today.

For the Unsaved

Ask that you will be an example in doing your part in cleaning up your world—and that God will use that as an opportunity to witness to the unsaved.

_____

_____

_____

_____

_____

JULY 2

Personal Prayer

Praise God as the one worthy of the worship of our entire lives (Rom. 12:1-2). Give thanks for God's mercy shown to you personally. Confess times of conforming to the pattern of this world. Commit yourself to the continual renewing of your mind. Ask God to be true to his promise that you will be able to test and approve what is his will.

For Your Family and Friends

Pray that your household and friends will be excellent worshipers in church services. Ask God to lead you from special worship times to the worship of daily devotion to him throughout the week.

For the Church

Pray for God to move in special ways throughout the world upon his gathered people. Ask him to help members remember that they belong to each other (12:5).

For the Kingdom

Pray that each of God's people will be reminded of the different gifts he or she possesses, according to the grace of God (12:6). Ask that they be further equipped through worship to use those gifts for God's kingdom (12:7ff.).

For the Unsaved

Ask God to love people to himself through your words and actions.

JULY 3

Personal Prayer

Praise God for meeting with his people in special ways through weekly worship services. Give thanks that you can continue to be with him today! Confess times of ignoring God during the weekdays. Commit yourself to a special time of worshiping God through personal devotions each day this week. Ask the Lord to remind you of his presence throughout this day.

For Your Family and Friends

Pray that you and those close to you may faithfully apply what God showed all of you through pastors and teachers in Sunday's worship. Ask God to help you be humble and gentle in this, encouraging each other rather than being judgmental.

For the Church

Pray for your local and international church leaders as they do their work this week. Ask God to prompt them to diligent use of their leadership gifts and positions (Rom. 12:8).

For the Kingdom

Pray especially for leaders of God's church who are highly visible through the news media. Ask God to give them humble courage and a consistently brilliant witness.

For the Unsaved

Pray that unsaved persons around the world will see that brilliant witness of Christian leaders and glorify God. Ask God to shine clearly and consistently through you in your sphere of influence.

JULY 4

Personal Prayer

Praise God verbally, saying, "Jesus is Lord" (Rom. 10:9). Thank Christ for fulfilling God's law for you and granting you his righteousness (10:4). Confess any attempts you are still making to earn righteousness and favor with God. Commit to a lifestyle of confessing the lordship of Jesus. Ask God to remove any lingering distrust (10:11).

For Your Family and Friends

Pray one by one for every member of your household to call on the name of the Lord and be saved (10:13). Ask God to help them believe through your witness.

For the Church

Pray for joyful and obedient involvement in the outreach ministries sponsored by your local church and your denomination. Ask God to give real wisdom to those involved in planning strategies to enable God's people to be more and more effective.

For the Kingdom

Pray for God's kingdom to come and his will to be done on your part of the earth as it is in heaven. Ask that the lordship of Christ, which we confess verbally, will be applied in just and righteous actions.

For the Unsaved

Thank God for those specially gifted and dedicated to bringing the good news (10:15). Ask him to use you in going and sending others (10:14).

Prayer Pointer

"Daily prayers lessen daily cares." —ANONYMOUS

_____

_____

_____

_____

JULY 5

Personal Prayer
Praise God for the depth of the riches of his wisdom and knowledge (Rom. 11:33). Give thanks that "from him and through him and to him are all things" (11:36). Confess times of thinking that God owes you favors or explanations (11:35). Commit yourself to thinking deeply about God until you come to the end of your ability to understand. Ask God to help you reach that point with wonder and amazement rather than doubt or cynicism (11:33-36).

For Your Family and Friends
Pray that the education of the children of your family and friends leads them to marvel at God's greatness. Ask God for teachers acutely aware of his design and involvement in all areas of creation.

For the Church
Pray for your church's educational program and personnel. Ask that God's church will also be faithful in supporting Christian education beyond its local ministries.

For the Kingdom
Pray that God will help all believers to be students of his ways with eyes to see and minds to understand more of his caring control. Ask that God's kingdom will soon come in fullness.

For the Unsaved
Pray for those who do not understand from a God-centered perspective. Ask God to open their hearts to his Word.

JULY 6

Personal Prayer
Praise God as the one who will soon crush Satan under your feet (Rom. 16:20). Thank him for revealing the mysteries of his salvation to you (16:25-27). Asking God to show you your sin, confess any ways in which you have been involved in causing divisions in Christ's people or have put up obstacles that impeded the spread of his Word (16:17-18). Commit yourself to being "wise about what is good, and innocent about what is evil" (16:19).

For Your Family and Friends
Pray for your family and friends to be personally involved in reaching the world for Christ. Ask God for a world-sized vision which also has your immediate neighborhood in view.

For the Church
Pray for workers to go into the harvest fields of the world. Ask God to prompt his people to abundant contributions of finances, prayer, and encouragement to send these missionaries.

For the Kingdom
Pray for cooperation between Christian denominations and mission personnel. Ask God to help believers seek his kingdom and righteousness above the growth of their own ministries.

For the Unsaved
Pray for the nations to believe and obey God, asking him to establish both "new" and "old" believers through the proclamation of Jesus Christ (16:26).

JULY 7

Personal Prayer

Praise God for his excellence in creation. Give thanks for the creation's variety and splendor. Confess ways in which you have misused parts of it. Commit yourself to the proper care and use of God's creation. Ask God to help you regard it as "clean" (Rom. 14:14), receiving it from him with thanksgiving.

For Your Family and Friends

Pray for healing for any family member or friend who is misusing drugs, alcohol, nicotine, or any other part of creation. Ask God to bring conviction of needed changes through his Spirit.

For the Church

Pray for sensitivity among Christians toward one another's beliefs about food, drink, religious observances, and other discretionary matters (Romans 14), so that fellowship and caring might not be hindered. Ask God to help you to "make every effort to do what leads to peace and to mutual edification" (14:19).

For the Kingdom

Pray that the world will be attracted by the loving care Christians show one another instead of being repulsed by in-fighting. Ask God to move his church to compassionate caring and healing without compromising his truth and methods.

For the Unsaved

Pray for anyone in your circle of contacts who is hurting. Ask God to show you a specific way in which you can show his care to that person or family.

JULY 8

Personal Prayer
Praise God as the one who again has supplied you with all you have needed this week. Thank him for putting some of his resources into your care. Confess any waste or mismanagement of those resources this week. Commit yourself to sharing with God's people who are in need (Rom. 12:13). Ask God to bring to mind the name of someone with whom he would have you share by showing hospitality (12:13).

For Your Family and Friends
Pray that your children and those of your friends learn principles of Christian stewardship from an early age. Ask God to make you an excellent example for them.

For the Church
Pray that those entrusted with the special spiritual gift of contributing to the needs of others will give generously (12:8). Ask God to give you and all members of your church a desire to lay up their treasures in heaven (Mt. 6:20).

For the Kingdom
Pray that God will keep prompting his people to overflow with love and good deeds. Ask that such generous love will result in people praising the Father in heaven (Mt. 5:16).

For the Unsaved
Pray for Christian missions to be so generously supported that they can focus on evangelism instead of fund-raising. Ask God to multiply their resources and effectiveness, bringing many into his family.

_____

_____

_____

_____

_____

JULY 9

Personal Prayer

Praise God for his everlasting love (Jer. 31:3), which has no end. Thank God for demonstrating his love for you by sending his Son to die in your place (Rom. 5:8). Confess any lack of love you have experienced toward God or other believers. Commit yourself to bearing the fruit of love by the power of the Holy Spirit (Gal. 5:22). Ask God to enable you daily to "put on love" (Col. 3:14).

For Your Family and Friends

Thank God for the love of your family and friends. Pray for any unbelieving friends or family members that they will experience the saving love of Christ (Eph. 2:4-5).

For the Church

As you gather with other believers for worship this week, pray that "being rooted and established in love . . . [you may] grasp how wide and long and high and deep is the love of Christ" (Eph. 3:17-18). Let this thought flood your mind in worship.

For the Kingdom

Ask that love will characterize the relationships of believers throughout the world and in your own denomination. Pray that the virtues of faith, hope, and love will be evident, but that love will be preeminent.

For the Unsaved

Think of one unsaved person. Name that individual and ask God to reveal his redeeming love in Christ in that person's life. Pray for an opportunity this week to share the good news.

JULY 10

Personal Prayer
Rejoice with the prophet Isaiah, who wrote, "I delight greatly in the LORD; my soul rejoices in my God. For he has clothed me with garments of salvation and arrayed me in a robe of righteousness" (Isa. 61:10). Thank God for producing such joy in your life. Confess any lack of Christian joy. Commit yourself to bearing the fruit of joy through the power of the Holy Spirit (Gal. 5:22). Ask God to fill you with an inexpressible and glorious joy (1 Pet. 1:8).

For Your Family and Friends
Pray for joy to fill your home. Ask God to root out anything that will rob your family of enjoying each other.

For the Church
Are your church leaders joyful persons? Pray that they will be so in their family life and work in the church. Pray especially that your pastor(s) will be "overtaken" with gladness and joy (Isa. 35:10).

For the Kingdom
Sin causes much gloom and sadness to blanket our world. Ask God to spare the church in every country from such sorrow. Pray that the church's joy will shine like a beacon light to those who are oppressed and joyless.

For the Unsaved
Pray for your own expression of joy in the Lord. Do unbelievers recognize it in you? Do they know the source of your joy? Ask God to make your joy genuinely contagious.

JULY 11

Personal Prayer

Praise the one who came as the Prince of Peace (Isa. 9:6). Thank Jesus for giving peace to his beloved ones (Jn. 14:27). Confess those times when you've allowed Satan to fill your soul with unrest. Commit yourself to bearing the fruit of peace by the power of the Holy Spirit (Gal. 5:22). Ask God to guard your heart and mind today with his peace (Phil. 4:7).

For Your Family and Friends

Peace is such a rare commodity in families today. Ask God to bring his peace into all of your family relationships. Pray also for peace among your friends.

For the Church

Intercede today for outreach ministries in your church or community which take the love of Christ into your neighborhood. Ask that their work will be richly blessed.

For the Kingdom

Warfare, bloodshed, strife, and turmoil mar every corner of the globe these days. But the good news is that Christ came "to reconcile to himself all things . . . by making peace through his blood, shed on the cross" (Col. 1:20). Pray for all those who seek to bring Christ's reconciliation to a restless world.

For the Unsaved

Pray for specific unsaved neighbors, that they will be justified by faith and enjoy eternal peace with God through Jesus Christ (Rom. 5:1).

JULY 12

Personal Prayer
Praise God for his patience. Thank the Lord for being patient with you and allowing you to come to repentance in Christ (2 Pet. 3:9). Confess impatience you have felt or expressed toward God or other people. Commit yourself to bearing the fruit of patience through the power of the Holy Spirit (Gal. 5:22). Ask God to fill you with his patience.

For Your Family and Friends
If you have small children, you know how quickly impatient words can surface in families. Pray for families who struggle with showing patience among family members.

For the Church
Remember the education committee of your church today. Pray for teachers, helpers, and learners in your education ministry. Pray especially for growth in your adult education classes.

For the Kingdom
Impatience is a hallmark of our me-first society. Pray that the church will have a softening influence, proclaiming and demonstrating a patient "Jesus-first" message. Ask that the church will be patient even in the midst of affliction (Rom. 12:12).

For the Unsaved
Claim God's promise toward the unsaved in 2 Pet. 3:9. While thanking God for his patience, pray that his salvation will be made known to many unbelieving people today.

Prayer Pointer
"A man prayed, and at first he thought that prayer was talking. But he became more and more quiet until in the end he realized that prayer was listening."
—SØREN KIERKEGAARD

JULY 13

Personal Prayer
Praise the God of everlasting kindness (Isa. 54:8). Thank him for exercising kindness, justice, and righteousness—and for delighting in them (Jer. 9:24). Confess any unkind deed or word or thought that has hurt another person. Commit yourself to bearing the fruit of kindness by the power of the Holy Spirit (Gal. 5:22). Ask God to add kindness to your faith (2 Pet. 1:5-7).

For Your Family and Friends
Ask God to help your family members and friends show kindness in all their relationships. Pray that kind words and deeds will become common in your household (Eph. 4:32).

For the Church
Pray for the outreach of your congregation and denomination to unbelievers in other countries. Ask that in all their gospel work, missionaries will be clothed with compassion, kindness, humility, gentleness, and patience (Col. 3:12).

For the Kingdom
Ask God to uphold Christian agencies which do kind deeds in the name of Christ for impoverished and hungry people. Pray that needs will be met for both giver and receiver.

For the Unsaved
Pray that your kind attitude will attract unsaved friends and coworkers to the Lord. Ask God to create natural opportunities for you to share your faith.

_____

_____

_____

_____

_____

JULY 14

Personal Prayer

Praise God for his marvelous goodness. Thank the Lord for being a refuge in times of trouble (Nah. 1:7). Confess your own failure to show goodness toward others. Commit yourself to bearing the fruit of goodness through the power of the Holy Spirit (Gal. 5:22). Ask God to enable you today to "taste and see that the LORD is good" (Ps. 34:8).

For Your Family and Friends

Pray for goodness to be evident in the lives of your family members and friends. Ask God to help each one to imitate the goodness of God.

For the Church

Intercede for individuals and groups in your congregation who reach out to persons "on the fringe" and promote Christian fellowship. Ask that the good which they do will be an example for others to follow.

For the Kingdom

Pray that good will win out over evil in every area of our society. Ask that righteousness and justice will permeate the fabric of our culture so that God will be glorified and praised.

For the Unsaved

Ask for an opportunity today to do good for an unbelieving friend. Pray that God will turn that encounter into a conversation of "good news."

Prayer Pointer

"Prayer is spoken of more often than any other activity of the gathered [New Testament] church." —KENT R. WILSON

JULY 15

Personal Prayer

Praise your covenant God for his abiding faithfulness (Deut. 7:9). Give thanks that even "if we are faithless, he will remain faithful" (2 Tim. 2:13). Confess any unfaithfulness you've allowed into your relationships with God and others. Commit yourself to bearing the fruit of faithfulness through the power of the Holy Spirit (Gal. 5:22). Ask God to help you be a faithful follower of Jesus Christ.

For Your Family and Friends

Pray that God's covenant love would extend through your generation and on to generations yet to come.

For the Church

Thank God for those in your congregation who evidence faithfulness in their financial management and liberal giving. Praise God for dedicated deacons who exercise responsible and godly stewardship in your church.

For the Kingdom

Pray that the church, Christ's body here on earth, will remain faithful to the Word and obedient to the Spirit. When persecution comes, ask that believers will "commit themselves to their faithful Creator and continue to do good" (1 Pet. 4:19).

For the Unsaved

Ask God to help you to be a faithful witness as he gives you opportunity in your everyday routine. Pray that in your relationships with unsaved people God will "strengthen and protect you from the evil one" (2 Thess. 3:3).

_____

_____

_____

_____

_____

JULY 16

Personal Prayer

In your heart sing to the Lord, your strength and song; praise the one who has become your salvation. Give thanks that with joy you can draw water from the wells of salvation (Isa. 12:2-3). Confess that your worship is sometimes lacking because you don't always remember the greatness of your salvation. Commit yourself to worshiping and singing with your whole heart; ask God to make you awake and alive to the power of his Word and the joy of music.

For Your Family and Friends

Ask God to minister to hurting family members or friends through the Word and through the supportive, caring comments of other church members.

For the Church

Pray for families with young children and teenagers, that the children may feel a sense of participation in worship this week and of belonging to the body of Christ.

For the Kingdom

Pray that worship may unite a "great multitude that no one could count, from every nation, tribe, people and language" in praise of the God of our salvation and the Lamb who sits upon the throne (Rev. 7:9-10).

For the Unsaved

Ask the Spirit to draw the unsaved on your street to a church where they can find hope and healing in the preaching of God's Word.

_____

_____

_____

_____

_____

JULY 17

Personal Prayer
Give praise to the one by whom all things were created, the one in whom all things hold together, the head of the church (Col. 1:16-18). Thank God for giving direction and purpose to your life in this day. Confess those times in the past few weeks when you've tried to take over the direction of your life. Commit yourself completely to Christ's leadership in this week. Ask him to help you find the time to listen for his voice at the beginning of each day.

For Your Family and Friends
Pray for those close to you who are struggling with finding some direction in their lives. Commit yourself to encouraging them to seek God's will.

For the Church
Intercede for the leaders in your congregation, that they may find the wisdom and courage to follow Christ's plan for your church without hesitating.

For the Kingdom
Ask the Spirit to guide church leaders in war-torn countries, that they may know what work Jesus has for their churches amid the ethnic tensions and political struggles of their people.

For the Unsaved
Pray that God will use your maturity in Christ to provide leadership for someone whose life is out of control and in need of spiritual direction.

_____

_____

_____

_____

_____

Personal Prayer

Praise the Lord Jesus, who will be "revealed from heaven in blazing fire with his powerful angels" (2 Thess. 1:7). Thank him that he will come to restore justice and righteousness in the earth. Confess the times when you have not lived in awareness of Christ's coming again in power and judgment. Ask him to help you desire and look forward to his coming, and commit yourself to preparing yourself and others for "the day he comes to be glorified in his holy people and to be marveled at among all who have believed" (1:10).

For Your Family and Friends

Pray daily for the salvation of any family members or close friends whose lives show that they do not truly believe that Christ is coming in power and judgment.

For the Church

Ask the Spirit to give the churches in your community a sense of urgency in bringing the good news of Jesus' death and resurrection to the unchurched and unbelieving in their neighborhoods.

For the Kingdom

Pray for the protection of Jesus' blood and the power of his cross over all North American missionaries who are working to reclaim those blinded by New Age religion, by materialism, or by drugs or sex addiction.

For the Unsaved

Ask God to change the hearts of those who don't love the truth, and to set them free from Satan's lies.

_____

_____

_____

_____

_____

JULY 19

Personal Prayer

Praise the Son of God, in whom are hidden all the treasures of wisdom and knowledge. Thank God for the depth of the riches of that wisdom and knowledge (Rom. 11:33). Confess those areas of your work or personal life for which you have forgotten to ask his wisdom and guidance. Commit yourself to calling out for insight and crying aloud for understanding, to looking for it as for silver and searching for it as for hidden treasure (Prov. 2:3). Ask God to let his discretion protect you and his understanding guard you.

For Your Family and Friends

Intercede for the parents you know who are struggling with raising their children, that God will open their hearts to his wisdom.

For the Church

Pray for the adult education classes at your church, that many more adults will be drawn to see that there is much more they can learn from the storehouse of God's wisdom.

For the Kingdom

Ask God's Spirit to equip and support those who are training Christian leaders from among tribes and peoples who have no previous Bible knowledge or background.

For the Unsaved

Claim the power of God in your unsaved acquaintances' lives to break down the strongholds of ignorance and to win them to the "foolishness" of the cross—the power and wisdom of God.

_____

_____

_____

_____

_____

JULY 20

Personal Prayer

Praise the God who knows the depths of your heart and sees all the secret places there. Give thanks that he hears the prayers of many people all over the earth and listens to all of our cries for help. Confess to God the days in this past week when you have not made sufficient time for prayer for yourself and others. Commit yourself to remembering his deep love for you and all people, and ask the Spirit to make that awareness grow into a habit of praying without ceasing "on all occasions with all kinds of prayers and requests" (Eph. 6:18).

For Your Family and Friends

Ask God to cause the parents you know to pray daily for their children, relying on God's protection and saving grace in their lives.

For the Church

Lift up to God the names of the world missionaries your church supports, asking that their specific needs for this day may be met.

For the Kingdom

Pray for the governments of countries in war or civil strife, that they may protect the missionaries and other Christians who are working for Christ within their borders.

For the Unsaved

Ask God to hear and answer the prayers of the unsaved, "so that all peoples of the earth may know [his] name and fear [him]" (1 Ki. 8:43). as a God who listens and responds.

_____

_____

_____

_____

_____

JULY 21

Personal Prayer
Glorify the Lord, who is gracious, full of compassion, and gentle with the weak (Ps. 116:5). Thank God for rescuing you during those times when you needed his help, even when you didn't ask for it (116:8). Confess the times when you have been impatient with others in need. Commit yourself to remembering throughout this day God's compassion for you and to reflecting that compassion to others. Ask God to help you fulfill this vow.

For Your Family and Friends
Intercede for those you know who are "overcome by trouble and sorrow" (116:3), that God will move them to call on his name and to rely on his compassionate help.

For the Church
Ask God to make the congregations in your community centers of kindness, where those in need will find the hands of Jesus ministering to them.

For the Kingdom
Pray for prison officials, that their administration of justice and punishment may be tempered with compassion and kindness.

For the Unsaved
Ask God to use your friendship with one unsaved person this week as a bridge to showing him or her the gracious love of God.

Prayer Pointer
"Prayer is the great engine to overthrow and rout my spiritual enemies, the great means to procure the graces of which I stand in hourly need." —JOHN NEWTON

JULY 22

Personal Prayer

Glorify God as the one who fills all of your desires and needs with his presence alone. Thank God for being sufficient for you even when every other source of joy or support is taken away. Confess your dependence on other people or situations to make you content and happy. Commit yourself to making Jesus your "pearl of great price," and ask him to make you willing to give up all you have for the sake of his kingdom, if necessary (Mt. 13:44-46).

For Your Family and Friends

Pray that God will lead them into a life-style that reflects a love for God, not a love for things.

For the Church

Ask God to pour his blessings especially on those members who, like the poor widow, are giving their very last dollar so that God's work can be accomplished in your neighborhood.

For the Kingdom

Pray for the hunger, agriculture, and disaster relief organizations around the world, that they may use the funds given them to the best possible ends.

For the Unsaved

Ask God to bring to your mind the material needs of an unsaved acquaintance so that you will be able to help meet those needs and bring that person closer to the kingdom.

JULY 23

Personal Prayer

Praise God for not leaving you "as orphans" but for giving another helper to be with you forever (Jn. 14:16, 18). Give thanks for God's presence and power, and trust him to continue to energize you, keeping you on the right course. Confess the times you are dissatisfied or frustrated in your walk with the Lord. Commit yourself anew to God and let his Spirit help you in your weakness, especially in prayer (Rom. 8:26). Ask him to reveal himself to you today in a new and fresh way.

For Your Family and Friends

Pray that your family and friends will have the joy, peace, and stability that comes from knowing God personally and spending time daily with him (Col. 3:15-17).

For Your Church

Pray for your church to excel in gifts that build it up by the enabling power of the Holy Spirit, demonstrated by effective preaching and fellowship that brings growth and harmony (1 Cor. 14:12).

For the Kingdom

Pray that the enabling power of the Holy Spirit will bring the coming of God's kingdom all over the world, beginning right where you are now (Acts 1:8).

For the Unsaved

Pray that the true witness of Christians in the "marketplace" will draw all people to Jesus (Jn. 12:32).

_____

_____

_____

_____

_____

JULY 24

Personal Prayer

Praise God for being the God of "burning bushes," calling you to respond and serve where he leads (Ex. 3:2). Thank God for revealing to you his call to service, and for your affirming response. Confess your deafness, blindness, hardheartedness, and excuses that keep you from hearing and responding to God's call (3:6, 11, 13). Commit yourself to being aware of God's presence every day and listening to his call to service, no matter how humbling that service may be. Ask him to give you a positive attitude in carrying out his call.

For Your Family and Friends

Pray that your family and friends will hold you accountable to fulfill God's calling for you.

For the Church

Pray that God will call forth leadership from your church who will "be careful" how they live, "not as unwise, but as wise" (Eph. 5:15).

For the Kingdom

Pray that you be hospitable, loving what is good, self-controlled, upright, holy and disciplined, holding firmly to the truth (Titus 1:8), thus growing God's kingdom on the inside.

For the Unsaved

Pray that God will use you to encourage others by sound teaching and the ability to refute those who oppose it (1:9), and so open doors of salvation to those for whom God has prepared it.

JULY 25

Personal Prayer

Praise God for his non-condemning attitude (Jn. 8:10-11), which gives you hope when you fail. Give thanks for help in seeing the "plank" in your own eyes before looking at the "specks" in another's (Mt. 7:3). Confess the many times you judge by appearance rather than by facts (Jn. 7:24). Commit yourself to God's judgment (1 Cor. 11:32), and be disciplined by him, learning from your mistakes (Heb. 12:10-11). Ask God to help you learn from other's judgments of you.

For Your Family and Friends

Pray for God's help to be generous in affirming your family and friends, rather than misjudging them or their motives (Ps. 119:66).

For the Church

Pray that your church will warmly welcome anyone, regardless of race, color, financial resources, etc., and take the lead in having all guests feel welcome (Heb. 13:1-2).

For the Kingdom

Pray that sound judgment and discernment will be preserved throughout God's kingdom (Prov. 3:21), resulting in kingdom growth.

For the Unsaved

Pray that your loving and nonjudgmental attitude toward one who has wronged you will give you opportunity to present Christ to that person, realizing God will bring every deed into judgment (Eccl. 12:14).

_____

_____

_____

_____

_____

JULY 26

Personal Prayer

Praise God for the example of servanthood given when Jesus washed the disciples' feet (Jn. 13:5-15). Thank Jesus for his promise that you will be blessed in being a servant, following his example (13:17). Confess those times you are quarrelsome and resentful, not wanting to be a servant (2 Tim. 2:24). Commit yourself to God as Samuel did and respond: "Speak, for your servant is listening" (1 Sam. 3:10). Ask God to reveal clearly his assigned task for you, even as he did for Paul (1 Cor. 3:5).

For Your Family and Friends

Pray that by faithfully obeying God's commands to be servants, your family members will see God's blessing in their lives and praise him always (Deut. 11:13-15).

For the Church

Pray that your church will faithfully learn the joy of servanthood in every area, fixing their eyes on Jesus, not growing weary or losing heart (Heb. 12:2-3).

For the Kingdom

Pray that Christians everywhere will "serve faithfully and wholeheartedly in the fear of the LORD" (2 Chron. 19:9).

For the Unsaved

Pray for an opportunity to be a witness today as a loving servant to an unsaved friend or neighbor (Gal. 5:13).

Prayer Pointer

"Simply to say prayers is not to pray; otherwise a team of properly trained parrots would serve as well as men in prayer." —C. S. LEWIS

_____

_____

_____

_____

JULY 27

Personal Prayer

Praise God, who teaches you to pray "not as I will, but as you will" (Mt. 26:39). Thank God for his counsel as you set the Lord always before you, thus keeping you from being shaken in any circumstance (Ps. 16:7-8). Confess your struggle with God's will when you are tempted to fail him as you see the world prospering (Ps. 73:1-22). Commit yourself to God anew today, knowing he holds you with his right hand, guides and counsels you, and will take you to glory (73:23-28). Ask the Lord for the assurance that whenever you come to him, he will never drive you away (Jn. 6:37).

For Your Family and Friends

Pray that you may see how God often works out his will for you by using family and friends. Give thanks for that (Es. 4:13-14).

For the Church

Pray that your church will challenge everyone who attends to seek God's will and counsel, resulting in a renewed interest in community outreach ministries as well as in world missions.

For the Kingdom

Pray that God's kingdom will be advanced by your willingness to do whatever God may require of you and to do it joyfully (Acts 21:13-14).

For the Unsaved

Pray that whenever you open your mouth, words will be given you so that you may fearlessly make known the gospel whenever the opportunity presents itself (Eph. 6:19).

JULY 28

Personal Prayer

Praise God for his compelling love (2 Cor. 5:14). Give thanks for that love that holds us as in a vice, never letting go (Jer. 31:3). Confess those times when you fight against God's love, wanting to go your own way or seek glory for yourself instead of for him. Commit yourself to being comfortable in that "love grip" of God so that you willingly live for him, serving him gladly (Prov. 3:3-6). Ask God to give you a greater appreciation of his eternal blessings and to be glad with the joy of his presence (Ps. 21:6).

For Your Family and Friends

Pray that your family and friends will not be threatened by God's compelling love but will rest secure in him as he shields them (Deut. 33:12).

For the Church

Pray that God's unfailing love will satisfy every member of the church so that all may "sing for joy and be glad all our days" (Ps. 90:14).

For the Kingdom

Pray that God's compelling love may keep believers from fear and lead them on in the daily work of ministry "in Jerusalem, and Judea . . . and to the ends of the earth" (Joel 2:21-27; Acts 1:8).

For the Unsaved

Pray that this love will give you boldness in being a witness of your joy in the Lord by word and in deed to many this week.

JULY 29

Personal Prayer
Praise God that birth and conception are miraculous and a special gift from God. Thank him for planning all your days before you were even born (Ps. 139:16). Confess any dissatisfaction over the gifts and abilities God has given you. Commit yourself to God daily and, like Paul, be content in whatever situation he has placed you (Phil. 4:11). Ask God to bring personal peace as a member of your family.

For Your Family and Friends
Pray that children in your family circle and among your friends may be blessed with godly parents who are good examples and who discipline them in love (Prov. 22:6).

For the Church
Pray that children's ministries may have an important role in your church and that children will happily invite their friends to participate in these activities with them.

For the Kingdom
Praise God for the children of missionaries, that they may share the love of Jesus among their friends.

For the Unsaved
Pray that unsaved children who attend Bible classes with friends will bring that gospel message to their own homes as well (Mt. 11:25).

Prayer Pointer
"Work as if everything depended upon work and pray as if everything depended upon prayer." —WILLIAM BOOTH

JULY 30

Personal Prayer

Praise "God, the Father Almighty, Creator of heaven and earth." Thank him for being your Father through Christ Jesus. Confess tendencies to act like a spiritual orphan. Commit yourself to more consistently remembering the responsibilities and privileges of being God's child. Ask him to help you bring honor to the family name.

For Your Family and Friends

Pray that all your friends and members of your family will truly be part of God's family. Ask God to help each one look beyond imperfect human parents to God as the perfect Father.

For the Church

Pray that your local congregation will bring pleasure to the Father through its weekly worship times. Ask God to help all members and regular attendees act with true family love toward one another.

For the Kingdom

Pray that the diverse groups of Christian believers will recognize that all are in the same family. Ask the Father to help believers to get along with brothers and sisters.

For the Unsaved

Pray that people throughout the world will acknowledge their Creator as their Father through Jesus Christ.

JULY 31

Personal Prayer
Praise "Jesus Christ, his only Son, our Lord." Thank him for his willingness to leave his heavenly home to live among sinners. Confess any way in which you have been unwilling to sacrifice in order to come alongside those in need. Commit yourself to having the attitude of Jesus (Phil. 2:5-11). Ask God to give you that selfless love.

For Your Family and Friends
Pray that you will consistently bring the presence of Jesus to those with whom you live. Ask Jesus to help you focus more on loving than on being loved.

For the Church
Pray that your local church will be known as a group where one can readily sense the presence, as well as the truths, of Jesus Christ. Ask Jesus to especially shine through your church's leaders.

For the Kingdom
Pray that the presence of Christ in his people will be a "salting" and "lighting" influence throughout the earth. Ask God to maintain full integrity in national and international media ministries.

For the Unsaved
Pray that the presence of Jesus through you will effectively draw an unsaved neighbor to him. Ask God to give you the right actions, words, and love in your community.

Prayer Pointer
"It is in recognizing the actual presence of God that we find prayer no longer a chore, but a supreme delight." —GORDON LINDSAY

AUGUST 1

Personal Prayer

Praise God for his power to do the miraculous. Give thanks for the miracle of Jesus being "conceived by the Holy Spirit and born of the virgin Mary." Confess any difficulties in believing that he has done what the Scriptures say he has done. Commit to believing in God's ability to do the miraculous in your life. Ask God to give you a bigger view of himself.

For Your Family and Friends

Pray that the mystery of God's power will produce awe in a family member or friend who seems a bit flippant about God. Ask God to lift up Jesus through you.

For the Church

Pray that Christ will be lifted up in your local church, drawing all people to himself. Ask God to call true believers away from any false religious practices and out of false churches.

For the Kingdom

Pray that Christ's people around the world will be faithful to move as his force into their communities. Ask God to move with supernatural power to bring whole groups to the divine Savior.

For the Unsaved

Pray that God will supernaturally increase the effectiveness of the outreach ministries of your local church. Ask him to use you in that great effort.

AUGUST 2

Personal Prayer

Praise Jesus as the suffering servant. Thank him for the love that brought him to the point where he "suffered under Pontius Pilate, was crucified, died, and was buried" and even "descended to hell" for you. Confess any lack of appreciation for such love. Commit yourself to never misusing the name of such a loving Savior. Ask him to guide you in giving your life in thankful response.

For Your Family and Friends

Pray that all of your close contacts will come to a deeper understanding of how much their sin cost Jesus. Ask God to save each one.

For the Church

Pray for those in the education ministries of your local church and broader church assemblies. Ask God to generate awe and love for Jesus through their teaching about his sacrifice.

For the Kingdom

Pray for the Christians whom God has called to be teachers throughout the week. Ask God to motivate them with the giving love of Jesus.

For the Unsaved

Pray that unsaved students will be drawn to the Savior through their teachers. Ask God to show them their unmistakable need for the one who was crucified to bring them real knowledge and real life.

Prayer Pointer

"Because God is the living God, he can hear; because he is a loving God, he will hear; because he is our covenant God, he has bound himself to hear."
—CHARLES H. SPURGEON

AUGUST 3

Personal Prayer

Praise Jesus as the one who "rose again from the dead" and "ascended to heaven" where he is "seated at the right hand of God the Father almighty." Thank God for access to him through Jesus the Intercessor. Confess any skepticism of God's willingness to hear your prayers. Commit yourself to living under the flag of King Jesus today. Ask the ascended King to rule over even the details of your life.

For Your Family and Friends

Pray that the children in your circle of close contacts will know that they belong to the King of heaven and earth. Ask God to help you model the dignity of living for Jesus.

For the Church

Pray for world missionaries who are calling groups of people to bow before Jesus. Ask that these groups' rulers and leaders also submit and begin to lead their people in Jesus' ways.

For the Kingdom

Pray for "all those in authority, that we may live peaceful and quiet lives in all godliness and holiness" (1 Tim. 2:2). Ask that the peaceful rule of Jesus might soon come in fullness.

For the Unsaved

Pray that unsaved acquaintances will submit to Jesus before he comes "to judge the living and the dead." Ask God to give you a sense of the urgency of bringing the good news to them.

_____

_____

_____

_____

_____

AUGUST 4

Personal Prayer

As one who professes to "believe in the Holy Spirit," praise God for his indwelling of all believers. Give thanks for his intimacy and power. Confess any tendency to rely on your own strength rather than God's. Commit to becoming more sensitive to God's ongoing presence. Ask God to increase your consciousness of continual companionship with him.

For Your Family and Friends

Pray that the Holy Spirit will fill each of your family and friends, bringing a deep sense of his presence. Ask him to fill your household with his power.

For the Church

Pray that we who have been richly blessed by the "fellowship with the Spirit" might be "like-minded, having the same love, being one in spirit and purpose" (Phil. 2:1-2). Ask God to move with power through any such spirituality.

For the Kingdom

Pray for God to move with his Spirit to bring true revival to your country. Ask God to move powerfully at your place of work.

For the Unsaved

Pray that the oneness of God's people will draw the unsaved to him. Ask the Spirit to convict unsaved acquaintances of their sin and convince them to turn in faith to God.

Prayer Pointer

"Prayers not felt by us are seldom heard by God." —PHILIP HENRY

AUGUST 5

Personal Prayer

Praise God as the Creator, Father, Savior, Lord, and indwelling Spirit of his church. Give thanks for "the holy catholic church, the communion of saints; the forgiveness of sins; the resurrection of the body, and the life everlasting." Reflecting with God on how you aid or damage his church, confess any sin he reveals. Commit to being a helpful member of God's community. Ask him to work through you to serve and enrich others.

For Your Family and Friends

Pray for each member of your household to forget what is behind and strain toward what is ahead, pressing on toward the goal to win the prize for which God has called them heavenward in Christ Jesus (Phil. 3:13-14).

For the Church

Pray for each member of Christ's body to excellently manage the treasures and gifts placed in his or her care. Ask God to prompt you to loving and generous service.

For the Kingdom

Pray for financial needs to be abundantly met in various efforts to advance God's kingdom around the world. Ask God for vision as well as finances.

For the Unsaved

Ask God to draw people to himself through your generous love.

_____

_____

_____

_____

_____

AUGUST 6

Personal Prayer
Read Ps. 47:5-8 and praise with joy your God, who has ascended amid the sound of trumpets. Thank him for being the King of all the earth, for reigning over the nations. Confess that you often do not think of God in such lofty terms. Commit yourself to praising God wholeheartedly today. Ask God to reveal himself to you as you praise him.

For Your Family and Friends
Does your family sing together in praise of God? Try it today! And pray that God will give each member of your family a joyful heart in praising God.

For the Church
"God is seated on his holy throne" (47:8). Pray that your congregation will have a true sense of God's holiness and majesty as they worship week by week. Pray that every part of your worship will be directed to this God.

For the Kingdom
Ask God to be in the midst of his people in every time zone as they bring a worldwide symphony of praise. Pray for an anointing of the Holy Spirit in every place of worship.

For the Unsaved
Ask God to touch the lives of unsaved people today. Pray that some will hear the gospel and fall in repentance and faith at the foot of the cross.

_____

_____

_____

_____

_____

AUGUST 7

Personal Prayer

Read Ps. 40:1-3 and praise your Redeemer and Savior. Thank God for lifting you up out of the mud and mire of sin. Confess those times you've desired to return to the slimy pit of sin. Commit yourself to living in such a way that others may "see . . . and put their trust in the LORD." Ask God to enable you to stand firm on the Rock of Jesus Christ.

For Your Family and Friends

Pray that Jesus the Rock will be the foundation and cornerstone of your family. Ask especially that teens you know will find a firm place to stand in Christ.

For the Church

Today pray especially for the leaders of your congregation. Ask God to put a new song in the mouths of your elders, deacons, and pastor(s), that they will show forth his glory in the church.

For the Kingdom

Pray for the Church in communist countries. Thank God for the many thousands of believers who remain faithful despite oppression. Pray that the strongholds of Satan will be demolished in those lands.

For the Unsaved

Ask God to draw an unsaved friend to himself. Pray that God will equip you to share the gospel with that person in an appropriate way. Seek opportunities this week.

_____

_____

_____

_____

_____

AUGUST 8

Personal Prayer

Read Ps. 73:23-26 and give praise to the one who holds you every day by your right hand. Thank God for guiding you by his wise counsel. Confess any time you have desired some earthly trinket more than the riches of your heavenly Father. Commit yourself to staying close to God today. Ask God to be "the strength of [your] heart and [your] portion forever."

For Your Family and Friends

Pray for any family members or friends who are straying away from God, who are trying desperately to pull free from God's loving handhold. Ask that they will turn back to God.

For the Church

Pray today for the outreach ministries of your congregation or denomination. Pray for those who lead these ministries. Ask that God will provide the funding necessary to reach out to those with spiritual and physical needs.

For the Kingdom

Ask for God's grace to fill those who minister comfort in the name of Christ to persons with AIDS. Pray that many who have contracted AIDS will find safety in the arms of Jesus.

For the Unsaved

Pray for any unsaved friends or relatives by name. Ask that they will embrace the peace that comes with having God hold them by the hand.

AUGUST 9

Personal Prayer

Read Ps. 86:15-17 and praise God for his marvelous compassion, grace, love, and faithfulness to you. Thank him for turning to you and having mercy on you. Confess any lack of appreciation for God's saving work in your life. Commit yourself to loving God wholeheartedly in response to his love for you. Ask God to give you a sign of his goodness.

For Your Family and Friends

Pray for God's mercy to be shown to any family member or friend in need. Ask the Lord to provide abundantly from his storehouses of grace.

For the Church

Ask God's blessing on the educational programs of your church. Pray for each teacher and helper. Ask God to show you how you might be involved in the instruction of others.

For the Kingdom

Pray that the enemies of God will be put to shame throughout his kingdom. Ask that the forces of the evil one will be destroyed and that justice, righteousness, and peace might prevail on the earth.

For the Unsaved

Ask that people in your neighborhood who do not yet know Jesus will be drawn to him by observing your Christlike behavior. Pray that they will have the boldness to ask about the faith they see in you.

Prayer Pointer

"God has chosen prayer as the key by which his church does its work. Through prayer we impact the world for God." —ANONYMOUS

_____

_____

_____

_____

AUGUST 10

Personal Prayer
Read Ps. 91:1-2 and praise the Most High, the Almighty, the Lord, your God. Thank him for providing shelter and shade from the heat of spiritual conflict in your life. Confess those times when you've sought shelter other than that provided by the Most High. Commit yourself to simply resting in God. Ask him always to be your refuge and fortress in every life situation.

For Your Family and Friends
Pray that your home will be a resting place, a shelter where you and your family can find peace, quiet, and safety. Ask that your children will sense the security of a home built on the love of Jesus.

For the Church
Pray for the work of missionaries throughout the world who carry the gospel in word and deed into sometimes hostile countries. Pray especially for those working in Muslim countries. Ask that they will be sheltered by the Most High.

For the Kingdom
Pray for those who take the liberating love of Christ into prisons throughout the world. Ask God to bless those prisoners who have trusted Christ, but must remain behind bars. Pray for their safety and testimony to other prisoners.

For the Unsaved
Ask God to be a refuge and fortress to many unsaved who are being blown about the wild winds of secularism. Pray that they will find shelter in Christ.

_____

_____

_____

_____

_____

AUGUST 11

Personal Prayer
Read Ps. 139:13-17 and praise the God who knit you together in your mother's womb. Give thanks for all of his wonderful works. Confess those moments when foolishly you've tried to hide from God. Commit yourself to living each day with the full assurance that God has written each one in his book. Ask that today you might be reminded of God's precious thoughts toward you.

For Your Family and Friends
Today thank God for your children or grandchildren. Think of how marvelously complex their bodies are. Pray for any of them who suffer from physical or mental impairments.

For the Church
Pray that caregiving and fellowship in your congregation will grow. Ask God to open the eyes of your church members to needs which they can meet.

For the Kingdom
Pray for those organizations throughout North America which promote the sanctity of human life. Ask God to put down the evil of abortion on demand. Pray that parents in your city or community who are considering abortion today will choose an alternative to preserve the life of their unborn child.

For the Unsaved
Pray for an unsaved friend by name. Ask God to enter into that person's conscience. Pray that he or she will become aware of God's plan of salvation through Jesus Christ. Ask God to make you ready to answer your friend's questions.

AUGUST 12

Personal Prayer

Read Ps. 148:7-14 and "let yourself go" as you praise God with all of creation. Thank God for his wonderful works, which join in praise to the Creator. Confess any times you have failed to value the creation or have misused it in any way. Commit yourself to maintaining an attitude of praise to God throughout this day. Ask that God's name will be praised throughout all the earth.

For Your Family and Friends

If you are married, intercede for your spouse. Pray for his or her walk with the Lord. Pray for marriages among your friends, asking that they will be grounded in Christ's love.

For the Church

Pray for the financial stewardship of your congregation. Pray that the members will have great joy in giving to the work of the Lord. Ask God's blessing on the deacons of your church as they manage financial resources.

For the Kingdom

Pray for all the schools of your community. Intercede for Christian teachers, school board members, and administrators in public schools. Ask God to prosper the work of Christian schools and colleges as well.

For the Unsaved

Pray that unsaved individuals you know will soon join "the people close to [God's] heart" (148:14) and the creation in praising the majestic name of the Lord.

AUGUST 13

Personal Prayer

Praise Jesus, who is "declared with power to be the Son of God by his resurrection from the dead" (Rom. 1:4). Thank the Father for having given us his "incomparably great power . . . the working of his mighty strength, which he exerted in Christ when he raised him from the dead" (Eph. 1:19-20). Confess the times when you have not taken into account the mighty power of God in your life. Commit yourself to meditating daily on the Scriptures and on the power of God (Mt. 22:29). Ask God to use your weaknesses to "show that this all-surpassing power is from God and not from us" (2 Cor. 4:7).

For Your Family and Friends

Ask God that your own reliance on his strength will be an encouragement and inspiration to family and friends who struggle with sin and weakness.

For the Church

Pray that those worshiping this Sunday may sense God's power moving in the worship service—to cleanse, to heal, to change lives.

For the Kingdom

Ask God to raise up preachers and teachers who will fearlessly proclaim his Word with power in all countries of the world.

For the Unsaved

Pray for God's power to be unleashed in the life of the unsaved people you know, that their eyes will be opened to God's love for them.

AUGUST 14

Personal Prayer

Praise God as the Father of the fatherless and the defender of the helpless. Give thanks that, even in large cities, God's eye is on the small and defenseless and alone (Jon. 4:11). Confess those times when you have not remembered by prayer or material aid those in your community who have needed your help (Mt. 25:35-40). Commit yourself to looking at others through the compassionate eyes of your Father. Ask him to pull you out of your comfort zone and into the needs of others.

For Your Family and Friends

Ask God to help you see where other family members feel helpless or alone and to allow you to bear their burdens with them (Gal. 6:2).

For the Church

Pray for your leaders, that they will model God's compassion in reaching out to the lonely and the helpless in your community.

For the Kingdom

Ask God to bless, financially and spiritually, his churches' programs in your area for the poor and homeless.

For the Unsaved

Pray that unsaved people in your community will be so moved by your church's compassion toward strangers and outsiders that they will be drawn into God's family.

Prayer Pointer

"No one is a firmer believer in the power of prayer than the devil; not that he practices it, but he suffers from it." —GUY H. KING

AUGUST 15

Personal Prayer

Praise God for his heart that is open, warm, loving, and kind toward all he has made. Thank God for reaching down to draw you to himself through his Son (Jn. 3:16). Confess the times when your heart has been unwilling to give to others the same out-reaching love that you have received from God. Commit yourself to learning the kind, patient love of God (1 Cor. 13:4). Ask him to fill you with a knowledge of the depth and breadth of his love (Eph. 3:14-19).

For Your Family and Friends

Pray for those marriages or parent/child relationships where love is lacking and where the home is a battleground. Ask God to heal their brokenness with his love.

For the Church

Ask God to make his love the hallmark of your church's outreach programs, so that neighbors will sense the genuine interest and care of the family of God.

For the Kingdom

Intercede for the specific caring ministries that your church or denomination is involved in worldwide, asking that broken lives and poverty-stricken families may be helped.

For the Unsaved

Ask God to show you what act of loving concern you can do this week for an unsaved friend or acquaintance.

_____

_____

_____

_____

AUGUST 16

Personal Prayer

Praise God, whose mind and imagination created the stars, the earth, and the life of all creatures. Give thanks for the reaches of God's knowledge, which far exceeds the limits of the human mind. Confess the times in this past week when you have leaned on your own understanding and not followed the teachings of the Lord (Hos. 14:9). Commit yourself to studying the Bible regularly to learn what God has to teach you. Ask the Lord to make his Word as sweet as honey (Ps. 19:10).

For Your Family and Friends

Pray for young adults and their parents, that the teaching of the Lord may be a living faith passed down from parent to child.

For the Church

Pray for each of your church education teachers, that they may be powerful examples by their words and behavior and may be aware of their great responsibility (Jas. 3:1).

For the Kingdom

Pray for the writers and editors of your church's education materials and those who train others to use them, that they may present God's teachings in a fresh way and inspire church education teachers to model their faith effectively in the classroom.

For the Unsaved

Pray that the Christian reading materials developed for adult beginning readers—the illiterate, refugees, immigrants, and others—may reach their hearts with the gospel.

AUGUST 17

Personal Prayer

From your heart give praise to God as the Father of all peoples, the one from whom every family on earth derives its name (Eph. 3:14-15). Thank him for having created such a wide variety of peoples and cultures, including your own. Confess those times when you have looked down on people simply because their culture or way of life is different from yours. Commit yourself to learning more about the people who live and work around you. Ask God to help you become genuinely interested in other people's perspectives as you pray for opportunities to share the good news with them.

For Your Family and Friends

Ask God to restore any breaches between the generations that you are aware of—frictions between grandparents and parents or grandchildren, and so on.

For the Church

Pray for your church's missionaries in war-torn countries, that they may remain safe and may present the light of hope and love in the midst of despair, hatred, and destruction.

For the Kingdom

Pray for the leaders of those countries, that they may acknowledge the lordship of Jesus Christ and his authority in their lives. Ask for justice and peace to be restored to their governments, along with an end to racial hatreds or prejudices.

For the Unsaved

Pray for the new immigrants to North America, that they may hear the gospel and be drawn into the church's fellowship.

AUGUST 18

Personal Prayer

Praise the one who is before all things, the one in whom all things hold together, the head of the church (Col. 1:17-18). Thank Christ for making peace between you and God by his blood shed on the cross. Confess those times when you have allowed something to come between you and another believer, weakening your unity in Christ. Commit yourself to seeking better understanding of that person's position and feelings. Ask God to help you see the unity that exists between all followers of Christ.

For Your Friends and Family

Pray for those families who have shut out unbelieving members. Ask for God's outreaching love to bring them back into the family circle.

For the Church

Ask God to reconcile differences in your congregation over worship style, outreach, and so on. Pray for a spirit of unity and humility (Phil. 2:1-4).

For the Kingdom

Pray that differences between denominations worldwide will not keep believers from praying and worshiping together and from working side by side in missions.

For the Unsaved

Pray for unbelievers in the media. Ask that God may allow them to see such unity in the church that they will have to acknowledge the reality of Jesus Christ (Jn. 17:23).

Prayer Pointer

"Make prayer the time to give yourself this day as a gift to God." —THE PRAYING CHURCH SOURCEBOOK

AUGUST 19

Personal Prayer

Give praise to Jesus as the manna that has come down from heaven, the bread of life who nourishes the hungry with himself (Jn. 6:48-51). Thank him for taking care of your spiritual as well as your physical needs. Confess those times during the past week when you have failed to come to Jesus in prayer in order to receive all that you need. Commit yourself to spending more time in his presence. Ask Jesus to show you his power to take care of all the desires of your heart (Mt. 6:33).

For Your Family and Friends

Ask God to give parents wisdom in teaching their children how to give a part of their income, no matter how small, to God. Pray that through this giving, children may learn to trust in their heavenly Father's ability to provide.

For the Church

Lay before God the financial needs of your congregation and ask God to show those who work with finances the best way to use the monies that have been offered.

For the Kingdom

Pray for generous giving to meet the desperate needs of those stricken with famine, earthquake, war, floods, or other disasters. Ask God to use such giving as a powerful witness to the gospel (2 Cor. 9:10-14).

For the Unsaved

Pray for the unsaved people you know who struggle with a shortage of money. Ask God to use these circumstances to turn them to him for help, through the generosity of the church.

AUGUST 20

Personal Prayer

Praise God that he promises to refresh you like the dew from heaven in order to blossom as the lily (Hos. 14:5). Give thanks for the beauty of flowers, a beauty to be reflected in the life of every Christian. Confess to God the times you disguise that beauty with outward circumstances which keep you from reflecting his image (Col. 3:5-10). Commit yourself to being clothed with compassion, kindness, humility, gentleness, patience, and especially love, which binds believers together in unity (3:12-14). Ask God to root out the weeds and let the beauty of Jesus be seen in you.

For Your Family and Friends

Pray that your family and friends may see the real inward beauty of your life reflecting Jesus, which makes your outward appearance beautiful at all times (1 Sam. 16:7).

For the Church

Ask that the beauty of your worship experiences will glorify God alone.

For the Kingdom

Pray that all teachers and preachers who handle the Word of God will preach and teach in God's strength, not with words of human wisdom, lest the cross of Christ be emptied of its power (1 Cor. 1:17).

For the Unsaved

Ask that you will not use flattery in your witness to unsaved friends, but rather honestly encourage and comfort them, urging them to be open to Christ (1 Thess. 2:4, 11-13).

_____

_____

_____

_____

_____

AUGUST 21

Personal Prayer
Praise God for his teaching on the tongue (Jas. 3:9). Give thanks that he promises protection from the lash of the tongue (Job 5:21) and healing from the tongue of the wise (Prov. 12:18). Confess those times your lips have spoken lies and your tongue muttered wicked things (Isa. 59:3). Commit yourself to God, who gives you the words that will sustain the weary (Isa. 50:4). Ask God to help you love not just with words or tongue but with actions and in truth (1 Jn. 3:18).

For Your Family and Friends
Pray that God will help you to be honest in all you do and say to your family and friends because "a lying tongue hates those it hurts and a flattering mouth works ruin" (Prov. 26:28).

For the Church
Ask that your church leaders will be good examples in their speech and conduct especially since "the mouth of the righteous man utters wisdom, and his tongue speaks what is just" (Ps. 37:30).

For the Kingdom
Pray that fear of speaking will not hold back Christians from being a witness. Ask that God will assure them as he did Moses, that he will help them speak (Ex. 4:10-12).

For the Unsaved
Pray that the testimony of your lips overflowing in praise and your tongue singing God's Word will be evident to non-Christians and point them to Christ (Ps. 119:171-172).

AUGUST 22

Personal Prayer

Praise God that even though you were once an enemy of God, he has reconciled you by Christ's physical body through death (Col. 1:21-22). Give thanks that you are now alive with Christ, without blemish and free from accusation (Col. 2:13). Confess your failure to live up to that holiness, praying, "God, have mercy on me, a sinner" (Lk. 18:13). Commit yourself to rejoicing when you are called to share in the suffering of Christ (1 Pet. 4:13-14). Ask God to help you see the victory you are given in Jesus as you trust the Holy Spirit to guide you in being his image-bearer (1 Cor. 15:57).

For Your Family and Friends

Some of your family may not sense victory in Jesus because of physical pain. Pray that the grace of Jesus will be sufficient for them (2 Cor. 12:9).

For the Church

All churches experience the pain of divorce, broken homes, and death. Pray that those who have overcome such difficult experiences as these may effectively reach out to others in similar situations.

For the Kingdom

Claim God's promise to defend the afflicted and to crush the oppressor (Ps. 72:4).

For the Unsaved

Pray for God to use some painful experience in your life as a means to reach an unbeliever with salvation (2 Cor. 1:3-7).

AUGUST 23

Personal Prayer

Praise God for his unconditional love (1 Corinthians 13). Thank him for showing you in Christ how to love others unconditionally. Confess your lack of love when you've failed to meet God's standards and requirements. Commit yourself to allowing his love to flow naturally through you, resulting in spontaneous acts of love (1 Jn. 3:18). Ask God to let the Holy Spirit work in you daily so that "love deeds" are a "natural" way of life.

For Your Family and Friends

Pray that God will use his love in you as a magnet to draw your family and friends closer to him and to each other.

For the Church

Pray that all your church staff may be rooted and established in love and have the power and ability to communicate God's love to all with whom they have contact (Eph. 3:17-19).

For the Kingdom

Ask that all kingdom workers serve together in love (Gal. 5:13) and communicate the important message that what really counts in life is faith expressing itself in love (5:6).

For the Unsaved

Pray that God will help you do something spontaneous today to reflect his love to one who is outside of the family of God (Lk. 6:27-31).

Prayer Pointer

"True prayer is a way of life, not just a case of emergency." —ANONYMOUS

AUGUST 24

Personal Prayer

Praise God that he is your stronghold in time of trouble (Ps. 9:9). Give thanks for God's promise that when you call on him in the day of trouble, he will deliver you (Ps. 50:15). Confess your failure to glorify and honor God when he does give you deliverance. Commit yourself to keeping the vows you make when you are in trouble (Ps. 66:13-16). Ask God to bring you to your knees in every situation, not just when special trouble surrounds you (Psalm 116).

For Your Family and Friends

Ask God to use your testimony of his faithfulness in time of trouble to help your family grow in God's love and see his purpose for their lives.

For the Church

Praise God for your church's efforts in supporting world missions. Pray that missionaries who must raise their own support will be rewarded for their trust in God to supply all their needs.

For the Kingdom

Pray that all Christians will see God's hand in trouble and trials knowing that "God . . . will pay back trouble to those who trouble you" (2 Thess. 1:6).

For the Unsaved

Pray that God will use a victory you've experienced to be a means of salvation for an unsaved friend this week.

Personal Prayer

Praise God that he sweeps away your offenses like the morning mist (Isa. 44:22). Give thanks that God is not unjust and will not forget your work and the love you have shown him as you help others (Heb. 6:10). Confess to him those secret things you do which you know are wrong but just haven't been able to confess (Ps. 44:21). Commit yourself to building others up with encouragement and ridding yourself of bitterness and anger, forgiving others as God in Christ forgives you (Eph. 4:29-32). Ask God to help you be an imitator of him, living a life of love (Eph. 5:1).

For Your Family and Friends

Pray that God will give you his strength to "right some wrong" that you have committed against a family member or friend.

For the Church

Pray that your church will be a forgiving, loving church that is open to receiving any who come, without judging them in any way (Mt. 7:1).

For the Kingdom

Pray for God's kingdom to grow in his people with a concern to love Jesus more and more, to read the Word faithfully, and not try to build self by judging others.

For the Unsaved

Ask that a positive act of forgiveness on your part will lead an unbelieving friend to attend church with you this week and seek faith in Christ.

AUGUST 26

Personal Prayer

Praise God that "though he brings grief, he will show compassion . . . for he does not willingly bring affliction or grief to the children of men" (Lam. 3:32-33). Give thanks for God's promise that your grief will be turned to joy (Jn. 16:20). Confess to him the times you let grief or affliction turn to bitterness or unconfessed sin. Commit yourself to allowing these trials or afflictions to be a stepping stone to a greater faith. Ask God to help you guard yourself in your spirit and do not break faith (Mal. 2:16).

For Your Family and Friends

Pray that your family will see that affliction can be good (Ps. 119:71), that in faithfulness God may afflict, and that his unfailing love will be their comfort (119:75-76).

For the Church

Ask that financial pressure in your congregation will draw you together in prayer and trust, and move you forward in faith as you share with those in need (Rom. 12:12-13).

For the Kingdom

Pray that God will continue to build his kingdom in areas of the world where there is oppression, hunger, and lack of resources.

For the Unsaved

Ask that God will use you today to give comfort to the afflicted who do not know Christ, assuring them that your God will supply all their needs (Phil. 4:19).

_____

_____

_____

_____

_____

AUGUST 27

Personal Prayer

Praise "God, from whom all blessings flow!" Thank him for making his blessings available to you in Christ Jesus. Confess that you are spiritually poor in yourself. Commit yourself to gratitude to God for replacing your poverty with all the treasures of "the kingdom of heaven" (Mt. 5:3). Ask for a renewed appreciation for this tremendous, gracious exchange.

For Your Family and Friends

Thank God for family members and friends who also have experienced God's exchange of their poverty for his riches.

For the Church

Pray that those worshiping God this week will come acknowledging, "Nothing in my hand I bring . . . helpless, look to Thee for grace." Ask for a profound sense of gratitude in your congregation's worship.

For the Kingdom

Pray that Christian believers throughout the world will truly celebrate what God does in Christ.

For the Unsaved

Pray for those caught in addictions to drugs, sex, self-reliance, etc., to admit that they are powerless to overcome these evils by themselves. Ask God to use you this week to point at least one person to him and his resources.

Prayer Pointer

"Prayer becomes a battleground where we wrestle with what it means to live God's life in the world." —MAXIE DUNNAM

AUGUST 28

Personal Prayer

Praise God, "the Father of compassion and the God of all comfort" (2 Cor. 1:3). Give thanks for God's comfort to you and all who truly mourn (Mt. 5:4). Confess any sin he shows you, truly mourning for the pain you have caused. Commit to receiving God's forgiveness. Ask the Lord to search your heart and thoughts, removing any offensive way and leading you "in the way everlasting" (Ps. 139:23-24).

For Your Family and Friends

Pray for those close to you to know God's comforting forgiveness. Ask God to effectively bring that to them through you.

For the Church

Pray that the leaders of your congregation and denomination will be persons who truthfully confront sin in themselves and in those they lead. Ask that they be clear channels of God's forgiving comfort.

For the Kingdom

Pray that the righteousness of Christ will be evidenced to your whole community through your church's leadership and membership. Ask God to help you keep his kingdom and righteousness your first priority.

For the Unsaved

Pray that the unsaved will not merely complain in the misery caused by their sins nor seek acceptance of their sins. Ask that they will be moved by God's Spirit to truly mourn in the sorrow of repentance and thereby be open to his healing and comfort.

AUGUST 29

Personal Prayer

Praise the Lord as the one who owns the earth and everything in it (Ps. 24:1). Thank him for making it part of the inheritance of the meek (Mt. 5:5). Confess aspects of your life where you do not have the meekness of submission to Christ's Lordship. Commit yourself to being filled and controlled by Christ. Ask him to properly bring the areas you influence under his influence.

For Your Family and Friends

Pray for any in your circle who are "out of control" or merely under the control of themselves. Ask God to reign in your home.

For the Church

Pray for outreach ministries, including various well-known evangelists, to be in proper accountability with God's people. Ask that the meekness of their submission to Christ's lordship far surpass their human appeal.

For the Kingdom

Pray that Christians in leadership positions in all walks of life be submitted to Christ. Ask that their meekness will allow those they influence to see past the human leaders to Christ.

For the Unsaved

Pray that the meekness of Christian leaders will pave the way for unsaved people to come to Christ.

_____

_____

_____

_____

_____

AUGUST 30

Personal Prayer

Praise Jesus as the righteous one. Thank God that "you are in Christ Jesus, who has become for us wisdom from God—that is, our righteousness, holiness and redemption" (1 Cor. 1:30). Confess any desire to dabble in unrighteousness in any corner of your life. Commit yourself to hungering and thirsting for righteousness, asking God to fill you (Mt. 5:6).

For Your Family and Friends

Pray for your family and friends to turn away from godless and evil television programs, videos, music, and magazines.

For the Church

Pray for church education personnel to excellently teach God's truth and model its application. Ask that right thinking with right living will be the trademark of your congregation's members.

For the Kingdom

Pray that the righteousness of Christ will shine through you so clearly and consistently that those around you "see your good deeds and praise your Father in heaven" (5:16).

For the Unsaved

Thank God for the gospel, the power of God for the salvation of everyone who believes (Rom. 1:16). Ask that a great hunger and thirst for Christ will be created in an unsaved person in your neighborhood.

AUGUST 31

Personal Prayer

Praise "God, who is rich in mercy" (Eph. 2:4). Give thanks that, in that great mercy, God has made you alive with Christ even when you were dead in transgressions (2:5). Confess situations where you've been unwilling to let God's mercy flow through you to someone who has wronged you. Commit to being merciful, knowing that this is where you also are shown mercy (Mt. 5:7). Ask God for the love and strength to be a merciful person.

For Your Family and Friends

Pray that your home will be a place dominated by compassion rather than severity. Ask God to cause his mercy to overflow from your home to your friends' homes.

For the Church

Pray for missionaries who are introducing people to the God who saves, not because of righteous human actions but because of his mercy (Titus 3:5). Ask God to make his mercy-bearing believers merciful to one another.

For the Kingdom

Pray for Christian relief workers and agencies showing compassion in the name of Christ. Ask for their safety in the midst of sometimes dangerous circumstances.

For the Unsaved

Pray that such forgiveness and compassion will prevail in the church that the world will know that Jesus has come with God's supernatural love (Jn. 17:23). Ask God to draw the unsaved to himself through that love.

SEPTEMBER 1

Personal Prayer

Praise the God of peace. Thank him for making available that "peace at all times and in every way" (2 Thess. 3:16). Confess ways in which you have added to an argument or refused to let God's peace be established between you and another person. Commit to being at peace with God and others by being both pure in heart and a peacemaker (Mt. 5:8-9). Ask God to spread the wholeness of his salvation through you.

For Your Family and Friends

Pray for any marriages or parent-child relationships among family and friends where God's peace is not being experienced right now. Ask God to help you know how and when to speak, be quiet, mediate, etc.

For the Church

Pray for the fellowship of your local church to be unhindered by strife and controversy. Ask God to also bring his peace to your denomination.

For the Kingdom

Pray for those who are peacemakers between nations in conflict. Ask God to prompt Christians to full involvement as peacemakers.

For the Unsaved

Pray that the willingness of Christians to resolve even difficult differences will be a brilliant display of God's love to the unsaved. Ask God to bring an unsaved friend into his family.

Prayer Pointer

"Front-line prayer meetings are battle stations in which the prayer warriors themselves are changed." —THE PRAYING CHURCH SOURCEBOOK

_____

_____

_____

_____

SEPTEMBER 2

Personal Prayer
Praise God for his indescribable love. Thank God for loving you so much that he would sacrifice his own son. Confess ways you have not been generous with your love in response. Commit to offering even your very body as a living sacrifice, holy and pleasing to God (Rom. 12:1). Ask him to help you not to be conformed to the world but to be transformed by the renewing of your mind (12:2).

For Your Family and Friends
Pray for Christian friends and family members to stand true for God no matter the cost. Ask that they be filled with God's joy in the midst of sacrifices.

For the Church
Pray for believers being persecuted for righteousness. Ask God to help them remember the heavenly reward, enabling all to rejoice and be glad even in the face of insults and false accusations for the sake of Christ (Mt. 5:10-12).

For the Kingdom
Pray that Christians giving sacrificially will be irresistible evidence of the presence and power of God. Ask God to multiply these sacrifices for the extension of his kingdom.

For the Unsaved
Pray that God will give you opportunities to give of your time and resources to help an unsaved acquaintance. Ask God to help you continue to share his love in spite of possible opposition.

_____

_____

_____

_____

_____

SEPTEMBER 3

Personal Prayer

This week, meditate on Psalm 42 each day. Today, praise God as the one who quenches your deepest spiritual thirst (42:1-2). Thank him for being the living water in your life. Confess times in your life when you've passed by God's streams of water and settled for Satan's stale pond instead. Commit yourself to quenching your thirst in the living God alone. Ask him to meet with you in prayer today.

For Your Family and Friends

Pray that your family will be a refreshing oasis of hospitality and warmth as you open yourselves to the needs of others.

For the Church

Do the members of your congregation thirst for God as they come to worship? Pray that they will. Pray also for God to prepare your own heart as you join with others in God's house this Sunday.

For the Kingdom

Pray for missionaries in many countries who share with hurting people not only the bread of life, but also cups of cold water in the name of Christ. Ask God's blessing on their labors.

For the Unsaved

Pray that your own thirst for a closer relationship with God might draw others to him. Ask God to get you out of the way so that they might see Jesus clearly and drink deeply of him.

Prayer Pointer

"Whether we like it or not, asking is the rule of the kingdom." —CHARLES H. SPURGEON

SEPTEMBER 4

Personal Prayer

Praise God for his constant presence with you every day. Thank him for always being near you even in times of extreme difficulty (Ps. 42:3). Confess those times when you've doubted God's loving presence. Commit yourself to seeking his face every morning in prayer and meditation. Ask God to go with you throughout this day.

For Your Family and Friends

Pray that believing members of your family will have a distinct sense of God's presence with them. Ask God to help them in times of distress.

For the Church

Pray for all the leaders in your congregation: your pastor, elders, deacons, ministry heads, and others who come to mind. Pray for God's obvious presence in their lives.

For the Kingdom

Ask God to provide the necessary funds for ministries dedicated to saving the lives of the unborn. Pray that believers will not lose heart in the battle against abortion.

For the Unsaved

Pray that the question "Where is your God?" might come home to an unbelieving friend or neighbor. Ask God to prepare you to speak a word of grace to that person.

_____

_____

_____

_____

_____

SEPTEMBER 5

Personal Prayer
Praise God for the privilege of coming to him in worship and praise today. Give thanks with "shouts of joy and thanksgiving" (Ps. 42:4) for God's many benefits. Confess your occasional lack of enthusiasm in devotion. Commit yourself to "festive" times of personal worship. Ask God to meet with you on those occasions.

For Your Family and Friends
Ask that the devotional experiences of your family and friends will be characterized by joy. Pray that the Spirit will enliven their walk with God.

For the Church
Ask God to bless the work of outreach ministries in your neighborhood or city. Pray that they will be empowered as they seek to bring the gospel to needy people.

For the Kingdom
Pray for any in your congregation who are unemployed or underemployed. Ask God to provide the work and financial resources needed. Ask him to grant encouragement to these people—perhaps through you.

For the Unsaved
Pray that an unbelieving neighbor might be led to question your joy in serving the Lord and thus provide an opportunity for you to share your faith. Pray for eyes to see and ears to hear these divine encounters.

Prayer Pointer
"Prayer is a shield to the soul, a sacrifice to God, and a scourge for Satan."
—John Bunyan

_____

_____

_____

_____

_____

SEPTEMBER 6

Personal Prayer

Praise God as the one who lifts your soul up from the depths of despair and discouragement (Ps. 42:5). Thank him for being your Savior and your God. Confess those times when you've chosen not to allow God to wipe away the tears of distress. Commit yourself to praising God every day for his tender mercies. Ask God to keep you from becoming downcast in your soul.

For Your Family and Friends

Pray for any close friends who struggle with depression or discouragement. Ask God to come close to them today and show them his marvelous love.

For the Church

Pray for the educational programs in your church. Thank God for those who write curriculum material. Intercede on behalf of teachers and helpers who instruct children and youth.

For the Kingdom

Intercede for Christian counseling agencies which help people find the healing light of Christ in the midst of a dark and dreary life. Pray that you will have greater compassion for those who suffer mental illness.

For the Unsaved

Ask God to cause many around the world today to "put their hope in God" (42:5) and thus be able to confess with believers in every land "my Savior and my God" (42:11).

_____

_____

_____

_____

_____

SEPTEMBER 7

Personal Prayer

Praise God as the one who protects you from life's roaring waterfalls and waves (Ps. 42:7). Give thanks that even in the stormy times of life God is always near. Confess those times when you've questioned God's presence or doubted his protection. Commit yourself to staying by his side no matter what comes your way. Ask God to lead and guide you through the stormy as well as the calm seasons of life.

For Your Family and Friends

Pray for any teens among your family or acquaintances who are weathering the all-too-common storms of abuse, parental divorce, or suicide. Ask for God's grace.

For the Church

Thank God for the work and witness of missionaries around the world. Pray that they will go on the wings of a praying church back home. Intercede especially for world missionaries supported by your church.

For the Kingdom

Pray for revival in the church in North America. Ask God to raise up faithful pastors and teachers. Pray that the gods of secularism and materialism will be cast out of our church families.

For the Unsaved

Think of one person with whom you could develop a friendship. It might be someone you see at work, or on the bus, or in your neighborhood. Ask God to create opportunities for you to share your faith—and then be ready to do so!

SEPTEMBER 8

Personal Prayer
Praise God for his love, which is with you both night and day (Ps. 42:8). Give thanks for the songs of praise which God brings forth from you. Confess that you sometimes don't feel like reveling in God's love or singing his praises. Commit yourself to living every day in the light of that love. Ask God to continue directing his love toward you.

For Your Family and Friends
Pray for the older members of your family—parents, grandparents, aunts and uncles. Pray that their later years of life will be filled with health and vitality. Intercede for any who are failing physically or mentally.

For the Church
Thank God for fellowship opportunities your church provides. Pray that caregiving and fellowship will extend outward, too, so that the needs of those in your neighborhood might be met through your church family.

For the Kingdom
Pray for believers in the federal governments of both the U.S. and Canada. Thank God that he has placed his people in and near the seats of highest political power. Ask that they will be enabled to make a difference because they serve the Savior.

For the Unsaved
Ask God to "direct his love" to a particular friend or acquaintance who does not yet know Jesus. Pray for an opportunity to share your faith with that person. Keep that one in your prayers throughout this week.

SEPTEMBER 9

Personal Prayer

Praise God for all his many blessings to you in your life (Ps. 42:11). Thank him that he is your God and that there is nothing that can ruin your relationship with him. Confess that you don't always feel like praising God. Commit yourself to living in hope every day. Ask God to surround you with his presence—and then respond to him with praise.

For Your Family and Friends

Pray for the youngest members of your circle of family and friends. Intercede for any infants or toddlers. Ask God to bless them with good health, with safe surroundings, and with loving parents who will teach them to love the Lord.

For the Church

Pray for the financial giving in your church. Ask that those who give generously will receive their reward for faithful stewardship. Ask that there will be a spirit of generosity among the members.

For the Kingdom

Pray for those who have the gift of evangelism and who use it in various ways. Ask that the proclamation of the gospel in cities, towns, and rural areas will be met with a harvest of souls.

For the Unsaved

Think of a world map and pray for the harvest among the nations. Ask for breakthroughs in countries that have been particularly resistant to the gospel. Ask God to touch the lives of people in every country around the world today.

SEPTEMBER 10

Personal Prayer
Praise God as your mighty, protective, and loving Father. Thank him for adopting you as his own son or daughter and for making you heir to all the promises given in Scripture (Gal. 3:26-29). Confess those times you have forgotten who you are—a child of the Most High God. Commit yourself to remembering each day that you have been born into God's family and have "clothed yourself with Christ" (3:27). Ask God to help you understand and appreciate your complete inheritance in Jesus Christ (Eph. 1:18).

For Your Family and Friends
Pray that the fathers you know will be able to reflect the Father's love, compassion, and wisdom to their children, so that the entire family will grow to trust and love God.

For the Church
Ask God to help your congregation welcome its neighbors and those who may be different in skin color, culture, economic class, or nationality, celebrating that "you are all one in Christ Jesus" (Gal. 3:28).

For the Kingdom
Pray that Christians in warring or oppressive countries may be shining lights of justice and compassion toward those who are being shunned or harmed.

For the Unsaved
Ask your Father to draw his wayward sons and daughters into his growing family.

SEPTEMBER 11

Personal Prayer

Praise God as the one who holds out his arms to the world in welcoming love and invitation. Thank God for having intervened in your life to bring you to a growing knowledge of his love for you. Confess your sins of this past week, trusting in the power of Jesus' blood to reconcile you with God. Commit yourself to becoming more aware of God's outreaching love toward your neighbors and friends. Ask him to make you a minister of reconciliation (2 Cor. 5:18-21).

For Your Family and Friends

Pray for those families who have been struggling with bitterness or alienation, asking God to bring reconciliation into their homes.

For the Church

Ask God to give the leaders of your church and denomination the ability to be effective "ambassadors of Christ," bringing a message of reconciliation to their communities. Pray also for unity and forgiveness where there are rifts in leadership.

For the Kingdom

Pray for reconciliation among foreign missionaries and local ministries where leaders are at odds with each other. Ask God to unify them with a single-minded vision for his kingdom.

For the Unsaved

Pray for those who have been raised in the church but who have never put their faith in Jesus and been reconciled to God. Ask that God will open their hearts to him before it's too late.

SEPTEMBER 12

Personal Prayer

Glorify God as the ruler over events both great and small, who knows not only the fate of nations but also the number of hairs on your head (Lk. 12:6-7). Thank God for hearing your prayers. Confess your struggles in prayer to God, and ask for his help and grace in this area (Heb. 4:14-16). Commit yourself to greater discipline in prayer for the needs of others. Ask God to give you wisdom as you pray for specific needs.

For Your Family and Friends

Ask God to strengthen the devotional time of families you know, that it may become a time of sharing, of learning from God's Word, and of prayer for each other.

For the Church

Pray that your church's outreach ministries may be undergirded with a strong foundation of prayer from gifted intercessors in your church, so that God's power will break through the strongholds of Satan in your community.

For the Kingdom

Pray for Christian churches around the world, that they may be known not as "houses of activity" but as "houses of prayer" (Mt. 21:13).

For the Unsaved

Pray today for one unsaved person you know, that God will use you to lead that person "to obey God by what [you] have said and done" (Rom. 15:18).

_____

_____

_____

_____

_____

SEPTEMBER 13

Personal Prayer

Give praise to God as the all-seeing one who knows the smallest detail of the future. Thank God for revealing some things to you about the future. Confess the ease with which you plan for the future without taking into account God's knowledge of what will happen (Jas. 4:13-15). Commit yourself to bringing your plans to him daily, asking his insight and guidance. Ask God to begin preparing you now for the challenges that lie ahead.

For Your Family and Friends

Pray for young people who are concerned about their future—and the elderly who are facing the unknowns of death in their future. Ask God to reassure them of his presence with them always.

For the Church

Pray that the church education program of your church will effectively prepare both adults and children to meet the challenges, work, and possible persecution of the years that lie ahead.

For the Kingdom

Pray for missionaries and teachers in developing countries, that they will have the necessary resources to adequately teach people to read and write and hear the gospel.

For the Unsaved

Pray for the opportunity to talk to someone who has wandered from the truth. Ask God to use you in bringing that person back to Christ (Jas. 5:19-20).

SEPTEMBER 14

Personal Prayer

Glorify God as the Lord who gathers his people from east and west, from north and south, to worship and serve him (Isa. 66:18-21). Thank God for including you as part of this family of varied cultures, races, and languages. Confess any tendency you have to put blinders on, so that you see God as interested only in one people or culture. Commit yourself to studying more about God's work in countries and cultures other than your own. Ask God to give you an opportunity to become involved in that work in some way— by prayer support, financial giving, letter writing, etc.

For Your Family and Friends

Pray for the gift of hospitality among Christian families you know, that they may reach out to people from other cultures or races.

For the Church

Pray that God's Spirit will help your church to move beyond its comfort zone in reaching out to those who are "unfamiliar"—of a different race, creed, or language. Ask God to give you plenty of opportunities to do so.

For the Kingdom

Pray for the day God will "gather all nations and tongues, and they will come and see [his] glory" (66:18). Pray for Christians who have made this vision their life's work.

For the Unsaved

Ask God to show you one person from a different religion whom you can pray for and befriend, perhaps eventually leading him or her to the one true God.

SEPTEMBER 15

Personal Prayer

Praise God as the fair judge and ruler who never lets wealth, appearance, or earthly power influence his decisions. Give thanks for God's constant concern for those in positions of weakness and poverty (Jas. 1:27). Confess those times when your support of the poor has been in word only and not in action (1:22-25). Commit yourself to seeing people as God sees them, not as our society sees them. Ask God to open your eyes to those who are "poor in the eyes of the world to be rich in faith" (Jas. 2:5).

For Your Family and Friends

Pray that the elderly members of these families may be well cared for and visited often, so that they may end their days in comfort and honor rather than loneliness and isolation.

For the Church

Pray for specific individuals and families in your church who may be having a hard time financially. Ask God what you can do to help (Gal. 6:9-10).

For the Kingdom

Ask God to bring relief and comfort to those in India who are treated as less than human because of their social status and circumstances of birth.

For the Unsaved

Pray that unbelievers will be drawn to faith in Christ because of the close-knit, unbiased, and loving fellowship they see in churches in your city or community.

_____

_____

_____

_____

_____

SEPTEMBER 16

Personal Prayer

Praise God as the source of all that you need, in both the spiritual and material realms. Thank God for giving you the ability to produce wealth and to meet basic physical needs. Confess those times when you have thought, "My power and the strength of my hands have produced this wealth for me" (Deut. 8:17-18). Commit yourself to envisioning each day the strength and power of God carrying you along in your work. Ask God to open your eyes to your utter dependence on him.

For Your Family and Friends

Ask God to help parents teach their children to find great enjoyment in giving money, energy, or creativity to the church's ministries. Pray that the parents may set a good example.

For the Church

Pray for those who are materially wealthy in your congregation, that they may be moved "to do good, to be rich in good deeds, and to be generous and willing to share." Thank God for his promise that this leads to a more sure treasure than material wealth (1 Tim. 6:17-19).

For the Kingdom

Intercede for the missionary workers in struggling South American countries, that God may fill them with joy as he supplies even their smallest financial and physical needs with donations and offerings from other churches.

For the Unsaved

Ask God to use even the financial situations of unbelievers to bring them into a dependent trust in his love and promises.

SEPTEMBER 17

Personal Prayer

Give highest praise to God as the all-sufficient one, "El-Shaddai." Thank God for being the strength of your heart and your inheritance forever (Ps. 73:26). Confess to him your reliance on material wealth or possessions to make you feel secure and satisfied. Commit yourself to saying, "Whom have I in heaven but you? And earth has nothing I desire besides you" (73:25). Ask God to help you grasp how completely his love and presence surround you in this day.

For Your Family and Friends

Pray for families who worship amid marital struggles or family tensions. Ask God to meet them in worship with compassion, power, and healing.

For the Church

Ask God to help your church make its worship services a place where unchurched neighbors and guests feel comfortable and welcome, so that they will want to stay and join God's family.

For the Kingdom

Pray for worship services all around the world, that God's Spirit might meet the needs of many hurting and spiritually hungry people who attend.

For the Unsaved

Ask God to reveal to you one person whom you should invite to worship this week or at least invite over for a meal or a cup of coffee.

Prayer Pointer

"It appears that God has so ordered life and the world that our praying is a vital part of his redemptive plan for individuals and the entire universe."
—MAXIE DUNNAM

SEPTEMBER 18

Personal Prayer

Praise God for the mystery of the Trinity—a model of love, unity, and oneness. Give thanks that God is able to bring a spirit of oneness among you and other believers, "so that with one heart and mouth you may glorify the God and Father of our Lord Jesus Christ" (Rom. 15:5-6). Confess any comments, thoughts, or actions that may have led to division, rather than unity, between you and another Christian. Ask God to make you humble enough to see your own fault in strained relationships and to seek forgiveness and peace.

For Your Family and Friends

Pray that parents may be unified as they teach and discipline their children, creating a God-glorifying harmony in the home.

For the Church

Ask God to put his special protection around the staff and leaders of your church, so that Satan will not be able to bring division through misunderstanding, pride, or self-interest (Phil. 2:1-3).

For the Kingdom

Pray that church leaders from all nations will "agree with each other in the Lord" over potentially divisive issues (Phil. 4:2).

For the Unsaved

Intercede especially for churches in racially mixed neighborhoods, that their witness and harmony may be so powerful that they draw unbelievers of all backgrounds into God's family.

_____

_____

_____

_____

_____

SEPTEMBER 19

Personal Prayer
Praise your Father as the head over the entire family of believers (Eph. 3:14-15). Thank God for the love he lavishes on you and others as he calls you "children of God" (1 Jn. 3:1). Confess those times when you have felt comfortable in your own circle of Christian brothers and sisters and forgotten to reach out to others beyond your own "family." Commit yourself this week to gaining at least one new brother or sister in Christ. Ask God to lead you to a person in your life who is ready to accept the gospel.

For Your Family and Friends
Pray for the believing teenagers you know, that they will be strong enough in their faith to witness to friends who are into drugs or premarital sex or rebellion toward God and their parents.

For the Church
Pray for the midweek outreach efforts of your congregation, that they may result in many neighborhood families coming to know Christ.

For the Kingdom
Ask God to fill all the outreach efforts of his church worldwide with his love, that Christians of all nations will "not love with words or tongue but with actions and in truth" (1 Jn. 3:18).

For the Unsaved
Pray that God will use you this week as the "salt of the earth"—in your actions as well as your words—to bring another person closer to the family of God.

_____

_____

_____

_____

_____

SEPTEMBER 20

Personal Prayer

Praise God as the source of all true wisdom and discernment (Col. 2:3). Thank him for supplying his church with the gifts of wisdom, knowledge, and the ability to distinguish between spirits (1 Cor. 12:8-10). Confess those times when you have failed to discern the cultural influences that try to choke out spiritual growth and fruitfulness. Commit yourself to testing the spirits to see whether they are from God (1 Jn. 4:1). Ask God to make you more aware of the reality of spiritual warfare in your life (Eph. 6:10-12).

For Your Family and Friends

Pray for acquaintances who may be exposed to the occult or New Age philosophy. Ask God to help them discern the falseness of these religions.

For the Church

Pray that God will raise up teachers in your congregation who are gifted in spiritual warfare and who can teach both children and adults how to use all the weapons of the faith against their enemy (6:13-18).

For the Kingdom

Ask God to lift the spiritual blindness from political leaders in your country, that they may make decisions that help create a wholesome and God-honoring society.

For the Unsaved

Pray for your unsaved family members and acquaintances, that God will protect them from false teachers and lead them to the truth.

_____

_____

_____

_____

_____

SEPTEMBER 21

Personal Prayer
Praise God as Jehovah-shammah, "the Lord who is there." Thank God for his immediate and all-encompassing presence in your life (Psalm 139). Confess the times this past week when you have doubted the Lord's presence or acted as though God were not surrounding you with his love and Spirit. Commit yourself to "practicing the presence of God" at all times. Ask him to give you signs of his presence every day this week.

For Your Family and Friends
Intercede for unborn children, that God's hand will be on them even in the womb, protecting and encompassing them with his love.

For the Church
Pray for specific missionaries that you know, that they may experience God's presence strongly as they watch prayers being answered and people brought to the Lord.

For the Kingdom
Ask for God's presence to linger as a fragrance on hospital chaplains as they minister to those facing illness and death.

For the Unsaved
Pray for the large Hindu population in India, that they may turn from dead idols to the living and true God.

Prayer Pointer
"Prayer is the key that opens the door to all that is good in life." —ANONYMOUS

SEPTEMBER 22

Personal Prayer

Give heartfelt praise to God as Jehovah-raah, "the Lord my shepherd." Thank God for leading you into quiet places and restoring your soul as you meet him daily in prayer. Confess those times when you have resisted the discipline and guidance of his shepherd's crook. Commit yourself to becoming so familiar with the Lord's voice that you will follow him without hesitation or fear (Jn. 10:3-5). Ask God to give you a shepherd's heart toward others.

For Your Family and Friends

Intercede for those families whose children are scattered "like sheep without a shepherd," without direction and purpose in their lives.

For the Church

Pray for the elders of your church as they care for those in your fellowship. Ask God to give them sensitivity and a caring heart.

For the Kingdom

Pray that Christian social workers may receive such nurture and care in their church fellowships that they are strengthened to face the difficult task of ministering to a broken world.

For the Unsaved

Pray that the unsaved people you know will come to meet and love their Savior, who wants them to "have life, and have it to the full" (Jn. 10:10).

Personal Prayer

Praise the name of Jehovah-jireh, "the Lord will provide." Thank God for having given you everything you need for life and health in this week. Confess to him the times when you have begrudged giving a kind word or encouragement or forgiveness to another person. Commit yourself to reflecting God's generosity and openhanded love to a difficult person in your life. Ask God to give you an extra portion of his Spirit as you strive to reflect his character.

For Your Family and Friends

If there is a specific need in your family that only God can provide, commit this need to him in the faith that he will supply it abundantly (2 Cor. 9:8).

For the Church

Intercede for the churches in your area which work in the inner city and struggle for funds to meet their budgets. Ask God to move the hearts of wealthier congregations to share with them.

For the Kingdom

Praise God for the way in which generous gifts from believers refresh the hearts and spirits of missionaries around the world (9:12-13).

For the Unsaved

Pray for organizations which supply Bibles to motels, hospitals, and foreign countries, that they may not lack funds to bring the Word of life to the unsaved.

SEPTEMBER 24

Personal Prayer
Praise the Lord, the source of all song, and make music to his name. Thank God for his love in the morning and for his faithfulness at night (Ps. 92:1-2). Confess that you sometimes sing by rote. Commit yourself to focusing on what you sing. Ask to feel God's presence through music today.

For Your Family and Friends
As you scan faces in church, ask God to soothe squirming children, sullen teens, and tense adults.

For the Church
Pray that through the music, message, prayers, and sacraments, your congregation will feel one in body and spirit (Eph. 4:3-4) as it gathers to worship.

For the Kingdom
Ask God to extend this spiritual bond so that your church feels one with believers around the world. Consider that believers are called to "one hope . . . one Lord, one faith, one baptism; one God and Father of all, who is over all and through all and in all" (4:4-6).

For the Unsaved
Pray to discern bridges between you or your church and those who are far from God.

Prayer Pointer
"We must try to converse with God in little ways while we do our work; not in memorized prayer, not trying to recite previously formed thoughts. Rather, we should purely and simply reveal our hearts as the words come to us."
—BROTHER LAWRENCE

_____

_____

_____

_____

SEPTEMBER 25

Personal Prayer
Praise God, the source of light and Light. Be thankful for the times you've felt the Lord's face shining on you (Ps. 80:3). Confess that you sometimes turn your face from God's. Commit yourself to seeking God's leading. Ask him for confirmation of new directions.

For Your Family and Friends
Petition God to channel peace and clarity through you to family and friends who flounder. Commit yourself to staying close to God, so your life models his leading.

For the Church
Intercede for leaders in your church, so they recognize and know how to carry out Christ's plan for your church. Pledge to express genuine appreciation; God may use your thanks to confirm something for a church leader.

For the Kingdom
Pray that Christian leaders around the world will be led by the Lord alone (Deut. 32:12), despite political, economic, and ethnic ties.

For the Unsaved
Ask God to show you one person who will welcome your spiritual maturity in their life.

Prayer Pointer
"Many pray with their lips for that for which their hearts have no desire."
—JONATHAN EDWARDS

SEPTEMBER 26

Personal Prayer

Praise the Son of Man, who cares about your material needs, your health, and your freedom. Thank him for including you in "proclaim[ing] the year of the Lord's favor" (Lk. 4:18-19). Confess that you give more thought to your family's needs than to the needs of those who have far less. Commit yourself to change. Ask God to open your eyes, heart, time, and finances to a specific person or outreach ministry.

For Your Family and Friends

Pray daily that together with family members or friends you will unite around a ministry cause. Ask for oneness of desire.

For the Church

Implore God to break down unspoken walls of behavior in your church. Resolve to reach out to someone who is overlooked because of his or her differences (Eph. 3:16-19).

For the Kingdom

Pray for courage and faithfulness for North American missionaries who see little results.

For the Unsaved

Ask God to help you care at least as much about unsaved people as you care about the church budget or the order of worship.

SEPTEMBER 27

Personal Prayer
Praise God, your Father and great Teacher. Give thanks for teachers and mentors who helped make your paths straight (Prov. 3:6). Confess that you sometimes focus more on their quirks than their virtues. Commit yourself to noticing the good in those who can teach you more about faith. Ask God how you can best support education in your church.

For Your Family and Friends
Pray that everyone in your church will find something to like in church school, youth group, or adult education. Listen to the experiences of your own children in these settings.

For the Church
Intercede for church educators who try to offer something worthwhile. Ask God to show you new ways to join in.

For the Kingdom
Pray that God's Spirit will lead teachers to discover fresh ways to instruct and disciple new Christians.

For the Unsaved
Claim the Holy Spirit's power to woo family members or friends who say Christianity makes no sense.

Prayer Pointer
"A man's state before God may always be measured by his prayers." —J. C. RYLE

SEPTEMBER 28

Personal Prayer
Praise the God of Abraham, Isaac, and Jacob. Thank him for including you among Abraham's spiritual descendants, for calling you to shine like a star in the firmament of glory (Gen. 22:17). Confess that sometimes your witness is dim. Commit yourself to connecting with and praying for other Christians who want to shine for God. Ask where you should begin.

For Your Family and Friends
Plead with God on behalf of children in your family and those around you. Pray that they will see the spiritual consequences of daily choices—and choose God.

For the Church
Ask God to translate parents' concern for their own children's salvation into passion to make disciples of every nation (Mt. 28:19-20).

For the Kingdom
Lift up missionary families, who often endure long separations from loved ones to share God's good news. Pray that they will enjoy results.

For the Unsaved
Ask God to honor the tentative prayers of those who aren't even sure there is a God—but are beginning to want one.

_____

_____

_____

_____

_____

Personal Prayer

Praise God, the Most Holy, worthy of all honor. Give thanks for gatherings where you can join in praise (Ps. 22:22, 25). Confess your reluctance to share such joys outside of Christian circles. Commit yourself to offering glimpses of God's grace to those outside the fellowship. Ask God to show you someone who craves the balm of Gilead (Jer. 46:11).

For Your Family and Friends

Invite God to reveal ways you neglect family or friends as you offer compassion to others. Pray for balance.

For the Church

Ask God to give your congregation joy in being Jesus' hands and feet. Pray for specific ways your church can help others meet their needs for food, income, housing, and transportation.

For the Kingdom

Intercede for North American social workers, who have more cases than time or funds. Ask God to guard them from burnout and cynicism.

For the Unsaved

Ask the Holy Spirit to prompt unbelievers to ask why Christians muck out flooded homes or run food pantries on their behalf.

Prayer Pointer

"The mightier any one is in the Word, the more mighty he will be in prayer."
—WILLIAM GURNALL

SEPTEMBER 30

Personal Prayer

Praise the Creator, who fills mountain springs, makes grass grow for cattle, and allows people to bring forth food from the earth (Ps. 104:10-14). Thank God for your food and shelter. Confess that all you have belongs to God. Commit to living as a steward, not a consumer. Ask God where to start in renewing your mind-set.

For Your Family and Friends

Ask God to help you find more joy in fresh air, pure water, and bird song than in manufactured goods. Model this among family and friends.

For the Church

Pray for members in your congregation who struggle with huge credit card bills or have trouble meeting their church offering pledge (Mt. 6:21).

For the Kingdom

Ask God to help Christian outreach agencies manage their budgets, so they can pay their employees justly and reach more people.

For the Unsaved

Pray that Christians—by caring more about people than things, by managing money well—will pique interest among non-Christians.

OCTOBER 1

Personal Prayer
Shout Hallelujah! to the Lord God Almighty. Praise God for his power and glory. Thank him for salvation (Rev. 19:1). Confess how rarely in recent days you have meditated on God's wisdom and strength. Commit yourself to thinking more about what you can do for God, rather than what God can do for you. Ask for a renewed sense of awe about God's character, for a greater hunger to know him.

For Your Family and Friends
Pray for family members or friends who hold God at arm's length. Plead for personal peace and joy in Christ, so they will want what you have.

For the Church
Pray that your worship leaders will be sensitive to those with unusual personalities or special needs. Many parts form Christ's body (1 Cor. 12:12-31).

For the Kingdom
Pray that Christians will be willing to examine and change even time-honored forms of worship—if such changes will draw unbelievers to the gospel.

For the Unsaved
Pray that unsaved people who feel empty will find salvation and fulfilling worship.

Prayer Pointer
"Prayer is not conquering God's reluctance, but taking hold of God's willingness."
—PHILLIPS BROOKS

_____

_____

_____

_____

_____

OCTOBER 2

Personal Prayer
Praise your Wonderful Counselor, Mighty God, Everlasting Father. Give thanks for the Prince of Peace (Isa. 9:6). Confess how often you'd rather make your own plans than think about what God might be telling you through church leaders. Commit to listening for God through others' words. Ask God to show you whether a specific leader has a word for you.

For Your Family and Friends
Pray for family and friends hurt by church leaders who have misused their influence.

For the Church
Pray for church leaders who must sometimes call for repentance before peace is possible (Josh. 7:1-26).

For the Kingdom
Intercede for leaders throughout the worldwide church. Ask on their behalf for character and integrity, so their actions reflect their convictions.

For the Unsaved
Claim Jesus' power to do your part in gathering in those who are like sheep without a shepherd (Mt. 9:35-38).

_____

_____

_____

_____

_____

OCTOBER 3

Personal Prayer

Praise Jesus, who welcomes the weary. Thank him for lifted burdens (Mt. 11:25-30). Confess that the way you fill your days often ignores Jesus' offer of rest. Commit to enjoying this rest yourself and sharing it with others. Ask God for a specific way you can eliminate something from your schedule in order to create time for resting in the Lord.

For Your Family and Friends

Pray for family and friends who spend much of their time and energy helping others. Ask that they will find their strength in God as they rest quietly in him (Ps. 37:7).

For the Church

Lift up church members who minister in rough schools, rural clinics, nursing homes, and disaster areas.

For the Kingdom

Pray that Christians will multiply God's infinite mercy by befriending people with disabilities, helping released prisoners find work, and sheltering refugees.

For the Unsaved

Pray that you will be more like the Good Samaritan than like the Levite as you meet unsaved people.

Prayer Pointer

"No time is so well spent in every day as that which we spend upon our knees."
—J. C. Ryle

_____

_____

_____

_____

_____

OCTOBER 4

Personal Prayer

Praise God, who calls believers into his kingdom. Thank him for giving you eyes to see and ears to hear the Word (Mt. 13:1-23). Confess that no matter how old you are, you have more to learn. Commit yourself to increasing your knowledge of the faith. Ask God where you should start—personal or group Bible study, church courses, support groups, memorization, singing through a hymnal . . .

For Your Family and Friends

Pray for a willing spirit among family and friends to let God into their lives.

For the Church

Pray that church education leaders will help class members handle tough questions with grace and tolerance.

For the Kingdom

Ask God to use church education programs as springboards to action. Plead for "faith and deeds" churches equal to the test (Jas. 2:1-16).

For the Unsaved

Pray that church school teachers will model the advantages of faith and remind children to pray for unbelievers.

_____

_____

_____

_____

OCTOBER 5

Personal Prayer

Praise God, who "so loved the world that he gave his one and only Son, that whoever believes in him shall not perish but have eternal life" (Jn. 3:16). Thank God for those who led you to Christ. Confess that you are sometimes afraid to introduce others to Christ. Commit yourself to building friendships with people who do not know Jesus. Ask God to help you identify a friend who might be open to conversion.

For Your Family and Friends

Resolve in prayer to talk more among friends and family members about how you as a group can support world missions (Mt. 18:19-20).

For the Church

Lift up missionaries from your church. Write to ask about their special prayer needs.

For the Kingdom

Pray for translators who wrestle with unfamiliar alphabets and languages to spread God's good news to every nation.

For the Unsaved

Ponder in prayer what it will be like when "all the ends of the earth will remember and turn to the LORD" (Ps. 22:27). Pray for the coming of that day.

Prayer Pointer

"Prayer is not merely an occasional impulse to which we respond when we are in trouble: prayer is a life attitude." —WALTER A. MUELLER

_____

_____

_____

_____

_____

OCTOBER 6

Personal Prayer

Praise the Lord, "our dwelling place throughout all generations" (Ps. 90:1). Thank God for the security you've found through faith. Confess ways you've rejected that security this week. Commit yourself to starting each morning satisfied with God's unfailing love (90:14). Ask how you might vary your morning routine to better begin the day with God.

For Your Family and Friends

Pray that God will fill your awareness, so you naturally speak of his care and fellowship in your family and among friends.

For the Church

Pray that Bible studies, households, and cell groups in your congregation will inspire members to deeper bonds and faith-directed action.

For the Kingdom

Lift up advocates for people in wheelchairs or without sight. They need prayers to rewrite laws, redesign buildings, and modify job requirements.

For the Unsaved

Ask God how you or your church could reach out to people with mental disabilities.

OCTOBER 7

Personal Prayer

Praise the Lord your God, who "goes with you; he will never leave you nor forsake you" (Deut. 31:6). Thank God for his presence in your life. Confess times when you think that just a little more money would make you even more content in God's presence (Heb. 13:5). Commit yourself to wanting what you have, rather than scrambling to have what you want. Ask God to simply supply your needs and to give you contentment with his choices.

For Your Family and Friends

Pray that you can teach your children to be generous with their time and money. Involve your friends' children in giving new and used toys to a battered women's shelter.

For the Church

Pray that your congregation will make wise decisions in allocating money for its own ministries, for other Christians, and for unbelievers.

For the Kingdom

Intercede for those who invest money on behalf of Christian agencies.

For the Unsaved

Pray for unbelievers whose poverty erects a wall between them and wealthier Christians.

Prayer Pointer

"Love to pray—feel often during the day the need for prayer, and take trouble to pray." —MOTHER TERESA

OCTOBER 8

Personal Prayer

Praise God for his sovereignty. Thank him for using ordinary people to prompt effectiveness in the Christian movement. Confess those occasions when you knew God was calling you to take a stand . . . and you didn't. Commit yourself to depending on God's power with renewed faith to act on those opportunities which shape the church of tomorrow (Col. 4:5-6). Ask, "Lord, what can I do to bring about positive change in your church?"

For Your Family and Friends

Pray that your family and friends will receive God's full forgiveness. Pray that they will experience the joy of extending grace to others more freely.

For the Church

Pray that your worship together reflects a celebration of who God is. Pray for the empowerment of all God's children to use their gifts and talents in service of the sovereign Lord.

For the Kingdom

Pray that those engaged in religious cults will recognize that forgiveness is experienced only through Jesus Christ.

For the Unsaved

Ask that unsaved people you know will experience a desire to question the things of our sovereign God.

OCTOBER 9

Personal Prayer
Praise Jesus, the gentle shepherd. Thank him for walking beside you and showing you the way. Ask God to make his presence obvious to you. Confess those times when you failed to recognize the Lord's guidance and protection. Commit yourself to thanking God for his quiet presence.

For Your Family and Friends
Pray that your quiet spirit will touch the hearts of those whom you love and those who are hard to love.

For the Church
Pray that your church leaders will lead your congregation in awe and respect for the gentleness of God.

For the Kingdom
Pray that people in positions of authority will see gentleness as a personal virtue and not a weakness.

For the Unsaved
Pray that the voice of the shepherd will break the hearts of those who desire to be led. Ask that you will be a reflection of his gentle nature (Phil. 4:5).

Prayer Pointer
"The more we receive in silent prayer, the more we can give in our active life."
—MOTHER TERESA

OCTOBER 10

Personal Prayer
Praise God, for his mercy endures to all generations. Thank him for receiving you without hesitation. Confess thoughts which prevent you from exploring God's mercy. Commit yourself to listening to his still, small voice. Jesus whispers, "Come unto me." Ask God to help you see the many ways he shows you his mercy.

For Your Family and Friends
Pray that God's mercy will be reflected in you in such a way that it becomes a magnetic power drawing your family and friends closer.

For the Church
Pray that God will create tender hearts in his people, the church. Pray for renewed passion to share Christ and his mercy.

For the Kingdom
Pray for Christian psychologists, psychiatrists, and social workers. Ask that they will eagerly share the life-changing, mind-altering power of the Lord Jesus Christ.

For the Unsaved
Pray that the mercy of God will flow through you to unsaved people you know.

_____

_____

_____

_____

OCTOBER 11

Personal Prayer

Praise God, the Creator of the heavens. Thank God for his awesome handiwork, for the beauty reflected in the stars, the moon, the clouds, and the sun. Confess those times when you wondered if God was real and you questioned if he loved you. Commit yourself to praising the Creator of the universe as you see the stars, sun, moon, and clouds. Ask him to provide you peace, knowing that he cares for you.

For Your Family and Friends

Ask God to help you let go of those you worry about. They, too, are in his hands.

For the Church

Intercede for church members who struggle to experience the reality of God. Pray that their faith will be affirmed as they see God in his creation.

For the Kingdom

Pray that those who explore the heavens and earth through science will find not only statistics, but the Creator.

For the Unsaved

Pray that unbelieving people who view the stars tonight will recognize a loving, creative God behind it all.

Prayer Pointer

"God shapes the world by prayer. The more praying there is in the world the better the world will be, the mightier the forces against evil." —E. M. BOUNDS

Personal Prayer

Praise God, who is the great physician. Thank him for healing broken hearts. Confess those times when you failed to help those who sought to experience the Savior's healing touch. Commit to serving God by serving them. Ask God to reveal names of individuals who suffer from pain, rejection, and spiritual death.

For Your Family and Friends

Pray that God will provide opportunity for you to support the healing of broken hearts through the power of Jesus Christ.

For the Church

Pray for missionaries in foreign countries where modern medicines are not readily available. Ask that God's healing power will become evident in the lives of many.

For the Kingdom

Pray that the physicians and nurses of the world will see human anatomy through the eyes of the great physician.

For the Unsaved

Pray that those experiencing pain will be moved to seek the healing power of the one who suffered pain, rejection, and brokenness for all humankind.

_____

_____

_____

_____

_____

OCTOBER 13

Personal Prayer

Give all your praise to God, for his faithfulness endures forever. In quiet reflection, thank God for his faithful presence during your times of greatest need. With humility, confess your attempts to manage life without him. With a desire to reflect God's faithfulness, commit to recognizing his power. Ask that you will see his faithfulness each day of your life.

For Your Family and Friends

God's faithfulness is communicated through you to others. Pray that you will reflect a sustaining, patient presence with those who observe God in you.

For the Church

Pray that caregivers will be a reminder of the God who empowers them to serve the broken. Pray that the fellowship within the church will be strengthened to reflect God's faithful promises to those he loves.

For the Kingdom

Pray for all marriages. Ask that God will strengthen the commitment between husbands and wives. Pray that our culture will once again embrace the sanctity of matrimony.

For the Unsaved

Pray that those who go to church faith-fully but don't know the faithful Father will hear his voice today and respond in faith.

Prayer Pointer

"To pray is nothing more involved than to open the door, giving Jesus access to our needs and permitting him to exercise his own power in dealing with them."
—O. HALLESBY

Personal Prayer

Praise your all-powerful God for conquering sin and death. Thank him for new life in Christ and for saving you from the torment of sin and the agony of eternal death. Confess to God any apathy toward his powerful love in your life. Ask him to develop moment-by-moment awareness of his love for you and a passion to share this love with unbelievers. Commit to praying regularly for unsaved friends, family members, and neighbors. Ask that God will use you to reflect his love, his life, his lordship.

For Your Family and Friends

Pray that the all-powerful God will extend strength to those in your family who call on his name.

For the Church

Pray that your congregation will recognize the importance of faithful stewardship to ministries which unleash God's power.

For the Kingdom

Ask that the effects of sin, death, destruction, and hatred will soon be overcome by the almighty power of the living God.

For the Unsaved

Pray that those who strive for earthly power will come face-to-face with its futility and surrender all to Jesus.

_____

_____

_____

_____

_____

OCTOBER 15

Personal Prayer

Praise God, who is the bread of life. Thank God for the strength he provides you to live each day. Confess those times when you have complained about weakness or yielded to the desire not to press on. Commit yourself to doing those things which nurture spiritual energy. Ask God to reveal to you ways by which he would have you offer "bread" to others.

For Your Family and Friends

Pray that God will provide the energy needed to deal with unexpected circumstances in your family life, remembering that he will sustain you.

For Your Church

Pray that when your congregation gathers around the communion table they will experience the bread as the body of Christ, broken for them.

For the Kingdom

Pray that the farmers across North America will see their fields of wheat and corn as a source of life provided by God.

For the Unsaved

Pray that our cultural spiritual malnutrition will develop into a hunger for the bread of life.

Prayer Pointer

"Set the tone of the day with early morning prayer, and spirituality then tends to prevail and prayer becomes easier." —ERNEST B. GENTILE

Personal Prayer
Praise God, the Father of all. Thank him for allowing you to call him "Abba"—Daddy. Confess your fear of seeing him as Father. Commit to seeking this attribute of God. Ask God to eliminate any barriers which complicate your ability to experience "Abba" as comforting.

For Your Family and Friends
Let go of the thoughts which hinder you from developing loving relationships with those who seek God.

For Your Church
Pray for sensitivity for those abused by fathers. Pray for ministries to develop which support their healing. Pray that as family units break down the church will be a place where people find family and the reality of God as their Father.

For the Kingdom
Pray for children who are being abused. Pray that their minds and hearts will be protected by the Father, who loves them dearly.

For the Unsaved
Ask God to reveal himself as a loving, welcoming Father to lost and lonely people you know.

_____

_____

_____

_____

_____

OCTOBER 17

Personal Prayer

Praise God, for he is truth. There is no deception in him. Thank God for his revealed redemptive plan. Confess those times when you have doubted the reality of God's righteousness. Commit to faith those things of God which are most difficult for you to accept as his truth. Ask God to help you see his truth revealed to you each day—in nature, in godly relationships, in the renewing of your mind through Christ Jesus.

For Your Family and Friends

Pray that your family and friends will see God's truth in a unique and meaningful way.

For the Church

Pray that your church's efforts to reach others with the gospel of Christ will be securely rooted in the truth of God's Word.

For the Kingdom

Pray that God will reveal the deceit and persuasive powers of false gods and cult leaders.

For the Unsaved

Pray that unbelievers will both respect and accept God's truth.

Prayer Pointer

"Prayer is for the helpless." —O. HALLESBY

OCTOBER 18

Personal Prayer

Praise God for his agape love, a liberating power, expressed through selfless acts. Thank God for times when you have experienced his unfailing love for you, his child. Confess those times when you failed to love him. Commit yourself to modeling God's love in all your relationships with others. Ask God to make you sensitive to those occasions when unconditional love can be expressed in your actions.

For Your Family and Friends

Pray that God will give you a vision for what he is accomplishing through the lives of those who are close to you.

For the Church

Thank God for godly mentors who patiently and selflessly teach you how to love and trust God.

For the Kingdom

Ask God to help you view every good and marvelous thing in our culture as his gift.

For the Unsaved

Pray that you will see those who are not yet Christians through the eyes of God—and love them even as he does.

OCTOBER 19

Personal Prayer

Praise God, for he is long-suffering. Thank God for his willingness to suffer for you. Confess those times when you failed to do so, for those times when you lacked patience with God's process. Commit yourself to being willing to suffer for his sake. Ask him for the ability to be long-suffering.

For Your Family and Friends

Ask for a patient, long-suffering attitude with family members or friends who may be especially irritating to you.

For the Church

Pray for missionaries who suffer for the cause of Christ. Pray that they will be encouraged in their task to raise high the cross of Christ.

For the Kingdom

Pray for those change agents who serve to liberate the oppressed.

For the Unsaved

Pray that Christians will be willing to be long-suffering in their service to those who seek Christ.

Prayer Pointer

"Praising God is the secret of having increased blessings in your life." —DON GOSSETT

OCTOBER 20

Personal Prayer
Praise God for his righteousness. Thank him for the consequences of sin which move you to repentance at the foot of the cross. Confess times of anger when you felt God was not fair. Commit to accepting your circumstances as God's justice at work which shapes his world. Ask God to help you see his righteous acts as acts of love, designed for you.

For Your Family and Friends
Ask God to help you trust his ability to judge those around you. He knows their hearts and their actions.

For the Church
Pray that the caregivers of your church will discern God's justice as it applies to affirming and discipling members of the congregation.

For the Kingdom
Pray for the judges in our courtrooms. Ask that their ability to discern truth will be strong and their wisdom to deal fairly with offenders will be of God.

For the Unsaved
Pray that God's justice will draw sinners to the Savior.

OCTOBER 21

Personal Prayer

Praise God for his comfort. Thank God that he holds you close and calls you his child. Confess those times when you have rejected God's love. Commit yourself to seeking God's comfort through the people in the church and his Word. Ask him to deliver you from your desire to handle your pain alone.

For Your Family and Friends

Pray that you will be a comfort to others within your family structure.

For the Church

Pray that the members of your congregation will reach out in ways which comfort those who are disheartened, discouraged, and depressed.

For the Kingdom

Pray for those who minister to the grieving. Ask that they will enjoy God's richest blessings.

For the Unsaved

Pray that unsaved people will search for and find the comfort that only Jesus can provide.

Prayer Pointer

"Far be it from me that I should sin against the LORD by failing to pray for you."
—1 Samuel 12:23

OCTOBER 22

Personal Prayer

Praise God, whose "every word . . . is flawless." Thank God for being "a shield to those who take refuge in him" (Prov. 30:5). Confess times of not believing or listening to his Word. Commit yourself to hearing God speak to you today. Ask him to truly be your refuge.

For Your Family and Friends

Pray that all those close to you will be especially open to God's Word as it is preached and taught. Ask God to especially use corporate worship times to encourage someone close to you who is struggling right now.

For the Church

As your church gathers for worship this week, pray that the leaders will help the congregation take refuge in God. Ask God's Spirit to lead all worshipers to focus beyond the forms of worship and the details of the service to him.

For the Kingdom

Pray for God's flawless Word to be clearly and practically preached throughout the world. Ask God's Spirit to open hearts so that his kingdom and righteousness may grow.

For the Unsaved

Pray that God will draw unsaved "seekers" to the worship celebrations of his people. Ask God to draw them through his people to himself.

_____

_____

_____

_____

Personal Prayer

Praise the Lord, who is able even to weigh your motives (Prov. 16:2). Thank God for times he has brought conviction to lead you to needed change. Confess any sinful actions, words, plans, or motives the Spirit brings to your attention. Commit to the Lord whatever you are planning to do, asking that he then make your plans succeed (16:3).

For Your Family and Friends

Pray for a pure heart as you lead your children and/or the children of your friends. Ask God to use you as a consistently good example.

For the Church

Pray that the leaders of your church will be motivated by love, faithfulness, and the fear of the Lord rather than pride (16:5-6). Ask God to keep your heart pure toward your leaders and to use you as an encourager for them.

For the Kingdom

Pray for integrity in the lives of Christians in all vocations. Ask God to place thoroughly righteous people in strategic leadership positions in your community and throughout the world.

For the Unsaved

Pray for Christians' consistent love, faithfulness, and fear of the Lord to provide a shining contrast to those caught in deceit. Ask God's Spirit to shine through you to bring someone to his light.

OCTOBER 24

Personal Prayer

Praise the Lord, whose name is a strong tower to which the righteous run and find safety (Prov. 18:10). Thank God for the safety he has brought to your life. Confess any area in which your walk is not consistent with bearing Christ's name. Commit to living all your life under God. Ask him to give you the courage that comes from knowing he cares for you.

For Your Family and Friends

Pray for those in your care to be under the strong tower of God's care. Ask God to assure them of their safety in his strong and tender presence.

For the Church

Pray for the outreach ministries of your local church and the church world-wide. Ask God to cause many unsaved persons to respond to this work, joining the righteous in running to him for safety and life.

For the Kingdom

Pray that the advances in media technology will be used to their best and fullest potential for spreading God's call to safety. Ask God to give his church innovative and visionary understanding of the possibilities for advancing his kingdom.

For the Unsaved

Pray for someone in your neighborhood who is not under the protection of God's name. Ask God for the courage and opportunities to lead that neighbor to your strong tower.

OCTOBER 25

Personal Prayer

Praise God, the source of knowledge (Prov. 1:7). Thank God for the wisdom to apply that knowledge in everyday situations. Confess times of leaning "on your own understanding," not acknowledging him (Prov. 3:5-6). Commit to acknowledging God in all your ways. Ask him to help you trust in him with all your heart.

For Your Family and Friends

Pray that God will open the eyes of children to see his involvement and care in all parts of his creation. Ask God to continually deepen the insights of the adults as well.

For the Church

Pray for your church's education programs. Ask God to lead all to a love for God that grows "more and more in knowledge and depth of insight, so that [they] may be able to discern what is best and may be pure and blameless until the day of Christ, filled with the fruit of righteousness that comes through Jesus Christ—to the glory and praise of God" (Phil. 1:9-11).

For the Kingdom

Pray for teachers and students in all schools to acknowledge God. Ask for special effectiveness for the Christians in these arenas.

For the Unsaved

Pray for neighbors who do not yet "fear the Lord." Ask God to open the eyes of their understanding to know him.

Prayer Pointer

"Through intercessory prayer God does something that would not otherwise be done." —MAXIE DUNNAM

_____

_____

_____

_____

OCTOBER 26

Personal Prayer

Praise God, the one who ultimately dispenses justice (Prov. 29:26). Thank him for leaders in your country and community who consistently hold up God's just standards. Confess ways in which you have not followed those standards in your own life. Commit to acting justly, loving mercy, and walking humbly with God (Mic. 6:8). Ask God to use you to help bring this way of life to your part of the world.

For Your Family and Friends

Pray for anyone close to you who is apparently not walking humbly with God in the way of justice and mercy. Ask God to establish the work of those who are living rightly with him (Ps. 90:17).

For the Church

Pray for your world missionaries. Ask God to remind them that "fear of man will prove to be a snare, but whoever trusts in the Lord is kept safe" (Prov. 29:25).

For the Kingdom

Pray that world missionaries and their agencies will work to promote God's ways of justice for the societies in which they work. Ask God to give them supernatural effectiveness.

For the Unsaved

Pray also for the individuals in those countries. Ask God to apply the merciful justice of Christ's sacrifice to their lives, leading them to a humble and grateful walk with him.

Personal Prayer

Praise God for being both high above you and intimately within you. Thank God for making you a friend of Jesus as you follow his ways (Jn. 15:14). Confess times of damaging that friendship by acting as if you didn't know Jesus and his ways. Commit to living in loving, obedient partnership with him (15:15). Ask Jesus to increase your appreciation of the gift of his friendship and fellowship.

For Your Family and Friends

Pray for those you love to continually "walk in the ways of good men and keep to the paths of the righteous" (Prov. 2:20). Ask God to give them discretion in choosing friends and associates.

For the Church

Pray for those who administer the caring and fellowship ministries of your local church. Ask God to show you someone who could be served by his care and friendship expressed through you.

For the Kingdom

Pray for Christians in all walks of life to carefully discern the counsel they receive so that they consistently "walk in the ways of good men." Ask God to encourage you through fellow believers to "keep to the paths of the righteous."

For the Unsaved

Pray for acquaintances who apparently are neither "good" nor "righteous." Ask God to convict them by his Spirit (Jn. 16:8-11) so that they turn to him.

OCTOBER 28

Personal Prayer

Praise the sovereign one who works out everything for his own ends (Prov. 16:4). Thank God for determining your steps (16:9). Confess any area where you may be doubting that his leading is best. "Commit to the LORD whatever you [are planning to] do," knowing that then "your plans will succeed" (16:3). Ask the Lord to alter any plans that are not fully in line with his best.

For Your Family and Friends

Pray for anyone close who seems more interested in the riches of this world than those of God. Ask God to help all to remember that it is far "better to get wisdom than gold, to choose understanding rather than silver" (16:16).

For the Church

Pray for Christians to give cheerfully and generously of this world's resources for leading many to the riches of God. Ask God to give great discernment to those managing ministry resources.

For the Kingdom

Pray for relief from poverty for one of the nations in the news. Ask God to bless the work of Christian relief agencies and others seeking to help.

For the Unsaved

Pray that Christians' generosity will shine beautifully in the darkness of our materialistic culture. Ask God to draw many through this light to exchange their trinkets for his true treasure.

_____

_____

_____

_____

_____

OCTOBER 29

Personal Prayer

Praise God for his faithfulness (2 Cor. 1:18). Give thanks that "no matter how many promises God has made, they are 'Yes' in Christ" (1:20). Confess any reluctance to trust God. Commit to consciously remembering that God has "anointed us, set his seal of ownership on us, and put his Spirit in our hearts as a deposit, guaranteeing what is to come" (1:21-22). Ask him to lead you in celebrating this faithfulness in worship.

For Your Family and Friends

Pray for a thankful, trusting spirit for your household. Ask God to increase the joy of fellow worshipers through your attitude.

For the Church

Pray for faithfulness to God by those who explain his Word. Ask God to clearly speak through them in a resounding affirmation of his "'Yes' in Christ" (1:18-20).

For the Kingdom

Pray for all who listen to God's Word explained. Ask God's Spirit to point out specific applications to people in all walks of life, showing them how to seek his kingdom and righteousness in their part of his world.

For the Unsaved

Pray for the actions and attitudes of God's people as they go out into your community to impact the unsaved. Ask God to use the faithfulness of his people to draw many to himself.

OCTOBER 30

Personal Prayer
Praise "the God and Father of the Lord Jesus, who is to be praised forever" (2 Cor. 11:31). Thank him for giving you spiritual leaders, past and present, who have led you in walking with God. Confess times of veering away on ungodly sidetracks. Commit yourself to following leaders who truly follow Christ, and ask God to use you as a godly leader for someone else.

For Your Family and Friends
Pray by name for those called to be the spiritual leaders in the households of your family and friends. Ask God's Spirit to prompt them to the diligence such a great responsibility requires.

For the Church
Pray for the leaders of your denomination and local church ministries. Ask God to give them vision, compassion for those they lead, and his strength to sustain them as they "face daily the pressure of [their] concern" for those under their care (11:28-29).

For the Kingdom
Pray for believers in all walks of life to be God-honoring leaders in their work environments. Ask God to strengthen them as they often must lead against the flow of cultural currents.

For the Unsaved
Pray for an unsaved person in your neighborhood. Ask God for the privilege of being a godly influence in that person's life, leading him or her to follow Christ.

OCTOBER 31

Personal Prayer
Praise Jesus Christ, the Lord, the image of God (2 Cor. 4:4-5). Thank God for making "his light shine in our hearts to give us the light of the knowledge of the glory of God in the face of Christ" (4:6). Confess times of disinterest in knowing God fully. Commit yourself to thinking daily about him and his glory. Ask God to make his light shine more fully in your heart.

For Your Family and Friends
Pray for God to shine through you to your family and friends, even though they know you well enough to see your weaknesses. Thank God that this shows even more clearly that the power is from him rather than you (4:7).

For the Church
Pray for God's light to shine in your community through your church's members. Ask God to help people focus on the glory of his light rather than on the failings of his light-bearers.

For the Kingdom
Pray for those working to begin new churches. Ask God to bring his light to more and more areas through these new communities of believers.

For the Unsaved
Pray for many unsaved people to be reached through small group Bible studies and Sunday school. Ask God to use you and other believers, in spite of frailties, to bring his light to many.

Personal Prayer

Praise the meek and gentle Christ, who has power to demolish strongholds (2 Cor. 10:1, 4). Thank God for his truth and power, which are so different from the world's. Confess times of placing ultimate reliance in mere human resources. Commit to putting your confidence and pride in the Lord (10:17). Ask God to guide you to live in such a way that you receive his commendation, no matter what the world says (10:18).

For Your Family and Friends

Pray for your households to be founded upon the principles of God rather than the mere "wisdom" of this world. Ask God to guide and protect your home with his truth.

For the Church

Pray for those in the church's education ministries. Ask God to give them the wisdom and courage to lead God's people to "demolish arguments and every pretension that sets itself up against the knowledge of God . . . [taking] captive every thought to make it obedient to Christ" (10:5).

For the Kingdom

Pray for God's people in all walks of life to "aim for perfection" (2 Cor. 13:11). Ask God to use their clear thinking to extend his kingdom and righteousness.

For the Unsaved

Pray by name for unsaved friends and neighbors. Ask God to break through ungodly thinking and replace it with the Truth who can set them free.

_____

_____

_____

_____

_____

NOVEMBER 2

Personal Prayer

Praise the sovereign God who opens doors for the gospel of Christ (2 Cor. 2:12). Thank God for leading you "in triumphal procession in Christ" and using you to spread "the fragrance of the knowledge of him" (2:14). Confess any lack of desire to be part of this procession. Commit to joining this great procession, and ask God to use you to bring "the knowledge of him" to your areas of influence.

For Your Family and Friends

Pray for each member of your household to be filled with God's missionary Spirit. Ask him to show your household how to be most effectively involved in mission work.

For the Church

Pray that God's missionaries "not peddle the word of God for a profit" but rather "speak before God with sincerity, like men sent from God" (2:17). Ask God to honor such selflessness.

For the Kingdom

Pray for the freedom to proclaim God's Word fully and openly in all countries. Ask for protection and great fruitfulness for missionaries who have left homelands to bring God's promise to the world.

For the Unsaved

Pray for those for whom "the aroma of Christ" in the "triumphal procession" is "the smell of death," asking God to work his grace into their hearts to change it to "the fragrance of life" (2:14-17).

_____

_____

_____

_____

_____

NOVEMBER 3

Personal Prayer

Praise "the God and Father of our Lord Jesus Christ, the Father of compassion and the God of all comfort" (2 Cor. 1:3). Thank God for coming to you with his compassion and comfort in your times of need. Confess insensitivity toward others who need you to be a channel of God's compassion and comfort. Commit to an openhearted lifestyle. Ask God to love someone through you this week.

For Your Friends and Family

Pray that the love among those close to you be that which comes from God. We often tend to be more compassionate to others than to those with whom we live on a daily basis, so ask especially for compassion toward those closest to you.

For the Church

Pray for the caregiving and fellowship ministries of your church. Ask God to provide visionary deacons to lead you and your local congregation in showing the love of Christ.

For the Kingdom

Pray for Christian relief agencies around the world. Ask God to give his supernatural strength to workers in the midst of intense need.

For the Unsaved

Pray for the unsaved to be warmed and opened by the compassion and comfort brought by God's people. Ask that they be moved to accept God's central compassion and comfort in the person of Christ Jesus.

_____

_____

_____

_____

_____

NOVEMBER 4

Personal Prayer

Praise God, who "is able to make all grace abound to you, so that in all things at all times, having all that you need, you will abound in every good work" (2 Cor. 9:8). Thank God for his abundant grace to you. Confess times of hoarding God's resources, as if his loving supply for you were not continuous. Commit to being "generous on every occasion," asking that such "generosity will result in thanksgiving to God" (9:11).

For Your Family and Friends

Pray for a generous spirit to be prominent and pervasive. Ask God to bring the joy of giving to even very young children.

For the Church

Praise God for believers who have "rich generosity," at times giving even beyond their normal ability in self-sacrificing love. Thank him especially for those who give themselves first to the Lord and then to each other, and ask that such generosity be multiplied in many others (2 Cor. 8:1-5).

For the Kingdom

Pray for the great array of Christian ministries seeking to meet needs around the world. Ask God to richly supply the resources needed.

For the Unsaved

Pray that Christians' generous "obedience that accompanies [their] confession of the gospel of Christ," will result in people praising God (2 Cor. 9:13). Ask God to draw the unsaved to himself through this joyful generosity.

NOVEMBER 5

Personal Prayer

Praise God for his Word that is so available for meaningful worship. Give thanks for the power to minister in God's name (Lk. 9:1-3). Confess those times when you neglect God's Word or fail to spend daily time with him (Lk. 18:1). Commit yourself to teaching, fellowship, and prayer (Acts 2:42). Ask God to bless you and to "enlarge [your] territory" with his power, presence, and protection (1 Chron. 4:10).

For Your Family and Friends

Ask God to use his Word in your life to teach, rebuke, correct, and train others in your family (2 Tim. 3:16).

For the Church

Pray that God will increase your faith through corporate worship. Ask that your pastor not compromise God's Word, even though methods of communicating that Word may change.

For the Kingdom

Ask God to enlarge the ministry and influence of Bible societies which make his Word available in lands around the world.

For the Unsaved

Pray that your knowledge of the Word will be used in love as you befriend an unbeliever.

Prayer Pointer

"Prayer is striking the winning blow; service is gathering up the results. You can do more than pray after you have prayed, but you cannot do more than pray until you have prayed." —S. D. GORDON

_____

_____

_____

_____

NOVEMBER 6

Personal Prayer
Praise God that he is coming with the clouds and every eye shall see him (Rev. 1:7). Give thanks that you have a personal relationship with God and will be with him for all eternity (1 Cor. 15:51-52). Confess your clinging to a sinful deed or habit that needs to be overcome. Commit yourself to being on guard and standing firm in your faith (Eph. 6:13-18). Ask God to hold that vision of glory before you, restraining you from strong attachment to earthly possessions.

For Your Family and Friends
Pray that those you love will recognize God's power and glory in his coming again, but also in their lives each day.

For the Church
Ask that the leaders of your church will be faithful examples of God's power, never being ashamed to testify of our Lord (2 Tim. 1:7-12).

For the Kingdom
Pray for every Christian to know and believe that godliness with contentment is great gain (1 Tim. 6:6).

For the Unsaved
Ask that you never be ashamed of the gospel of Jesus Christ for it is the power of God for salvation (Rom. 1:16). Share that salvation today with a non-Christian.

Prayer Pointer
"If I commit myself for the day to the Lord Jesus, then I may rest assured that it is his eternal, almighty power which has taken me under its protection and which will accomplish everything for me." —ANDREW MURRAY

NOVEMBER 7

Personal Prayer
Praise God that he is the Chief Shepherd, preparing for you the crown of glory that will not fade (1 Pet. 5:4). Thank him for leading you like a shepherd to well-watered gardens. Confess those times you stray like a lost sheep and forget God's commands (Ps. 119:176). Commit your life to doing what is pleasing to God (Heb. 13:20-21). Ask him to help you recognize false prophets who come to you in sheep's clothing, but inwardly are ferocious wolves (Mt. 7:15).

For Your Family and Friends
Many have family members who are like sheep without a shepherd (Mt. 9:36). Pray that God will use you as a shepherd in some way today.

For the Church
Pray that your church will reach out in love and not judgment to members who have strayed. Ask that they again may find the security of the good shepherd (John 10).

For the Kingdom
Jim Elliott wrote: "He is no fool who gives what he cannot keep to gain what he cannot lose." Pray that you will be a sharing and giving person in God's kingdom.

For the Unsaved
Pray that by "giving something that you cannot keep" to one in need today, another may receive the gift of salvation.

Personal Prayer

Praise God for his command to serve him faithfully with all your heart, considering what great things he has done for you (1 Sam. 12:24). Thank God for the greatest of all gifts, salvation in Jesus Christ (Jn. 3:16). Confess your lack of faith as you attempt to flee from God in the midst of trying circumstances (1 Kings 19). Commit yourself to growing in the knowledge and grace of God, giving him the glory (2 Pet. 3:18). Ask God to show you daily how your faith is a Fantastic Adventure In Trusting Him.

For Your Family and Friends

Pray for God to increase your faith as well as the faith of all those close to you, reflecting how God takes care of the grass and flowers, and even more so of you (Mt. 6:26-30).

For the Church

Pray that every teacher in your church will be a living example of great faith because of something God has done or is doing in his or her life right now (Heb. 11:1).

For the Kingdom

Pray that joy and gladness may be found throughout God's kingdom, with thanksgiving and songs of gladness for God's faithfulness to all generations (Isa. 51:11).

For the Unsaved

Pray that the joy and gladness of an active faith in Christians throughout the world will speak to the hearts of the unsaved, so their desire will be to serve the Lord (Jas. 2:14, 17).

NOVEMBER 9

Personal Prayer

Praise God that he speaks in ways that even the lonely, anguished, and defeated can understand (2 Cor. 1:3-4). Give thanks that all things are possible in God (Mt. 19:26). Confess the many times you are tempted to work things out yourself, or are enmeshed in self-pity (Rom. 8:28). Commit to God all who are defeated and lonely. Ask God to help you remember that all you do is to be done in the name of Jesus, giving thanks and glory to him (Col. 3:17).

For Your Family and Friends

Trust God to instill in you the desire to share your physical and spiritual possessions with family members or friends in need (1 Jn. 3:17; Heb. 13:15-16).

For the Church

Pray that God will give your church a heart for reaching the nations of the world for Christ, through encouragement of missionaries, through giving, and through prayers.

For the Kingdom

Pray specifically for the distribution of Bibles throughout the world and for the financial means to continue this important work.

For the Unsaved

Ask God to use these Bibles as a means of salvation for many who receive them as they are given in the name of Jesus with much prayer.

NOVEMBER 10

Personal Prayer

Praise God for his teaching to be of good cheer even in a world of tribulation (Jn. 16:33). Thank God for being your shelter in times of trouble (Ps. 91:1-2). Confess personal burdens that you haven't committed to him and which rob you of that "good cheer" (2 Cor. 5:4). Commit yourself to trusting Christ in every situation (1 Cor. 10:13). Ask God to reveal himself in a special way to his children who feel distant from him today.

For Your Family and Friends

Intercede for any of your family members or friends who are suffering intensely today. Ask God not to withhold his mercy. Pray that his love and truth will protect them (Ps. 40:11).

For the Church

Pray that God will use you and other compassionate people in your church to help those with special needs today.

For the Kingdom

There are so many sheep in God's kingdom. Pray for God to gather them in by using his people everywhere to feed, care for, and love them (Jn. 21:15-17).

For the Unsaved

Ask God to give you sensitivity to any unsaved person who asks you about our troubled world. Pray for eyes to see that as an opportunity to speak of the hope you have in Jesus (1 Tim. 6:17-19).

Prayer Pointer

"Praying for people will bring you to love them. Loving them will lead you to serve them. Serving them will be the open door through which God can move in to save, heal, and make whole." —MAXIE DUNNAM

NOVEMBER 11

Personal Prayer

Praise God whose kingdom is not a matter of eating and drinking but of righteousness, peace, and joy in the Holy Spirit (Rom. 14:17). Thank God for his kindness and love in Jesus, who saved you by the shedding of his own blood (Titus 3:4-7). Confess those times of subtle boasting of how much you do for the Lord and his church (2 Cor. 11:21-30). Commit yourself to quietly helping another person through prayer, encouragement, or deed without self-recognition. Ask God to keep you from pride (Rom. 11:20).

For Your Family and Friends

Pray for your family and friends to spend quality time together, building firm foundations in their faith (1 Cor. 3:8-17).

For the Church

Ask that your church will spend time encouraging and equipping members, warning those who are idle, helping the weak—being the best possible stewards of time as well as money (1 Thess. 5:11-21).

For the Kingdom

Pray that impoverished Christians all over the world will continue to teach the "financially fit" that happiness and eternal joy are found in Jesus, not in "things."

For the Unsaved

Pray that God will give you an opportunity (and that you will use it) to share with one who is "rich" in this world but "poor" in spirit (Mt. 5:3).

_____

_____

_____

_____

_____

Personal Prayer

Praise your great, mighty, and awesome covenant-keeping God (Neh. 9:32). Thank God for strengthening those whose hearts are fully committed to him (2 Chron. 16:9). Confess those times when you depend on your own strength rather than God's (Eccl. 5:7). Commit yourself to spending time daily reflecting on God's awe, his faithfulness, and might (Ps. 89:6-8). Ask God's forgiveness for neglecting him when hardships arise.

For Your Family and Friends

Pray that God will reassure your family that he does care for them and will restore their fortunes even as the great day of the Lord draws near (Zeph. 2:3, 7).

For the Church

Pray that your congregation will reflect on the Lord's righteousness and justice in worship this week (Zeph. 3:5).

For the Kingdom

Pray that God's kingdom will grow as oppressed people recognize God's awesome majesty and come to him in faith.

For the Unsaved

Pray for God to use you today to lead an oppressed unbeliever to recognize God's awesome majesty.

Prayer Pointer

"Worship is intended to introduce God's kingdom power throughout the church and extend that power through the church." —JACK HAYFORD

NOVEMBER 13

Personal Prayer

Praise God that your sighing is not hidden from him (Ps. 38:9). Give thanks that you can cast all your care on him because he cares for you (1 Pet. 5:7). Confess to God the many times you worry, are fearful, or trust in something other than God (Ps. 37:5-6). Commit yourself to daily food from God's Word and time with him in prayer. Ask God for victorious faith that overcomes the world (1 Jn. 5:4).

For Your Family and Friends

Ask that your family will be reminded of God's goodness and faithfulness through your example of giving him all the glory in every situation.

For the Church

Pray that your church will be living proof of the fact that God fulfills the desires of those who fear him (Ps. 145:19).

For the Kingdom

Pray that you will be a consistent example of God's love today and always—and thereby help to advance God's kingdom on earth.

For the Unsaved

In whatever difficult circumstances you find yourself, pray for God to use you as a springboard for the salvation of an unbeliever.

_____

_____

_____

_____

_____

NOVEMBER 14

Personal Prayer

Praise God that you are his temple (1 Cor. 3:16). Thank God for the work he's given you to build up Christ's body, the church (Eph. 4:16). Confess those times you do not honor God with your body, as he has purchased you with the price of his blood (1 Cor. 6:19-20). Commit yourself to Jesus' cleansing of your total being (Jn. 13:8-10). Ask God to reveal to you daily the mystery of his glorious riches (Col. 1:26-27).

For Your Family and Friends

Pray that your family and friends will not dwell on outward beauty but on the unfading beauty of the inner self, a gentle and quiet spirit (1 Pet. 3:3-4).

For the Church

Pray that your church's outreach ministry to the needy in your community will be a beautiful example of Christian servanthood.

For the Kingdom

Pray for many more full-time kingdom workers all over the world and for Christians to respond to God's call saying, "Here am I, send (use) me" (Isa. 6:8).

For the Unsaved

Ask that your love, which comes from a pure heart, good conscience, and sincere faith, will be instrumental in leading unsaved friends to Christ (1 Tim. 1:5).

Prayer Pointer

"Prayer enlarges the heart until it is capable of containing God's gift of himself. Ask and seek, and your heart will grow big enough to receive him and keep him as your own." —MOTHER TERESA

Personal Prayer

Praise God for choosing the foolish things of the world to shame the wise and the weak things to shame the strong (1 Cor. 1:27). Thank God that your salvation does not depend on your wisdom but on his grace alone (Eph. 2:8-9). Confess your self-sufficiency (Lk. 16:11-13). Commit yourself to doing what the Lord requires of you to act justly, love mercy, and walk humbly with your God (Mic. 6:8). Ask God to show you clearly the depth of the riches of wisdom and knowledge of God (Rom. 11:33).

For Your Family and Friends

Pray for family members who live outside the family of God. Ask that they will come to know the wisdom of God found only in Christ Jesus.

For the Church

Pray that your church leaders will show God's wisdom by their godly lives and deeds done in the humility that comes from wisdom (Jas. 3:13).

For the Kingdom

Pray for godly wisdom to be given in great abundance to leaders of worldwide mission agencies. Pray that they will be kept from making wrong choices as they seek to advance God's kingdom throughout the earth.

For the Unsaved

Ask that God will clearly show you the place he would have you serve so that you might be an effective witness to the unsaved (Eph. 5:1).

_____

_____

_____

_____

_____

NOVEMBER 16

Personal Prayer
Praise Jesus, who is the gate of salvation (Jn. 10:7-10). Thank him for bringing you through that gate and for the security you find inside. Confess those times when you seek security in something other than Jesus. Commit yourself to being a doorkeeper in the house of God rather than dwelling in the tents of wickedness (Ps. 84:10). Ask God to use you to attract those outside of Christ to enter into a saving relationship with him.

For Your Family and Friends
Pray that those close to you will have thankful hearts in every situation.

For the Church
Pray that your church will march triumphantly against the hosts of Satan, with the assurance that the gates of hell cannot prevail against God's church (Mt. 16:18).

For the Kingdom
Pray for the protection of God's people throughout the world. Ask that they will strongly resist Satan's attacks (Jas. 4:7).

For the Unsaved
Pray that you will open your doors of love to those outside of Christ, that some may yet gain entrance to the door of heaven.

Prayer Pointer
"Do not be anxious about anything, but in everything, by prayer and petition, with thanksgiving, present your requests to God. And the peace of God, which transcends all understanding, will guard your hearts and your minds in Christ Jesus." —PHILIPPIANS 4:6-7

NOVEMBER 17

Personal Prayer

Praise God for his glorious grace freely given in his Son, Jesus Christ (Eph. 1:6). Thank him for an outpouring of the Spirit of the Lord (2 Cor. 3:17). Confess those times when the exercise of your freedom has become a stumbling block to the weak (1 Cor. 8:9). Commit yourself to walking in the freedom of God's Word (Ps. 119:45). Ask God to make you a slave of righteousness (Rom. 6:18).

For Your Family and Friends

Pray that the Lord will set your family and friends free from painful memories.

For the Church

Pray for the caregivers of your church to be especially helpful to believers who are in unhappy marriages with unbelievers (1 Cor. 7:14).

For the Kingdom

Praise God that believers are all baptized by the Spirit into one body—whether Jew or Greek, slave or free—and are all given the same Spirit (1 Cor. 12:13).

For the Unsaved

Pray for people you know who are still slaves to sin. Ask God to show them through you that he has not deserted them but is waiting patiently for salvation to come to their house (Acts 16:29-32).

NOVEMBER 18

Personal Prayer

Praise God for the good gifts he gives to those who ask him (Mt. 7:11). Give thanks, even in the midst of pain all around, that God's gifts are good. Confess your lack of quality time spent with God in prayer (Rom. 8:26). Commit yourself to modeling Jesus' example of praying in solitary places (Mk. 1:35). Ask God to give you a real devotion to prayer—being watchful and thankful, making the most of every opportunity (Col. 4:2-5).

For Your Family and Friends

Pray for family members and friends who are facing the imminent death of a loved one. Ask that they will sense the real comfort that prayer offers in such times.

For the Church

Pray that your church members will generously give of their time and money so that pleas for more will not be necessary (2 Cor. 9:6-7).

For the Kingdom

Pray that God will instill in Christians around the world the desire to pray faithfully and fervently (Prov. 15:8, 29).

For the Unsaved

Ask God to use emergency or crisis situations in the lives of unsaved people to bring them to the foot of the cross. Pray for eyes to see how you can help in such situations.

Prayer Pointer

"One of the most common weaknesses of our prayer lives is the vagueness of our focus. . . . Petition saves us from that. It forces us to be specific, to be precise, to clarify our wants and desires." —MAXIE DUNNAM

_____

_____

_____

_____

NOVEMBER 19

Personal Prayer

Praise God, the one who is your "refuge" and your "fortress" (Ps. 91:2). Thank him for taking care of you in every storm of life. Confess times when you've sought refuge in some thing or someone other than God. Commit yourself to placing all your trust in this powerful and loving God. Ask God to protect and defend you against Satan's schemes.

For Your Family and Friends

Ask God to make your home a spiritual refuge from the temptations of this world. Pray that your children will find strength, peace, and security there. Pray for harmony among the members of your family.

For the Church

Pray for the worship of your congregation. Intercede for all who lead and for all who participate. Ask God to keep your church's worship focused solely on him.

For the Kingdom

Ask God to break down human barriers and fortresses designed to shut out the gospel throughout the world. Pray for believers who live and worship under the oppression of godless governments. Pray that God will be their refuge.

For the Unsaved

Ask God to open your eyes to the needs of unbelieving people around you. Pray for opportunities to befriend them and to share your faith.

NOVEMBER 20

Personal Prayer
Praise God, the one who is your dwelling place (Ps. 90:1). Thank him for giving you a wonderful inheritance in Jesus Christ, "an inheritance that can never perish, spoil, or fade" (1 Pet. 1:4). Confess moments during the past day or week when you've looked for other "dwelling places." Commit yourself to living under the authority and love of your heavenly Father. Ask God to show you today why his "dwelling place" is the best.

For Your Family and Friends
If you come from a line of believers, give thanks to God for being the dwelling place of generations past. Pray for his grace to be shown to generations yet to come.

For the Church
Intercede for the families of your pastor(s), elders, and deacons. Ask that God will be their dwelling place, too. Pray that these church leaders will find great joy both at home and in their work in your congregation.

For the Kingdom
Pray that God will gather together all those throughout the world who are searching for him as their dwelling place, and will bring them into the light of his marvelous, redeeming grace. Ask God to use you in that great gathering worldwide.

For the Unsaved
Pray that you will be enabled to show to an unbeliever by your word and deed why it is that you trust God as your dwelling place.

NOVEMBER 21

Personal Prayer

Praise God, the one who is your "light" and your "salvation" (Ps. 27:1). Thank him for shining his saving light in your darkness. Confess times when you've preferred to live in the darkness of sinful actions and habits rather than in the light of Jesus. Commit yourself anew to living in his light. Ask God to surround you every day this week with his light and salvation.

For Your Family and Friends

Pray for opportunities to spread God's light in the lives of any family member or friend who does not know Jesus as Savior and Lord. Ask God to touch their lives with the gospel.

For the Church

Intercede for the outreach ministries of your church and denomination. Pray that their financial needs will be met. Ask that they will clearly show forth the light of the good news through their ministries.

For the Kingdom

Pray for Christian ministries which bring healing light into some of our society's darkest corners. Pray for those who work with the homeless, with substance abusers, with the poor, with persons in mental institutions, and others. Ask that the love of Jesus will soothe every hurting heart.

For the Unsaved

Pray by name for someone you know who has not yet committed his or her life to Christ. Ask God to reveal how you can be a spiritual help to that person.

NOVEMBER 22

Personal Prayer

Praise God for all his mighty works (Ps. 46:8-10), for his power, his majesty, his magnificent splendor over all the earth. Thank God for this psalm's very clear and uplifting picture of God's grandeur. Confess that you sometimes live as if God were small, powerless, and expendable. Commit yourself to serving this grand and glorious God with humility and reverence. Ask God to reveal something of his splendor in your life this week.

For Your Family and Friends

Pray that believers among your family and friends will have this same view of God. Pray that their lives will reflect his majesty.

For the Church

Intercede for the educational ministry of your church. Pray for those who teach and for those who are learners. Ask God to raise up dedicated and gifted teachers in your congregation. Thank him for quality curriculum materials.

For the Kingdom

Pray for evangelical seminaries and Bible schools in the U.S. and Canada which are training pastors, evangelists, and teachers for the work of ministry. Ask God to meet their financial needs. Pray for more young Christians to study and train for pastoral ministry.

For the Unsaved

Pray that "the works of the Lord" might be so evident as to draw unbelievers to saving faith in Jesus Christ. Ask for spiritual blinders to be removed.

NOVEMBER 23

Personal Prayer
Praise God, the one who is never far away from his children. Thank him for being close to you when you feel brokenhearted or crushed in spirit (Ps. 34:18). Confess your own unwillingness to have a God so near. Commit yourself to drawing near to God in daily prayer and fellowship (Jas. 4:8). Ask him to bless you by his presence throughout your life.

For Your Family and Friends
Pray that believing family members and friends also will draw near to God. Uphold them in their personal devotional lives.

For the Church
Intercede for the great worldwide mission effort of the church. Ask God to raise up more workers to enter the harvest around the world. Pray specifically for missionaries whom you know or support financially.

For the Kingdom
Thank God for the work of chaplains who minister in God's name in prisons, hospitals, schools, and the armed forces throughout North America. Ask God to bless their work and witness.

For the Unsaved
Ask God to enable an unsaved friend you know to reach out to him in faith. Thank God for the promise that those who seek him with a believing heart will find him (Acts 17:27).

Prayer Pointer
"God does nothing on earth save in answer to believing prayer." —JOHN WESLEY

NOVEMBER 24

Personal Prayer
Praise God, the one who strengthens and helps you (Isa. 41:10). Give thanks for God's promise to be with you when you "pass through the rivers" or "walk through the fire" (Isa. 43:2). Confess those times when you've doubted God's loving presence and care. Commit yourself to trusting in God to protect and defend you. Ask him to increase your faith.

For Your Family and Friends
Pray for the marriages of your family and friends. Intercede especially for any who are pursuing divorce. Pray that those marriages will be healed.

For the Church
Ask God to make your congregation a warm and loving church to all. Pray for a spirit of concern and humility as you reach out to the needs of other members and beyond.

For the Kingdom
Pray for the political leaders of your country. Ask that they will be men and women of integrity and honor. Pray that their primary allegiance will be to God alone.

For the Unsaved
Ask God to encourage those who are seeking. Pray that they soon will come to God in repentance and faith.

Prayer Pointer
"We are now in the beginning stages of the greatest movement of prayer in living memory." —C. Peter Wagner

Personal Prayer

Praise God, the one who keeps you in perfect peace (Isa. 26:3). Give thanks for peace which is far beyond your understanding (Phil. 4:7). Confess that you sometimes look to the world to bring you peace rather than to God. Commit yourself to living in peace with others (1 Thess. 5:13). Ask God to give you a peaceable spirit.

For Your Family and Friends

Pray for the peace of God to spread throughout your home. Ask him to bring about peaceful resolution to any ongoing strife in your family.

For the Church

Ask that God's peace will reassure those who tithe regularly and give sacrificially in your church. Pray that they will not suffer due to their commitment to financial stewardship.

For the Kingdom

Pray for peace in various denominations of Christ's church where Satan is causing division. Pray for your own denomination. Ask for repentance and renewed commitment to follow Jesus.

For the Unsaved

Jesus promises to give his peace to those who believe in faith (Jn. 14:27). Pray for one unsaved person you know to receive Jesus' precious peace.

_____

_____

_____

_____

_____

NOVEMBER 26

Personal Prayer
Give praise to God who is the ruler of all things (1 Chron. 29:12). Thank him for his mighty and powerful acts. Confess times when you've questioned God's power by trusting in your own strength. Commit yourself to exalting God in everything you do this week. Ask him to give you strength to live for him.

For Your Family and Friends
Uphold members of your family who are in special need, who have suffered loss of some kind, or who need encouragement.

For the Church
Pray for the children who worship regularly in your congregation. Ask that they will sense the important role they play in the life of your church.

For the Kingdom
Give thanks to God for the spread of the gospel throughout the world. Pray that worshiping churches will be pleasing to him.

For the Unsaved
Pray by name for an unsaved friend, relative, or coworker. Ask God to open this person's spiritual eyes to the wonder of new life in Christ.

Prayer Pointer
"Prayer is obedience! God's command and promise is our motive for prayer."
—JOHN CALVIN

NOVEMBER 27

Personal Prayer

Praise the infinite God who has no beginning and no end. Thank God that with him all things are possible (Lk. 1:37). Confess any lack of faith concerning God's ways and works. Commit yourself anew to living obediently before God. Ask him to keep your eyes focused on Jesus.

For Your Family and Friends

Pray today for any who are newly married among your family or friends. Ask that their love will grow strong and that they will base their relationship on the solid rock of Christ.

For the Church

Ask God to give joy to the elders and deacons of your church. Pray that the many meetings they attend and the extra responsibility they carry will not be burdensome to them.

For the Kingdom

Pray for justice and righteousness to come to the nations of this world which seek to block the work of the Lord (Ps. 2:1-2). Ask that their rulers will bow to Jesus and begin to serve him (2:10-11; Isa. 60:3).

For the Unsaved

Pray for the work of godly evangelists around the world who fearlessly preach the gospel to lost people. Ask that their labors be rewarded.

_____

_____

_____

_____

_____

NOVEMBER 28

Personal Prayer
Praise God as the one whose arm is "not too short to save, nor his ear too dull to hear" (Isa. 59:1). Thank God for the promise to hear you when you come to him in prayer. Confess any sin which may result in his not hearing your prayers (59:2). If you are struggling in this area, commit yourself to regular, daily times of prayer and fellowship with God. Ask him to draw close to you as you fellowship with him.

For Your Family and Friends
Pray for any in your circle of Christian friends whose prayer life has grown thin. Ask that they will be reminded that God does hear and answer prayer.

For the Church
Ask God's blessing on the evangelism committee members of your congregation. Pray that they will be effective in helping your church to reach out more.

For the Kingdom
Pray for the work of prayer ministries throughout North America. Pray that they will receive the financial support needed to keep the work of prayer before the church.

For the Unsaved
God has long arms when it comes to salvation. No one is beyond his reach. Thank him for that truth and pray for one unsaved person you know.

Prayer Pointer
"Ministry without prayer becomes work in the power of the flesh. Prayer without ministry is complacent Christianity." —ANONYMOUS

_____

_____

_____

_____

_____

NOVEMBER 29

Personal Prayer

Praise the God who loves even the little children (Lk. 18:16). Give thanks for God's promise in Prov. 22:6 to help parents train their children in the right way. Confess any lack of love or any impatience you have experienced toward your children or others. Commit yourself to a renewed appreciation for the place children have in God's sight. Ask for wisdom to train your children in his ways.

For Your Family and Friends

Pray for the training of covenant children in your congregation. Ask God to bless their nurture at home and in the church. Pray also for their parents.

For the Church

Pray for God's blessing on the children's educational programs in your congregation. Pray for the teachers in the church school and leaders of children's clubs.

For the Kingdom

Ask God to "turn the hearts of the fathers to their children, and the hearts of the children to their fathers" (Mal. 4:6) throughout his kingdom.

For the Unsaved

Pray that people who do not yet trust in Jesus will have a sincere desire to become children of the living God.

Personal Prayer

Praise the God who knows your sinful ways, but is still there to heal, guide, and comfort you (Isa. 57:18). Give thanks for God's constant faithfulness. Confess any sinful deeds or thoughts that have remained unconfessed. Commit yourself to seeking the guidance of the Holy Spirit every day. Ask him to walk close beside you today.

For Your Family and Friends

Pray for any family member or friend who is in need of God's comfort in a special way. Ask for opportunities to minister his healing grace to them.

For the Church

Pray for God's blessing in worldwide missions. Intercede for missionary families known to you. Pray that they will experience the joy of the harvest. Ask that Satan's schemes may be thwarted.

For the Kingdom

Ask God to expand his kingdom throughout the world as people are brought to him one by one. Pray for a clear sense of God's purpose for you in his kingdom.

For the Unsaved

Pray for an opportunity in the next day to share your faith with someone who does not know Jesus. Ask God to give you courage and boldness in your witness.

Prayer Pointer

"The church's greatest deficiency today is in power—not in programs, strategies, materials, or ideas. And power for ministry can be released only through prayer." —ANONYMOUS

_____

_____

_____

_____

DECEMBER 1

Personal Prayer

Praise God, who is a refuge for the poor and needy (Isa.25:4). Thank him for caring about those who are in desperate circumstances. Confess times when you have not shown compassion to the needy. Commit yourself to serving others in new and stretching ways. Ask God to provide those opportunities for you.

For Your Family and Friends

Thank God for being a shelter from the storm for your family (25:4). Pray that teens will seek that shelter rather than taking refuge in the world.

For the Church

Ask God to anoint the fellowship in your congregation with the Holy Spirit. Pray that any friction between members will be addressed and healed. Pray that newcomers will find a refuge in your congregation.

For the Kingdom

Intercede for ministries which bring Christ's compassion to the poor and needy throughout the world. Ask that their needs will be met as they bring hope to thousands.

For the Unsaved

Pray that one unsaved person you know will see and desire the shelter which Jesus offers. Ask that God will use you to guide that person into eternal safety.

_____

_____

_____

_____

_____

DECEMBER 2

Personal Prayer

Praise God, who is "holy, holy, holy" (Isa. 6:3). Give thanks for God's glory, which is seen throughout the whole earth. Confess any sin which keeps you from experiencing the holiness and glory of God. Commit your life anew today to seeking God's holiness and glory. Ask him to reveal himself to you as you seek his glory in your life.

For Your Family and Friends

Pray that your family will have a renewed sense of God's glory in all areas of your family life—our work, relationships, conversation, leisure time, and so on.

For the Church

Ask God to bless your congregation financially. Pray that members will give like the Macedonians gave to the ministry of the apostle Paul—yond their ability (2 Cor.8:3), but first to the Lord.

For the Kingdom

Pray for all gospel preachers throughout God's kingdom. Ask him to prosper their work as they labor in the harvest field. Pray that the Lord of the harvest will add his blessing to the proclamation of the good news.

For the Unsaved

Pray for any unsaved single parents you may know. Ask God to show you how you can help them in their child rearing. Pray for opportunities to share the gospel of Jesus Christ.

Prayer Pointer

"The ministry of intercession is very demanding. To be serious about intercession is to be ready to give ourselves for the sake of others." —MAXIE DUNNAM

DECEMBER 3

Personal Prayer

Praise God for his overruling love (2 Cor. 5:14). Give thanks that God's love compels you to do things which please him. Confess those times when you have chosen not to listen to God's words and direction. Commit yourself to worshiping God, for his power over those things that destroy love. Ask God to reveal his overruling love in your daily life.

For Your Family and Friends

Pray that your family and friends will make decisions today which reflect the love of God in their lives.

For the Church

Pray that through the worship of God your church family will be moved to more fully appreciate and experience God's power.

For the Kingdom

Pray that Satan's opposition will be bound so that men and women of all nations will see God's powerful love.

For the Unsaved

Ask that the love of God will compel you to take the risks necessary to share the gospel with someone who has not yet heard.

_____

_____

_____

_____

_____

DECEMBER 4

Personal Prayer
Praise God for his everlasting power and goodness. Thank him for sharing his power with you in Christ. Confess those times when you tend to trust in your own power and strength. Commit yourself to focusing on God's power at work within you. Ask God to fill you with a renewed awareness of his presence within you.

For Your Family and Friends
Pray that your family and friends who know Jesus will seek his power for daily living.

For the Church
Pray that your church leaders will recognize that God's power is greater than that of Satan and act accordingly, knowing they have nothing to fear.

For the Kingdom
Pray that the contrast between good and evil will become very distinct so that God's everlasting power will be made known to all.

For the Unsaved
Ask God to enable you to show unconditional love to people who do not yet know Christ and his everlasting power.

Prayer Pointer
"No day is well spent without communication with God." —ANONYMOUS

DECEMBER 5

Personal Prayer

Praise God for the creativity and imagination with which he has gifted you. Thank him for giving you the desire to live for Christ. Confess those times when you have allowed your thoughts and imagination to stray into sin. Commit yourself to setting your mind on all the fullness of God. Ask God to expand your thoughts of him as you consider the width and depth and breadth of his glory.

For Your Family and Friends

Pray that your family and friends take time to rest from their busy schedules in order to reflect on God's creativity in nature.

For the Church

Pray your church's outreach efforts will also reflect the imagination and creativity of your church members. Ask that the outreach will be effective in reaching your community.

For the Kingdom

Thank God for the beauty of his creation throughout the world. Ask that natural beauty will be protected from the harm which sin inflicts on the creation. Pray that people around the world will see and say, "What an awesome God!"

For the Unsaved

Pray that unsaved people will gain a sense of God's creative power as they consider the complexity of the human body. Ask that such thoughts will lead them to seek the Savior.

DECEMBER 6

Personal Prayer

Praise God as the one who speaks "in your language." Give thanks for God's ongoing communication with you through his Word. Confess the fact that sometimes God speaks, but you disobediently choose not to listen. Commit yourself to the active obedience of young Samuel, who said, "Speak, for your servant is listening" (1 Sam. 3:10). Ask God to give you ears to hear his message.

For Your Family and Friends

Pray that those close to you will also have the desire to listen to God and to obey his Word.

For the Church

Pray that the teachers working in your Christian education program will speak on behalf of God as they teach and apply his Word among students of all ages.

For the Kingdom

Pray for the ministry of gospel broadcasting agencies who use the airwaves to send God's message in many languages throughout the earth.

For the Unsaved

Pray that the contrast between good and evil will be so distinct that even those with the weakest spiritual hearing will hear the good news of Jesus Christ.

Prayer Pointer

"An hour of prayer at the beginning of the [council] meeting actually shortens the overall meeting time by bringing a greater spirit of unity, by emphasizing spiritual priorities, and by opening people's hearts to the Spirit's guidance."
—ANONYMOUS

_____

_____

_____

_____

_____

DECEMBER 7

Personal Prayer

Praise God even in your weakness, believing that in Christ, when you are weak, then you are strong (2 Cor. 12:10). Thank God for opportunities to serve him with perseverance and purpose. Confess those times when you chose to believe that spiritual power comes from within you. Commit yourself to appropriate "boasting" in your weaknesses so that Christ's power might be made even more evident in your life (12:9). Ask God to help you "delight" even in the tough times of life.

For Your Family and Friends

Pray for spiritually and physically weak members of your family or friends. Ask that God's Spirit will empower and strengthen them.

For the Church

Ask the Holy Spirit to empower missionaries who preach and teach the gospel in countries and cultures very different from your own (Acts 1:8).

For the Kingdom

Pray that Christians in every part of the globe will be strengthened to do battle with the evil spiritual forces that are at work in our world. Pray for an outpouring of God's power throughout his church worldwide.

For the Unsaved

Pray that the life-giving power of Jesus Christ will be revealed to unsaved people you know. Pray for them by name.

DECEMBER 8

Personal Prayer

Praise God for confiding in those who love him (Ps. 25:14). Give thanks for this developing relationship God has established with you. Confess those times when you have refused to share intimately with God. Commit yourself to seeking his companionship daily. Ask God to create within you a desire for intimacy, total honesty, acceptance, and joy in his presence.

For Your Family and Friends

Pray that God will bring fulfillment to those who are suffering from the pain of unfulfilled dreams.

For the Church

Pray that true intimacy will be demonstrated by the children of God in a way that is appealing and attractive to unbelievers who are observing.

For the Kingdom

Pray that those who have suffered sexual, emotional, and/or physical abuse will be helped to understand and experience intimacy.

For the Unsaved

Ask God to give you the opportunity and courage to befriend a person seeking a meaningful friendship. Ask that Jesus will be the center of your relationship.

Prayer Pointer

"It is not possible to explain the power and effectiveness of the New Testament church without reference to prayer." —ANONYMOUS

_____

_____

_____

_____

_____

DECEMBER 9

Personal Prayer

Praise the God who lays claim to the entire world and all that live in it (Ps. 24:1). Thank him for the food, shelter, and clothing that sustains you and gives comfort to your life. Confess the times when you have failed to acknowledge God's riches in your life. Commit yourself to examining your acts of stewardship. Ask God to give you a heart of liberality, knowing that all you have comes from him (1 Chron. 29:14).

For Your Family and Friends

Ask God to show your family new and creative ways to share the abundance of your lives with families who have much less.

For the Church

Pray that your church will take seriously the stewardship of God's resources. Pray for those who make decisions regarding finances in your church. Ask for wisdom.

For the Kingdom

Ask God's blessing among Christian communities where there is poverty, hunger, and deprivation. Pray for justice where there is economic injustice.

For the Unsaved

Pray that your own giving spirit toward others will speak volumes concerning Christ's generous gift of salvation to all who believe.

DECEMBER 10

Personal Prayer

Praise God for the diversity of his creation. Give thanks for your heritage and unique attributes which add to the abundance of God's diverse creation. Confess those times when you failed to accept and love people unlike yourself. Commit yourself to learning about and thanking God for other cultures. Ask God to stretch your understanding of who he is and what he desires of you.

For Your Family and Friends

Praise God for each family member and friend. They are so different in personality. Thank God for their diversity.

For the Church

As you worship God this Sunday, take a mental tour of the pews near you. Silently pray for the people sitting in those pews. Again thank God for their diversity—and for your church's unity.

For the Kingdom

Pray that cultural diversity will be recognized as a gift of God.

For the Unsaved

Ask God to open doors of opportunity for you to share the gospel with someone from a differing background or culture. Pray that God will prepare you for that divine encounter this week.

Prayer Pointer

"God's power enters our human programs through the door of prayer. Unless the church's ministry is bathed in prayer, it remains merely a human endeavor."
—Anonymous

DECEMBER 11

Personal Prayer

Praise God for his marvelous plan of redemption worked out through history. Thank God for the significant leaders he called to make a difference in the growth of the Christian movement. Confess times when God called you to lead in some way, but you chose rather to follow. Commit yourself to discovering how the use of your gifts can influence others to follow Jesus. Ask God to give you courage and insight as he calls you to go and bear fruit that will last (Jn. 15:16).

For Your Family and Friends

Pray that your family members and friends will recognize and use their gifts for the growth of God's kingdom.

For the Church

Pray that leaders in your church will have the burden and ability to seek and disciple others.

For the Kingdom

Pray that political leaders throughout the world will recognize Jesus Christ as Lord. Ask that repentance and revival will come to nations which have not yet honored him.

For the Unsaved

Pray that gang leaders will see their influence transformed to a positive affect. Pray that their desire for control and acceptance will be satisfied through the power and blood of Jesus Christ. Pray that God will give them a vision for their potential to lead a broken generation.

DECEMBER 12

Personal Prayer
Praise God for caring for you (1 Pet. 5:7). Thank him for being so interested in your welfare that he even knows the number of hairs on your head (Lk. 12:7). Confess those times when you failed to take his care seriously. Commit yourself to imitating God's care by caring selflessly for others. Ask him to fill your heart and mind with a sense of his deep love for you.

For Your Family and Friends
Thank God for those who reach out to you with acts of kindness. Thank him for acts of kindness shown by members of your own family.

For the Church
Pray that your church's evangelistic efforts will be caring efforts. Ask God to show your church how to minister to more than just the spiritual needs of those who don't have a saving relationship with Christ.

For the Kingdom
Pray that communication specialists throughout the world will work together to increase opportunities for thousands of people to learn about Jesus.

For the Unsaved
Ask God to help you show a sincere, caring attitude toward one unsaved person today. Look for opportunities to share the gospel with that person.

Prayer Pointer
"Life's best outlook is a prayerful uplook." —ANONYMOUS

DECEMBER 13

Personal Prayer

Pray Daniel's words of praise: "Praise be to the name of God for ever and ever; wisdom and power are his" (Dan. 2:20). Thank God for guiding you to make wise choices in life. Confess times when you chose to follow the foolishness of this world's wisdom rather than the wisdom of God. Commit yourself to seeking the "Spirit of wisdom and of understanding" (Isa. 11:2). Ask God to give to you the "wisdom that comes from heaven" (Jas. 3:17).

For Your Family and Friends

Pray for students among your family and friends. Ask that they will gain knowledge in their studies, but more, that they will gain the wisdom which comes from trusting in the Lord (Job 28:28).

For the Church

Pray that your church's education program will focus on matters of the heart as well as of the head.

For the Kingdom

Ask God's blessing on Christian scientists as they explore the mysteries of God's wisdom displayed in the natural realm. Ask that God's clear fingerprints will be seen in all their experiments and discoveries.

For the Unsaved

Pray for the ability to keep your testimony simple and genuine as you cross paths with people who are trying to understand the things of God.

DECEMBER 14

Personal Prayer

Praise God for choosing you "before the creation of the world to be holy and blameless in his sight" (Eph. 1:4). Thank him for choosing the poor in the world's eyes to be rich in faith (Jas. 2:5). Confess the times when you have felt apathetic toward God's lordship. Commit yourself to living in his promises as revealed in the Word. Ask God to help you live a holy and blameless life.

For Your Family and Friends

Thank God for ancestors who loved the Lord and passed down the stories of the Christian faith to their children and grandchildren. Pray that you will do the same in your family.

For the Church

Ask God to prosper the work of world missionaries which your church supports. Pray for them and their families by name.

For the Kingdom

Pray for aviation and transportation agencies which support the work of the gospel overseas. Ask for personal safety and the financial resources needed to carry on their ministries.

For the Unsaved

Pray for the advance of the gospel among the baby boomer generation. Ask that they will find the answer to their desire for purposeful living in Jesus Christ.

Prayer Pointer

"It is in private prayer that we most easily get in touch with our spiritual selves."
—ANONYMOUS

_____

_____

_____

_____

_____

DECEMBER 15

Personal Prayer

As you praise God today, focus on his great mercy (Ps. 108:4). Thank him for taking delight in surrounding you with his mercy (Mic. 7:18). Confess that in the busyness of life you sometimes forget his mercy to you. Commit yourself to extending that same kind of loving mercy to others who are in need. Ask God to grant you his peace and fellowship as you live for him this day.

For Your Family and Friends

Thank God for showing his mercy to your family. Pray that any unbelieving family members will turn from sin to the Lord.

For the Church

Pray that your church will also extend God's mercy to the needy and impoverished members of your community. Ask that God will open eyes to see opportunities for service.

For the Kingdom

Ask that the church will increasingly become a haven of hope and healing for some who seek answers only in the psychiatrist's office.

For the Unsaved

Pray that unsaved people you know will discover that God really is full of mercy, and that that is what they ultimately need!

DECEMBER 16

Personal Prayer

Praise God, who is the creator of both rich and poor. Thank him for giving you the ability to produce wealth (Deut. 8:18). Confess any time you have put your trust in your earthly possessions rather than in the spiritual riches of God (8:13-14). Commit yourself to living contentedly with all that God has provided. Ask him to give you a generous heart toward those who have less.

For Your Family and Friends

Pray that God will meet physical and financial needs among your family members and friends. Pray for opportunities to give what you can to meet their need.

For the Church

Pray that God will add his blessing to the stewardship of your congregation. Pray also for the wise distribution of funds to meet various needs.

For the Kingdom

Ask God to open the pocketbooks of church members worldwide. Pray that there will be an outpouring of generosity equal to that of the Macedonian Christians (2 Cor. 8:2) in Paul's day.

For the Unsaved

Pray that unsaved people will view believers as unselfish and giving. Ask that they will be drawn to Christ as they observe selfless acts of service.

Prayer Pointer

"If I could hear Christ praying for me in the next room, I would not fear a million enemies. Yet distance makes no difference. He is praying for me."
—Robert Murray McCheyne

DECEMBER 17

Personal Prayer

Praise the God of truth, whose words are trustworthy (2 Sam. 7:28). Thank Jesus for being the only way, truth, and life (Jn. 14:6). Confess the times you've chosen to believe the lies of Satan rather than the true promises of God. Commit yourself, as a member of Christ's body, to speaking truthfully in all your relationships (Eph. 4:25). Ask God to buckle the belt of truth around your waist.

For Your Family and Friends

The Bible says that God detests lying lips (Prov. 12:22). Ask God to guard the lips of you and your children at home, school, and work.

For the Church

As you gather for worship this week, pray that the one who brings God's message will set "forth the truth plainly" and not "distort the word of God" (2 Cor. 4:2).

For the Kingdom

Pray that truth will be honored by your local government officials—supervisors, mayors, commissioners, judges. Ask that they will be committed wholeheartedly to advancing truth in the public square (Zech. 8:16).

For the Unsaved

The devil is "a liar and the father of lies" (Jn. 8:44). Ask that Satan's empty schemes will be exposed and that unsaved people will believe in Jesus.

DECEMBER 18

Personal Prayer

Praise your God, whose right hand is filled with righteousness (Ps. 48:10). Thank him for being righteous in all his ways and loving toward all he has made (Ps. 145:17). Confess your own sinfulness, especially times in the last day when you have acted in an unrighteous way toward others. Commit yourself to being "filled with the fruit of righteousness that comes through Jesus Christ" (Phil. 1:11). Ask God to keep you in close communion with him throughout this day.

For Your Family and Friends

Ask God to enable believing teens among your family and friends to "say 'No' to ungodliness and worldly passions, and to live self-controlled, upright and godly lives" (Titus 2:12).

For the Church

Pray for the elders of your congregation by name. Ask God that they will be models of right living for your congregation.

For the Kingdom

Pray for all efforts to bring godliness and righteousness to the great institutions of our society. Intercede for Christian leaders in business, education, and government.

For the Unsaved

Ask God to touch the hearts of unbelievers who are living for themselves, that they will come to their senses and stop sinning (1 Cor. 15:34).

_____

_____

_____

_____

_____

DECEMBER 19

Personal Prayer

Praise God who has invited you into his circle of fellowship through Jesus Christ. Thank him for his invitation to love him with your whole being (Mk. 12:33). Confess to God that sometimes you don't love and honor him as you should. Commit yourself to Deut. 10:12: "To fear the LORD your God, to walk in his ways, to love him, and to serve [him] with all your heart and with all your soul." Ask God to enable you fulfill that commitment today.

For Your Family and Friends

Think of the oldest and the youngest members of your family. Ask God to meet the special needs of those two people. Thank God that his love spans many generations.

For the Church

Pray that the evangelistic outreach of your church will be driven simply by a genuine love for people. Ask that any pride or self-will will be confessed.

For the Kingdom

Pray that the knowledge of Christ will spread throughout the whole world, even as a tiny seed grows into a large and vigorous plant (Mk. 4:31). Pray for faithful preachers of the gospel (Mt. 24:14).

For the Unsaved

Ask God to make you more alert to the needs of unsaved people you know. Pray that God will show you practical ways you can minister to them and ultimately show them how to believe.

DECEMBER 20

Personal Prayer

Praise God for the humility which Christ displayed in coming to earth and going to the cross for you (Phil. 2:8). Thank Jesus for modeling true humility as he washed his disciples' feet (Jn. 13:5). Confess the pride which keeps you from wholeheartedly submitting to Jesus' lordship. Commit yourself to drawing near to your Lord at the foot of the cross. Ask him to give you a servant's heart.

For Your Family and Friends

Pray that God will give you opportunities this week to serve those close to you. Ask that all your actions will be fueled by humility and not false pride.

For the Church

Thank God for the teachers in your church's adult education program. Give thanks also for curriculum materials and Christian publishers who provide quality instructional materials.

For the Kingdom

Ask for God's blessing on Christian artists and musicians who bring praise and glory to God through their creative expressions.

For the Unsaved

Ask God to search your heart concerning unsaved persons you know. Pray that any attitude of superiority will be rooted out of your life so that you can humbly and genuinely present the claims of Christ.

Prayer Pointer

"Any church without a well-organized and systematic prayer program is simply operating a religious treadmill." —JOHN BILLHEIMER

DECEMBER 21

Personal Prayer

Praise the God of faith, hope, and love (1 Cor. 13:13). Thank him for the "new birth into a living hope through the resurrection of Jesus Christ" (1 Pet. 1:3). Confess those times when you have given in to discouragement rather than hoping in God. Commit yourself to taking hold of the hope which God freely offers to you (Heb. 6:18). Ask that you will have opportunity to share your hope with another person today.

For Your Family and Friends

Pray for any member of your family who is downcast and despairing. Ask that the God of hope will bring a measure of comfort and peace.

For the Church

Pray for missionaries by name who serve in other countries. Ask God to bless their labors, to spare them from discouragement, and to remind them of many reasons to hope in God.

For the Kingdom

Ask God's anointing of Christians who bring Jesus' comfort and peace to those afflicted with terminal illnesses. Pray for those ministering in Christ's name to people suffering from the effects of AIDS.

For the Unsaved

Ask God to help you live in such a way that your unsaved friends will ask "you to give the reason for the hope that you have" (1 Pet. 3:15). Then be ready with your answer!

DECEMBER 22

Personal Prayer

Praise your God, who alone is holy (Rev. 15:4). Thank him for the glorious promise that one day all nations will come and worship him. Confess sins which keep you from drawing close to God. Commit yourself daily to exalting and worshiping your holy God. Ask God to help you keep his command to "be holy, because I am holy" (Lev. 11:45).

For Your Family and Friends

In all your family relationships, pray that the truth of Heb. 12:14 will be central: "Make every effort to live in peace with all men and to be holy."

For the Church

Pray that the members of your congregation will welcome guests to your church with warmth and hospitality. Ask God to remove apathy and indifference.

For the Kingdom

Pray that believers throughout the world will conform their wills to God in order to "live holy and godly lives" (2 Pet. 3:11).

For the Unsaved

Pray that unsaved people you know will be drawn to Jesus because of the attractiveness of your holy living.

Prayer Pointer

"If family worship is neglected, other attempts at prayer are like sprinkling the foliage of a plant while leaving the roots dry." —ANONYMOUS

DECEMBER 23

Personal Prayer
Praise "the Father of the heavenly lights, who does not change like shifting shadows" (Jas. 1:17). Thank God for remaining the same throughout all eternity (Ps. 102:27). Confess that sometimes you are not as consistent as you would like to be in your walk with God. Commit yourself to remaining true to that which does not change, the eternal God (2 Cor. 4:18). Ask God to glorify himself in your life.

For Your Family and Friends
Pray that in the midst of life's many changes, those closest to you will remain true to God and his Word. Pray for balance and harmony in each life.

For the Church
Pray that the stewardship of resources in your congregation will please God. Ask that members will be willing to give generously of their time and talents as well as their finances. Pray that they will experience joy in giving.

For the Kingdom
Ask God to change the hearts of men and women and children who hear the good news spoken by evangelists around the world. Pray for a great worldwide harvest of souls this year.

For the Unsaved
Pray for God to open your eyes to one person who needs the gospel. Prepare your heart by asking God to give you the words to say and the confidence to say them when God opens the door.

_____

_____

_____

_____

_____

DECEMBER 24

Personal Prayer

Focus on Jn. 15:1-17 for the next few days. Praise your Father, who is the gardener of your soul. Thank Jesus for being the true vine which nourishes and gives life to the branches. Confess moments when you've tried to sever your relationship to Jesus in some way. Commit yourself to welcoming God's pruning in your life despite the pain it might bring. Ask God to make you more fruitful as you live for him.

For Your Family and Friends

Ask God to make the "garden" of your family members a fruitful and abundant place. Pray for his tilling and planting and nurturing of faith among those close to you.

For the Church

Ask the true vine to take root in every family represented in your home church. Pray that the joy of union with Christ will be evident in your worship.

For the Kingdom

Pray that the true vine will flourish throughout the world, as Jesus draws people of every nation to himself in repentance and faith.

For the Unsaved

Ask that your fruit-bearing will be attractive to unsaved people you know. Pray that they will "taste [of that fruit] and see that the LORD is good" (Ps. 34:8).

Prayer Pointer

"God rules the world through the prayers of his people." —ANONYMOUS

DECEMBER 25

Personal Prayer

Praise Jesus, the true vine, for the privilege of being one of his branches. Thank him for the promise of union with himself (Jn. 15:4). Confess the times when you have proudly thought of yourself as the vine rather than as a branch. Commit yourself to remaining in the true vine. Ask God to keep you firmly attached to the vine so that you can bear much fruit.

For Your Family and Friends

Pray for childless friends who desire to have children. Ask God to give them this desire of their heart. Pray that they will have patience to wait on the Lord and to submit to his timing.

For the Church

Pray that the leaders of your congregation will be fruit-bearing branches. Pray that a vital union with Christ will be evident in the lives of elders, deacons, and other church leaders.

For the Kingdom

Ask God to bless the fellowship of local church bodies where members are challenged to "remain in Christ." Pray for unity among such Christians in neighborhoods and communities around the world.

For the Unsaved

Pray that your wholehearted commitment to Christ will be attractive to one unsaved person you know. Ask God to give you an opportunity to share your faith with that person.

DECEMBER 26

Personal Prayer

Praise God as the one who makes it possible for you to bear much fruit (Jn. 15:5). Thank him for the promise of a great spiritual harvest in your life. Confess sins which stunt the development of spiritual fruit in your life. Commit yourself to daily devotional habits which will stimulate the growth of such fruit. Ask God to help you produce the kind of harvest which will give him the glory and praise.

For Your Family and Friends

Pray that the teenagers in your family or among your friends will commit themselves to being fruit-bearing young people. Pray that they will learn that "apart from [Jesus, they] can do nothing" (15:5).

For the Church

Pray for fruitfulness in the evangelistic efforts of your congregation. Ask that an increasing number of members will join in "seeking the lost" in your neighborhood. Pray for the outreach leaders.

For the Kingdom

Ask God to pour out his blessing on his church throughout the world. Pray for fruitfulness among those who remain faithful to God and are firmly united to Jesus, the true vine.

For the Unsaved

Pray by name for any unsaved friends in your work place or neighborhood. Pray that they will have the courage to ask you about your faith. Ask God to prepare you for that conversation.

_____

_____

_____

_____

_____

DECEMBER 27

Personal Prayer

Praise your God, who is the giver of all good gifts (Mt. 7:11). Thank him for his promise to give you "whatever you wish" (Jn. 15:7) if you remain in him. Confess times when you have failed to thank God for his many spiritual and temporal gifts to you. Commit yourself to imitating God's generosity as you give to others and to God. Ask him to help you freely give as you have freely received (Mt. 10:8).

For Your Family and Friends

Pray that parents of small children will give of their time to their children while they are young. Ask that family time will be viewed as a sacred trust and not as a burden.

For the Church

Thank God for the teachers in your church's adult education program. Pray that they will have a sense of God's call to this important work. Ask that they will be firmly united to Christ.

For the Kingdom

Pray for colleges and universities around the world which honor the name of Christ in their education. Ask God to prosper their influence in the lives of thousands of students worldwide.

For the Unsaved

Ask God to use you to lead a person to the most important gift of God, which is eternal life through Jesus Christ (Rom. 6:23).

DECEMBER 28

Personal Prayer
Praise Jesus for the depth of his redeeming love, which sent him to the cross for you (Gal. 2:20). Thank him for dying on your behalf. Confess any lack of love you feel toward a brother or sister. Commit yourself to remaining in Jesus' love by keeping his commandments (Jn. 15:10). Ask God to show his love to you in new ways today.

For Your Family and Friends
Ask for God's love to permeate all of your relationships with other family members and friends. Pray that Jesus' peace will heal any tension or discord in those relationships.

For the Church
Pray that world missionary organizations will be effective in preaching and teaching the love of God in Christ to people who have never heard the gospel before. Ask that the mission personnel will be "rooted and established in love" (Eph. 3:17).

For the Kingdom
Pray that all of God's children throughout his kingdom will exult in the great love which God has lavished on those who believe (1 Jn. 3:1).

For the Unsaved
Ask that the redeeming love of God will come gently to an unsaved person you know. Ask God to reveal a glimpse of his unconditional love through you.

Prayer Pointer
"Nothing lies beyond the reach of prayer except that which lies beyond the will of God." —ANONYMOUS

DECEMBER 29

Personal Prayer

Praise God that the Christian life includes periods of "complete" and unbridled joy (Jn. 15:11). Thank Jesus for being your joy-filled Savior (Lk. 10:21). Confess any sin that stands in the way of your experiencing the fullness of joy which Jesus provides. Commit yourself today to rejoicing in the Lord, to being joyful in God your Savior (Hab. 3:18). Ask Jesus to make his joy in you complete.

For Your Family and Friends

Is there joy in your home? Ask God to show you ways you can bring joy to others in your family or to your friends. Pray for a joyful spirit as you think creatively.

For the Church

Ask that joy will characterize the fellowship of your congregation. Pray that it will flow out to embrace those on the edges of your church who are hurting or wandering.

For the Kingdom

Thank God that his kingdom is full of "righteousness, peace and joy in the Holy Spirit" (Rom. 14:17). Commit yourself to being a joyful citizen of that kingdom in all that you do.

For the Unsaved

Pray that the joy which Christ offers will attract many whose unconfessed sin keeps them in sadness and despair.

DECEMBER 30

Personal Prayer
Praise Jesus for calling you his friend (Jn. 15:15). Thank him for giving you a job to do in his kingdom—that is, to "bear fruit" (15:16). Confess those times when you've sought to do your own work rather than God's work. Commit yourself to bearing fruit that will last. Ask Jesus for the strength and wisdom you need to carry out his commands.

For Your Family and Friends
Praise God for family members and friends who also have been called by him to bear fruit. Thank Jesus for his friendship with them. Pray that they will seek to nurture that friendship with their Savior.

For the Church
Pray that the friends of God in your church will be generous in their financial contributions to his work. Pray that ministries of your congregation will not suffer from lack of funds.

For the Kingdom
Ask that Jesus' appointing of his disciples to "go and bear fruit" will capture the hearts and minds of Christians worldwide. Ask God what part you can play in his plan of fruit-bearing.

For the Unsaved
Pray that Jesus, who was called a "friend of . . . sinners" (Mt. 11:19), will befriend an unsaved person you know. Ask Jesus how you, too, might become a friend of sinners in order that they might come to Christ in faith.

_____

_____

_____

_____

_____

DECEMBER 31

Personal Prayer

As you come to the end of the year, lift your voice in praise to the one who is a prayer-hearing and prayer-answering God. Thank him for the tender talks you have had with him over the past year. Confess those times when you foolishly doubted the power of prayer. Commit yourself to maintaining a daily prayer time in the coming year. Ask God to keep you accountable to him.

For Your Family and Friends

Take a few moments to recount all the blessings your family has enjoyed over the past year. Thank God for those. Recall also the sorrows. Pray for anyone who is still hurting.

For the Church

Thank God for your local church, especially for numerical and spiritual growth among members. Pray for peace in your church in the coming year. Ask God's blessing on your pastor and other leaders.

For the Kingdom

Pray for God's kingdom to come in the coming year. Ask that believers throughout the earth will be bold witnesses for Christ so that all people everywhere might have the opportunity to hear the gospel.

For the Unsaved

Ask God to bring in any unsaved friend or family member who yet remains outside of Christ. Give thanks for wandering sheep he has rescued in this past year.

_____

_____

_____

_____

_____

A TWO-YEAR
BIBLE READING PLAN

Bible Books: All 66 books of the Bible
Reading Pace: Read two chapters a day, 6 days per week. Some short chapters are combined.
Suggested Plan: Alternate between Old and New Testament.

GENESIS
1 2 3 4 5 6
7 8 9 10 11 12
13 14 15 16 17 18
19 20 21 22 23 24
25 26 27 28 29 30
31 32 33 34 35 36
37 38 39 40 41 42
43 44 45 46 47 48
49 50

MATTHEW
1 2 3 4 5 6
7 8 9

EXODUS
1 2 3 4 5 6
7 8 9 10 11 12
13 14 15 16 17 18
19 20 21 22 23 24
25 26 27 28 29 30
31 32 33 34 35 36
37 38 39 40

MATTHEW
10 11 12 13 14 15
16 17 18 19 20

LEVITICUS
1 2 3 4 5 6
7 8 9 10 11 12
13 14

MATTHEW
21 22 23 24 25 26
27 28

LEVITICUS
15 16 17 18 19 20
21 22 23 24 25 26
27

MARK
1 2 3 4 5 6
7 8

NUMBERS
1-2 3 4 5 6 7
8 9 10 11 12 13
14 15 16 17 18 19
20 21 22 23 24 25
26 27 28 29 30 31
32 33 34 35 36

A TWO-YEAR
BIBLE READING PLAN

MARK
9 10 11 12 13 14
15-16

DEUTERONOMY
1 2 3 4 5 6
7 8 9 10 11 12
13 14 15 16 17

LUKE
1 2 3 4 5 6
7 8

DEUTERONOMY
18 19 20 21 22 23
24 25 26 27 28 29
30 31 32 33 34

LUKE
9 10 11 12 13 14
15 16

JOSHUA
1 2 3 4 5 6
7 8 9 10 11 12
13 14-15 16-17 18 19 20
21 22 23 24

LUKE
17 18 19 20 21 22
23 24

JUDGES
1 2 3 4 5 6
7 8 9 10 11 12
13 14 15 16 17 18
19 20 21

JOHN
1 2 3 4 5 6
7

RUTH
1 2 3 4

1 SAMUEL
1 2 3 4 5 6
7 8 9 10 11 12
13 14 15

JOHN
8 9 10 11 12 13
14

1 SAMUEL
16 17 18 19 20 21
22 23 24 25 26 27
28 29 30 31

JOHN
15 16 17 18 19 20
21

A TWO-YEAR
BIBLE READING PLAN

2 Samuel
1 2 3 4 5 6
7 8 9 10 11 12
13 14 15 16 17 18
19 20 21 22 23 24

Acts
1 2 3 4 5 6
7

1 Kings
1 2 3 4 5 6
7 8 9 10 11

Acts
8 9 10 11 12 13
14

1 Kings
12 13 14 15 16 17
18 19 20 21 22

Acts
15 16 17 18 19 20
21

2 Kings
1 2 3 4 5 6
7 8 9 10 11 12
13 14 15 16 17 18
19 20 21 22 23 24
25

Acts
22 23 24 25 26 27
28

1 Chronicles
1-9 10 11 12 13 14

Romans
1 2 3 4 5 6
7 8

1 Chronicles
15 16 17 18 19 20
21 22 23-27 28 29

Romans
9 10 11 12-13 14 15-16

2 Chronicles
1 2 3 4 5 6
7 8 9 10 11 12
13 14 15 16-17 18

1 Corinthians
1 2 3 4-5 6 7
8-9

2 Chronicles
19 20 21 22 23 24
25 26-27 28 29 30 31
32 33 34 35 36

A TWO-YEAR
BIBLE READING PLAN

1 CORINTHIANS
10 11 12 13 14 15
16

EZRA
1-2 3 4 5 6 7
8 9 10

NEHEMIAH
1 2-3 4 5 6 7
8 9 10 11 12 13

2 CORINTHIANS
1 2-3 4 5 6 7
8-9 10 11 12-13

ESTHER
1 2 3 4 5 6-7
8 9-10

JOB
1 2 3 4 5 6
7 8 9 10 11 12
13 14 15 16 17 18
19 20 21

GALATIANS
1 2 3 4 5-6

JOB
22 23 24 25 26 27
28 29 30 31 32 33
34 35 36 37 38 39
40 41 42

EPHESIANS
1 2 3 4 5 6

PSALMS
1-2 3-4 5 6 7 8
9 10 11-12 13-14 15-16 17
18 19 20-21 22 23-24 25
26 27 28-29 30 31 32
33 34 35 36 37 38
39 40

PHILIPPIANS
1 2 3 4

PSALMS
41 42-43 44 45 46-47 48
49 50 51 52 53-54 55
56 57 58 59 60-61 62
63-64 65 66 67 68 69
70 71 72 73 74 75
76 77 78 79 80

COLOSSIANS
1 2 3 4

A TWO-YEAR
BIBLE READING PLAN

PSALMS
81 82 83 84 85 86
87 88 89 90 91 92-93
94 95 96 97 98-99 100-101
102 103-104 105 106 107 108
109 110-111 112 113 114 115
116-117 118 119:1-48
119:49-96 119:97-144 119:145-176
120-121

1THESSALONIANS
1-2 3-4 5

2 THESSALONIANS
1-2 3

PSALMS
122-123 124-125 126-128
129-130 131-132 133-134
135 136 137-138 139 140 141
142 143 144 145 146 147
148 149-150

PROVERBS
1 2 3 4 5 6
7 8 9 10 11 12
13 14 15 16 17 18
19 20 21 22 23 24
25 26 27 28 29 30
31

1 TIMOTHY
1-2 3-4 5 6

ECCLESIASTES
1 2 3 4 5 6
7 8 9 10 11 12

SONG OF SONGS
1 2 3 4 5 6
7 8

2 TIMOTHY
1 2 3 4

ISAIAH
1 2 3 4-5 6 7
8 9 10 11 12 13
14 15 16 17 18 19-20
21 22 23 24 25 26
27 28 29 30 31 32
33 34 35 36

TITUS
1 2-3

ISAIAH
37 38-39 40 41 42 43
44 45 46 47 48 49
50 51 52 53 54 55
56 57 58 59 60 61
62 63 64 65 66

PHILEMON
1

A TWO-YEAR
BIBLE READING PLAN

JEREMIAH
1 2 3 4 5 6
7 8 9 10 11 12
13 14 15 16 17 18
19 20 21 22 23 24
25 26

HEBREWS
1 2 3-4 5-6 7

JEREMIAH
27 28 29 30 31 32
33 34 35 36 37 38
39 40 41 42 43 44
45 46 47 48 49 50
51 52

HEBREWS
8 9 10 11 12 13

LAMENTATIONS
1 2 3 4 5

EZEKIEL
1 2-3 4 5 6 7
8 9 10 11 12 13
14 15 16 17 18 19
20 21 22 23 24

JAMES
1 2 3-4 5

EZEKIEL
25 26 27 28 29 30
31 32 33 34 35 36
37 38 39 40 41 42
43 44 45 46 47 48

1 PETER
1 2 3 4-5

DANIEL
1 2 3 4 5 6
7 8 9 10 11 12

2 PETER
1 2 3

HOSEA
1 2-3 4 5 6-7 8
9 10 11-12 13-14

1 JOHN
1 2 3 4 5

JOEL
1 2 3

AMOS
1 2 3 4 5 6
7 8 9

OBADIAH
1

A TWO-YEAR
BIBLE READING PLAN

JONAH
1-2 3-4

2 AND 3 JOHN
1 1

MICAH
1 2 3 4 5 6
7

NAHUM
1 2 3

JUDE
1

HABAKKUK
1 2 3

ZEPHANIAH
1 2 3

REVELATION
1 2 3 4-5 6 7

HAGGAI
1 2

REVELATION
8 9 10-11 12 13 14

ZECHARIAH
1 2-3 4-5 6 7 8
9 10 11 12-13 14

MALACHI
1 2 3-4

REVELATION
15-16 17 18 19 20 21
22

A ONE-YEAR
BIBLE READING PLAN

Bible Books: Psalms, Proverbs, Ecclesiastes, and the New Testament
Reading Pace: Read one chapter a day and two on Sunday (448 total).
Some short chapters are combined.
Suggested Plan: Alternate between Old and New Testament.

FIRST MONTH

MATTHEW
1 2 3 4 5 6 7 8
9 10 11 12 13 14 15 16
17 18 19 20 21 22 23 24
25 26 27 28

PROVERBS
1 2 3 4 5 6 7 8
9

SECOND MONTH

MARK
1 2 3 4 5 6 7 8
9 10 11 12 13 14 15-16

PSALMS
1-2 3 4 5 6 7 8 9
10 11-12 13-14 15-16 17 18 19 20-22
23-24

THIRD MONTH

LUKE
1 2 3 4 5 6 7 8
9 10 11 12 13 14 15 16
17 18 19 20 21 22 23 24

PROVERBS
10 11 12 13 14 15 16 17
18 19 20 21 22

A ONE-YEAR
BIBLE READING PLAN

FOURTH MONTH

JOHN

1 2 3 4 5 6 7 8
9 10 11 12 13 14 15 16
17 18 19 20 21

PSALMS

25 26 27 28-29 30 31 32 33
34 35 36 37 38 39 40 41

FIFTH MONTH

ACTS

1 2 3 4 5 6 7 8
9 10 11 12 13 14 15 16
17 18 19 20 21 22 23 24
25 26 27 28

PROVERBS

23 24 25 26 27 28 29 30
31

SIXTH MONTH

ROMANS

1 2 3 4 5 6 7 8
9 10 11 12 13 14 15 16

PSALMS

42-43 44 45 46-47 48 49 50 51
52 53 54 55 56 57 58 59
60-61 62 63-64

SEVENTH MONTH

1 CORINTHIANS

1 2 3 4-5 6 7 8-9 10
11 12 13 14 15 16

A ONE-YEAR
BIBLE READING PLAN

2 CORINTHIANS
1 2-3 4 5 6 7 8 9
10 11 12-13

PSALMS
65 66 67 68 69 70 71 72

COLOSSIANS
1 2 3 4

7

EIGHTH MONTH

GALATIANS
2 3 4 5-6

EPHESIANS
1 2 3 4 5 6

PHILIPPIANS
1 2 3 4

PSALMS
73 74 75 76 77 78 79 80
81 82 83 84 85 86 87 88
89

8

NINTH MONTH

1 THESSALONIANS
1-2 3-4 5

2 THESSALONIANS
1-2 3

1 TIMOTHY
1-2 3-4 5 6

2 TIMOTHY
1 2 3 4

TITUS
1 2-3

PSALMS
90 91 92-93 94 95 96 97 98-99
100-101 102 103 104 105 106

9

A ONE-YEAR
BIBLE READING PLAN

TENTH MONTH

PHILEMON

HEBREWS
 1 2 3-4 5-6 7 8 9 10
 11 12 13

JAMES
 1 2 3-4 5

PSALMS
 107 108 109 110-111 112 113 114 115
 116-117 118 119:1-48 119:49-96 119:97-144
 119:145-176 120 121 122-123 124-125

10

ELEVENTH MONTH

1 PETER
 1 2 3 4-5

2 PETER
 1 2 3

1 JOHN
 1-2 3 4 5

2 JOHN-3 JOHN-JUDE

PSALMS
 126-128 129-130 131-132 133- 134 135

ECCLESIASTES
 1 2 3 4 5 6 7 8
 9 10 11 12

11

TWELFTH MONTH

REVELATION
 1 2 3 4-5 6 7 8 9
 10-11 12 13 14 15 16 17 18
 19 20 21 22

PSALMS
 136 137-138 139 140 141-142 143 144 145
 146 147 148 149-150

12

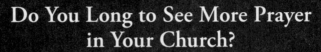